THE WITCH'S GUIDE TO RITUAL

Also by Cerridwen Greenleaf

Moon Spell Magic for Love: Charms, Invocations, Passion Potions, and Rituals for Romance

Moon Spell Magic: Invocations, Incantations & Lunar Lore for a Happy Life

Dark Moon Magic: Supernatural Spells, Charms, and Rituals for Health, Wealth, and Happiness

The Magic of Crystals & Gems: Unlocking the Supernatural Power of Stones

The Magic Oracle Book: Ask Any Question and Discover Your Fate

The Practical Witch's Spell Book: For Love, Happiness, and Success

5-Minute Magic for Modern Wiccans: Rapid Rituals, Efficient Enchantments, and Swift Spells

THE WITCH'S GUIDE TO RITUAL

Spells, Incantations, and Inspired Ideas for an Enchanted Life

CERRIDWEN GREENLEAF

CORAL GABLES

For permission requests, please contact the publisher at:

Mango Publishing Group
2850 Douglas Road, 2nd Floor
Coral Gables, FL 33134 USA
info@mango.bz

For special orders, quantity sales, course adoptions and corporate sales, please email the publisher at sales@mango.bz. For trade and wholesale sales, please contact Ingram Publisher Services at customer.service@ingramcontent.com or +1.800.509.4887.

The Witch's Guide to Ritual: Spells, Incantations, and Inspired Ideas for an Enchanted Life

Library of Congress Cataloging
ISBN: 9781642501704

BISAC: OCC028000—BODY, MIND & SPIRIT / Magick Studies

LCCN: 2019948630

Formerly published as *Rituals for Myth and Meaning* by Mango Publishing, an imprint of Mango Media, Inc.

Printed in the United States of America

Table of Contents

FOREWORD

By Arin Murphy-Hiscock

People hunger for ritual. As children, we create complex rituals of play and interaction. As adolescents, we engage in awkward social rituals to test and define our identities. As adults, we pass certain milestones such as marriage, first house, and first child, yet these traditional milestones reflect only a small portion of the moments we feel ought to be marked in some fashion

In the twenty-first century, many people feel spiritually adrift as the world moves ever faster. Important events seem to go by, unnoticed and unremarked. You can, however, mark these events when you create your own rituals. You can celebrate the successes, mourn the losses, and shout out the accomplishments. You can design a ritual for family, a community, or just yourself.

Ritual provides a sense of connection and a sense of comfort. It strips away the barriers we raise to shield ourselves in everyday life. Performing a ritual with someone dear to you for the first time is an incredibly moving experience, as I discovered years ago when my husband and I came together to do ritual instead of each of us practicing alone. I recently learned the lesson again when my mother asked us to perform a waxing moon ritual in her backyard when we visited. It was her first nontraditional ritual experience with others, and it was an honor to be there with her as she allowed the beauty and simplicity of the ritual to touch her.

A large part of ritual through the ages has revolved around lowering the defensive barriers we raise and reaching out to one another and to something greater than ourselves. Whether you choose to call that something greater than ourselves God, Goddess, Spirit, Cosmic Light, or the Universe, uniting with that something greater than the sum of its parts is an essential element of ritual. Ritual strengthens our own identity, purifies our energies, and brings us into harmony with the energies flowing through our lives.

As a priestess, I facilitate ritual for others. As a teacher, I teach them how to create their own rituals, lead others in rituals they create, and fully experience them. People who attend my workshops are surprised to learn that when they light a candle in gratitude or supplication to a higher power, they are in fact performing a ritual. Rituals may be complex and dramatic, or they may be as simple as floating a single blossom on the surface of a bowl of water. What matters is your *intention* as you perform your action. Being aware of your intentions and the meaning behind your practice brings a deeper meaning to your actions. This is what creates ritual it is a way to discover the self, to discover the world around you.

Crafting and performing rituals creates the opportunity to restore balance and harmony in your life. Performing ritual also gives you a method of self-expression and a safety valve for blowing off emotional steam. Designing ritual is a wonderfully creative experience that offers everyone the opportunity to try something different. It is important to remember that rituals are fluid and flexible; this book isn't one of those books that will tell you what you must or must not do every time you set up a ritual. A personal ritual benefits us the most when it adapts to our current needs. There are times for traditional ritual as well, but the rituals in this book are designed to supplement them, not supplant them.

This book was created for intermediate practitioners. This means certain things have been assumed: that you have read an introductory book on rituals before or have at least some experience with ritual. Cerridwen doesn't spend a lot of time going over the basics. Instead, she emphasizes rites and rituals from several cultures, offers templates to get your mind going, and provides information to help you design your own rituals. You'll discover that by drawing certain things together—a feather, a candle, a flower—you can create an atmosphere that enhances your mood. Play with color on the altar and in your ritual clothing. Research deities from various mythologies and discover their spheres of influence. Ask for the help of Mother Nature or the spirits of the four elements. The examples in this book provide you with wonderful ideas to experiment with and to serve as a starting point for your own explorations.

These practices are meant to be accessible to people of all faiths and paths who seek to enrich their spiritual practices and add meaning to their lives. You hold in your hands a treasure trove of information gathered from ceremonies throughout history and from all over the world. Let this information inspire you and excite you. Let your imagination take flight. Trust your intuition, go with your instincts, and listen to your heart. By following these three simple guidelines, you will be able to craft beautiful, and more important, meaningful rituals to enrich your life, provide comfort, and maintain harmony and balance in your life.

Welcome to *The Witch's Guide to Ritual.*

CALLING THE CIRCLE

I once had the pleasure of attending a talk by Huston Smith, a preeminent scholar of the world's religions who first came to the attention of the world when he brought a young Tibetan Buddhist monk—His Holiness, the Dalai Lama—to America for the first time. Smith spoke about the continuing impact of religion in our world, most notably, the strife in the Middle East over religious differences. He was at his most joyous when he spoke about his own spiritual practices, which he described to us. They were beautiful in their simplicity. Smith said that, upon rising each day, he did Hatha yoga for some minutes, followed by reading a few pages of sacred text, after which he meditated or prayed for at least five minutes. He would finish his morning ritual by doing a bit of yard work and some composting, which resulted in rich, dark soil and a beautiful garden that he greatly enjoys.

The entire audience smiled as they listened to this great and humble man describe the simple spiritual practices with which he began each day. These were Huston Smith's personal morning rituals. I loved the irony that this premier academic, who has such a deep understanding of all the religious rituals throughout history, had created such an uncomplicated practice for himself. I left the talk inspired and soon felt compelled to write a book of rituals that add meaning into our lives.

Whether people are conscious of it or not, our lives are centered upon ritual. The Wednesday night pizza and movie with the kids is a family ritual. It could be greatly enriched by adding a spiritual aspect—perhaps children could share the highlight of their week so far, and photos or memories could be added to a family album to be treasured for generations to come. The Saturday night date is a romantic ritual, knitting circles are a growing trend, and doing yoga is replacing going to the gym as a spiritual and physical workout. People need ritual to inform and enrich their lives, to deal with stress, and above all, to create meaning in their lives.

Becoming conscious of the possibilities of ritual is the first step in *The Witch's Guide to Ritual.* Daily spiritual practices and seasonal rituals create a life filled with blessings. Many of us were brought up with specific religious practices. Although I was brought up as a First Day Adventist, when I studied history, I kept discovering practices from the past that I felt were just as relevant today. One ancient ritual I discovered was bibliomancy, which is a form of divination developed when books were precious objects made of papyrus or vellum. Bibliomancy is a simple ritual that I have incorporated into my daily life for inspiration "from the gods." You simply open a book at random and let a word or phrase come to your attention. You thus become inspired in the true meaning of the word, which is simply to breathe in.

The beauty of knowing history is that we can learn from the past and take the best to heart by applying it to our lives. Ritual is very much a part of our history and should be studied and applied to our lives today. Ritual gets us out of or heads and back into our bodies. It gets us into a place of spirit. By participating in rituals on a regular basis, you can grow in wisdom and feel an increasing sense of your aliveness.

Chapter 1

FOR THE GOOD OF ALL: THE HISTORY AND USE OF RITUAL

Noted anthropologist Margaret Mead states in her groundbreaking text *Ritual and Social Crises* that "throughout human history man has employed ritual behavior," that ritual is an important part of the socialization of our species. In his excellent *Magic of Ritual,* author and ritual scholar Tom Driver states that "everything points to the supposition that our remote ancestors were ritualizing before they became human. This activity became a pathway to our human condition." Other great thinkers like Ludwig Wittgenstein agree with Driver's theory, but also emphasize the importance of ritual in human history with a link to the expressive and performing arts. In addition, there are interesting theories that rituals honoring the gods and goddesses were the progenitors to the arts. Ritual is a source of culture for the religions of the world as well as for speech.

Medieval historian J. Huizinga claimed that ritualizing play provided a foundation for culture. Huizinga is most noted for his seminal text, *The Autumn of the Middle Ages*, in which he asserts that ritual and play were given an important role in the Middle Ages and kept people connected to each other. "Every event," he writes, "every deed was defined in given and expressive forms and was in accord with the solemnity of marriage, death—by virtue of the sacraments, basking in the radiance of the divine mystery. But even the lesser events—a journey, a labor, a visit—were accompanied by a multitude of blessings, ceremonies, sayings and conventions."

The great academic Roy Rappaport undertook some of the most thorough studies of rites and ceremony among the tribes in Papua, New Guinea. Based on extensive research, he found that ritual stemming from the marking of time in the context of cyclical celebrations is based on the natural world, and creates and maintains order in societies. Rappaport calls this "context making" and states that "annual rounds of festival" surely distinguish the seasons from each other more clearly than the weather does. Rappaport goes so far as to say that the seasonal festivals and their accompanying ceremonies created the foundation and ordering of our lives and communities. He states most emphatically, "I take ritual to be the basic social act."

We are experiencing a renaissance of ritual at the beginning of the twenty-first century. Perhaps a new society is emerging from the creative kiln of ritual. Ritual processes regulate our lives, individually and as groups. Anthropologists, psychologists, and other students of the human race have shown that ritual has existed since the dawn of humanity and has always played an important role in culture. Scholars of the psyche, including Freud, who eloquently addressed the role of ritual, speak of the power of ritual and how it brings people together physically and emotionally. Ritual creates "communities" from which spring a sense of unity, harmony, and belonging. Rituals are outside of time. In ritual, we are in a moment when we can shed the normal conventions of behavior. We all have habits or idiosyncrasies that are not generally accepted—clapping hands, shouting out with joy, ululating, ecstatic dancing, and talking to spirits to name a few. None of this is shocking within the context of a shared ceremony where everybody has stepped out of the routine of ordinary day-to-day behavior and is embracing life itself.

Ritual is work, play, song, dance, and an embrace of the spirit. Ritual is change and forward movement, an affirmation of life. Ritual is a set of symbolic acts that represent a higher state of being. It is a raised consciousness and the glue that binds people together. It is time spent with the sacred, elevating us above our workaday duties to a holy place within and without. Rituals are freedom, the power of love, and the joy of release through participation. From Haiti to India to the Vatican, ritual is a vital part of people's lives. The benefits of ritual are many: aesthetic, moral, personal, and communal. Being conscious of the power of ritual offers many benefits on an individual level, for groups and communities, and even globally. Our contemporary culture is in urgent need of spiritual renewal, and ritual can replace the void of meaning in people's lives. Ritual can even relieve the modern symptom of isolation that has so many people spending so much time alone and feeling lonely. In troubled times, ritual can heal hearts and restore peace and harmony. We can enact rituals that liberate our souls, open our minds, and transform our lives and communities.

The human heart longs for ritual. To be fully alive and whole, we need to engage creatively in ritual. We should be active participants in rituals, whether they are rites of passage for birth, adulthood, marriage or death; ceremonies of healing, grieving, or celebrating; or political performances aimed at changing society.

This book is intended as a tool for you to engage more creatively in ritual than you have in the past. The lore and lessons have come to use from history. *The Witch's Guide to Ritual* can guide you down the path until you feel ready to take that leap of faith and begin to design rituals of your own.

I have listened to and learned from many masters of the craft of ritual, and the message is clear: Rituals are the rhythm of life When you design your own rituals; you are designing your own destiny.

While this book focuses largely on rituals for the good of all, it also reminds us of ritual's power to do harm. Harm can be avoided, however, with mindfulness to intention and awareness of the short and long-term effects of the energy being raised and managed.

We have all read frightening urban myths about "ritual abuse," where well-intentioned folks fall victim to the manipulation of a misguided ritual leader. This "danger zone" cannot be glossed over. Sadly, ritual abuse can occur not only in cults and covens, but history has shown that it has also taken place in churches, synagogues, and temples. As people crave ritual for the sense of connection and spirit, ritual can be used to influence and control. Keep this in mind, and if you feel uncomfortable with any aspect of a group ritual, excuse yourself and leave that circle far behind you.

The creation and performance of rites and ceremonies are some of the very best activities human life has to offer. Rituals are similar to works of art in that their power may not be in sync with morality. Keeping this awe-inspiring strength to move the human spirit in mind and being aware of the potential downside of power will go a long way in preventing trouble.

Ritual has been used to change the world in dramatic ways. Mahatma Gandhi used ritual Hindu meditation to help gain India's independence. Gandhi applied his ritual fasting, the labor of his hands through the art of weaving, and his devotion to utter truth to help further his revolutionary goals. The Reverend Martin Luther King's civil rights movement consisted of rituals, songs, and chants that started in southern black churches, where people were called upon to turn the tide and create reforms in civil rights. King and his followers used spirituals as a shield, chanting their gospel songs while facing down the police and soldiers. Nelson Mandela, born into the Xhosa tribe in the Cape Nguni region of Africa, ousted apartheid in South Africa in an equally inspired way. In his biography, Mandela recollected about his childhood that his "life, and that of most Xhosas at the time, was shaped by custom, ritual, and taboo. This was the alpha and omega of our existence, and went unquestioned." Recently, we have seen suppressed traditions such as Wicca and other traditions of Witchcraft becoming popular. Wicca has a wonderfully straightforward approach to the subject of ethics through a strong code based on moral and personal responsibility. A brief outline of the three principles of the Wiccan way follows.

The Wiccan Rede

In his book, *The Meaning of Witchcraft,* Gerald Gardner states, "An ye harm none, do as ye will." This statement encourages the individual freedom to do as you see fit so long as it does not affect anyone negatively. While you pursue your own interest, that is, think of how what you do affects others. This applies to all aspects of life, but especially with ritual and spell work because you are working with energies that have wide-ranging powers. This rule requires real attention and a high degree of consciousness in terms of assessing the repercussions of any action in regard to all the possible physical, spiritual, emotional, and psychological consequences as a result of all ritual work.

The Threefold Law

"What you do comes back to you threefold" resembles the Buddhist principle of karma. the Threefold Law is a directive to always think of the consequences of personal actions, including rites, ceremonies, and spells you perform. Negativity comes back to you three times over, so attention to attitudes and thoughts is absolutely essential. The flip side of this law is that positive energy also comes back to you threefold. Kindness, love, and generosity are all magnified. This is also a reason to do ritual work for long-distance healing and for global issues such as peace, the environment, and world hunger. Send good works and helpful intentions out to others and you yourself will benefit.

The Golden Rule

"Do unto others as you would have others do unto you." Many people might find it amazing that Neo-Pagans and Christians share this basic rule of morality that places personal responsibility at the highest level. In other words, the "right action" is up to you and is of ultimate importance. The Bible tells us that "whatsoever a man soweth, that shall he also reap" (Galatians 6:7).

You don't have to be Wiccan to appreciate these basic principles for responsible use of ritual. These few, simple guidelines are universal in nature and can apply to any walk of life and to any spiritual practice. It is also vital to respect the diversity of religions. Respect others as you wish to be respected. In their ability to impact others, magic and ritual are serious undertakings. With good intentions and heightened awareness about managing energy, you can learn to become a responsible ritualist. Anne Niven, publisher of the excellent *SageWoman, PanGaia,* and *newWitch* magazines, recently related a story of a writer who was unintentionally teaching a less than responsible ritual. This writer's recommendation was for teenage girls to go for a walk near a body of water and invoke the spirit of a suicidal banshee there to help work through their depression. To work with such an unbalanced spirit while in an extreme emotional state is potentially dangerous. We need to think our rites through in regard to short-term effects, long-term effects, and how we and others will be affected by our ritual work. Careful consideration will go a long way toward increasing the effectiveness of your work. A simple rule of thumb is to trust your instincts and do your research really well. Also, never take the gods and goddesses lightly, as these ancient energies are very powerful. To protect yourself, learn as much as you can about the deities, as well as the herbs, flowers, oils, and essences you intend to use. Honoring the earth and caring for our precious environment is absolutely essential as well. Ritual requires consciousness and integrity, traits that will serve you well in every path of your life. As a ritualist, you should walk your talk and act responsibly in all your work.

Chapter Two

THE ESSENTIAL TOOL KIT: EVERYTHING YOU NEED FOR RITES AND RITUALS

Magic resides inside of us; we create it with our thoughts and actions. It is our deepest personal power, and we are all born with it. This is the energy we draw upon each and every day of our life. The goal of ritual is to bring about needed change. It is how we make things better for ourselves, for the people in our lives, and for our world. From an inner place of intention, we are working to bring about change for peace, prosperity, love, health, home, spirituality, and other areas in our lives that are always in need of improvement.

When you establish a sacred space and use your magical tools in it, you can create a place where the mundane world is left behind. It can be in your home or your backyard where, despite the noise of the day-to-day, you can touch the sacred. There is no need to ascend to the top of a mountain or to a silent retreat in search of the scared; anywhere you choose can become a place of magic where you cast the circle.

The magic circle is created by "casting," or drawing in the air with concentrated energy. Inside this circle, energy is raised, rituals are performed, and spells are worked. The sacred space is also where you call upon the gods and goddesses and become attuned to your own special desires. With attention and focus, working in the circle can be a truly intense experience. All your senses will come alive. You will feel, see, and hear the energies that you invoke. You will have created a tangible sphere of power.

You can cast a circle anywhere—out in the forest, on a beach, or in the comfort of your own home. Wherever the circle is cast, that space becomes your temple. If you are in your kitchen or living room, stack the chairs against the wall to define the limits of your circle. The Wiccan tradition specifies that the circle must have a diameter of nine feet. That said, a circle could actually be any size to accommodate a large group of people or just yourself. Many Wiccans and other Pagans case a circle for spell work and to enclose every seasonal sabbat celebration.

In truth, casting a circle is only limited by the imagination or the function you ascribe to it. The magic begins at your altar with your sacred tools. To be fully imbued with energy, your tools of magic and ritual should reside upon your altar. Collecting your ritual tools should be a pleasant search that can take months or even years. Although making ritual tools is satisfying, you can also find them in flea markets, at antique stores, and craft fairs around the country. Nowadays, the Internet and several terrific mail-order catalogs such as *The Pyramid Catalog* and *Mystic Trader* also offer superb tools for sale. Always make sure you cleanse and purify your new tools, whether they are antique or just made, to ensure that the energy is yours and yours alone. Think of your ritual tools as energy conductors that absorb and project energy of the environment and the ritual work that you perform.

Ritual Tools

Every ritual tool is sacred to the individual who is performing the ritual act. Whether your find your tool in a store or whether it is given to you as a gift, each tool should hold special meaning and should feel absolutely perfect to you as you use it.

Athame

Pronounced "a-THAW-may," this is your magical knife. It can also be a ritual dagger or sword, and I have even seen a Tibetan *dorje* (the thunderbolt of the god) used as an athame. The athame represents and contains yang energy, or the male aspect of the gods. Ritual knives are also associated with the element of fire. For these two reasons, your athame should be placed on the right side of your altar. The athame is used to direct the energies raised in your ritual. Because it is not used for cutting but rather for the manipulation of the forces involved in the work of enchantment, an athame is usually a dull blade. Some Wiccan traditions specify that the handle of the athame should be black or very dark in color, since black is the color that absorbs energy. A dark-handled knife thus becomes quickly attuned to the ritualist.

Bolline

The bolline is a (usually) white-handled knife that is used for making other tools and for cutting materials such as cords and herbs within the magic circle.

You can create your magical wand, for example, by cutting off a tree branch with your bolline. This increases the energy held within it and creates a magical tool by using a magical tool. You should also use your bolline for carving symbols and names into your candles and wands as well as your other tools. A bolline generally has a curved blade and a white handle to distinguish it from the athame. It is similar to the athame in that it also embodies the yang, or male, energy.

Book of Shadows

Your Book of Shadows (BOS) is your record of ritual work. At its finest, it should be a history of all your rituals, energy work, circles, spells, and all the magic you have manifested. It should be a journal of all that you have practiced and wrought. In your BOS, you should keep a record of your research and the lore you have discovered. Is there a particular phase and sign of the moon that works especially well for you? Document it here, and you will be building a practice that you can apply to future rituals. This will also be a great help in recording your ritual work and evolving and developing as a ritual designer. All the astrology, herb lore, crystal information, and other knowledge that I share in this book comes from the detailed notes I keep in my own BOS. I have discovered that the new moon in Pisces, for example, is the best moon phase for me to work rituals of change. After documenting this information and performing both new and traditional, time-tested rituals and spells with the new moon in Pisces, I learned from a professional astrologer that it is my natal placement—the moon is in the same phase and sign in which is positioned at the time of my birth. Thus this moon phase and sign accords with my own energy and creates a time when my personal power is at its peak. Through trial, experimentation, and much practice, you will discover secrets of the universe for yourself and record what you learn in your own BOS.

The Book of Shadows can be a tremendous aid if you use it daily or as often as possible. Whenever you come upon a bit of wisdom regarding the nature of ritual or magical work, write it down. This should also be a book of inspiration, filled with your own thoughts, poetry, and observations. Most importantly, it should be a record of results. If you track the effectiveness of a ritual, you can use this information and newfound wisdom in the future. Your BOS should be a book you turn to again and again. It can be a gorgeous, hand-crafted volume of handmade paper and ribboned bookmarks or a simple three-ring binder. Just make sure it appeals to *you* so that you will use it often and well.

Broom

As a magical tool, the broom was born of the practical magic of sweeping the ritual area clean before and after casting a spell. With focus and intention, you can dispel negative influences and bad spirits from the area and prepare a space for ritual work. In bygone days, pagan marriages and Beltane trysts took place with a leap over the broom, an old traditional element of handfasting, or pagan wedding. While this happens more rarely now, the broom has grabbed the popular imagination as the archetypal symbol of witches.

Your broom is an essential tool for energy management. Obtain a handmade broom from a craft fair, not a machine-made plastic affair from the supermarket. A broom made of wood and woven from straw will be imbued with the inherent energies of those natural materials. Also, do *not* use your ritual broom for housework, as this would mix up energies in your home and sacred space. Many of you may well consider your home to be sacred space in its entirety. Keep your regular household implements separated from your ritual tools nonetheless. This is a matter of protecting yourself and the energy of your sacred space. Any of your cleaning implements, such as a broom, can very easily have chemicals from regular housecleaning remaining on them. In general, it is not advised to use tools such as a ritual knife to debone a chicken, for example, as this reduced the effectiveness of your ritual tools and risks a confused blending of mundane and magical energies. If you treat your ritual tools with the utmost respect, they will serve you well. Over time they will become deeply imbued with magical energy through exclusive use in your workings. The Wiccan tradition holds brooms in high regard, and some witches have an impressive collection of brooms, each named to distinguish between their roles as "familiars," or kindred spirits.

Candles

Nowadays, the popularity of candles has reached an all-time high. Candles are used by folks of all walks of life for relaxation, meditation, and aromatherapy. This simple yet profound tool can make powerful magic. Notice how candlelight transforms a dark room and fills the air with the energy of magical light. Suddenly the potential for magic is evident.

Candles contain all four of the elemental energies:

Air—Oxygen feeds and fans the candle flame.

Earth—The solid wax forms the candle.

Water—Melted wax is the fluid elemental state.

Fire—The flame sparks and blazes.

How to Charge a Candle

"Charging" a candle means instilling it with magical intent. A candle that has been charged carries that intention through all four elements and up to the heavens. It fills the very air with your magic. Ritual candles are chosen for their correspondences, carved, and "dressed," or anointed, with the energy of an essential oil.

Candle Color Correspondences

Black: banishing, absorbing, expulsion of the negative, healing serious disease, attracting money

Brown: home, animal wisdom, grounding, healing

Dark Blue: change, flexibility, the unconscious, psychic powers, healing

Gold: solar magic, money, attraction, the astral plane

Gray: neutrality, impasse, cancellation

Green: money, prosperity, growth, luck, jobs, gardening, youth, beauty, fertility

Light Blue: patience happiness, triumph over depression, calm understanding

Orange: attraction, success with legal issues, mutability, stimulation, support, encouragement

Pink: love, faithfulness, friendships, goodness, affection

Purple: healing, ambition, business success, stress relief, power

Red: strength, protection, vitality, sexuality, passion, courage, power, love, good health

White: purification, peace, protection, truth, binding, sincerity, serenity, chastity, happiness, spirit

Yellow: mental power and vision, intelligence, clear thinking, study, self-assurance, prosperity, abundance, divination, psychism, powers of persuasion, wisdom, charisma, sound sleep

Once you clarify your intention, cleanse your candles by passing them through the purifying smoke of sage or incense. Further charge your candle by carving a symbol or sigil into the wax. You can warm the tip of your ritual knife using a lit match and carve your full intention into the candle wax. As you engrave the appropriate magical words onto the candle, you are charging it with energy and intention. Next, you should "dress" your candle with specific oil. Every essential oil is imbued with a power that comes from the plants and flowers of which it is made. The appendix gives correspondences that you can use. You can also use oils to anoint yourself at the crown of the head or at the third eye to increase mental clarity. By using the inherent powers of essential oils, you are increasing the effectiveness of your rite and "doubling" the energies by anointing both your tool—in this case, the candle—and yourself.

Essential oils are highly concentrated extracts of flower, herb, root, or resin extract, sometimes diluted into base oil. Try to ensure that you are using authentic essential oils instead of perfume or fragrance oils, which are synthetic versions. Always treat the oils with great care, as some are highly irritating to those with sensitive skin. For this reason, some people choose to wear clean cotton gloves when handling oils. Use droppers to measure the oils carefully, and avoid touching your face and especially eyes when working with them. Never drink your essential oils and use caution when inhaling them, as some of the stronger ones can have a negative effect on your sinuses. Different people have different reactions to various essential oils. My friend Nancy, for example, gets migraine headaches any time amber oil is in use. If possible, find an herbalist who will guide you as you experiment with oils in rituals and workings. I am fortunate in that I may consult with Randy, my trusted oil mixer at San Francisco's The Sword and the Rose. He is extremely knowledgeable and generous with his wisdom. Research and explore the wide varieties of essential oils now available, and eventually you will discover those that work for you.

Essential Oil Magical Correspondences

Astral Projection: jasmine, benzoin, cinnamon, sandalwood

Courage: geranium, black pepper, frankincense

Dispelling Negative Spirits: basil, clove, copal, frankincense, juniper, myrrh, pine, peppermint, rosemary, sandalwood, Solomon's seal, yarrow, vetiver

Divination: camphor, orange, clove

Enchantment: ginger, tangerine

Healing: bay, cedar wood, cinnamon, coriander, eucalyptus, juniper, lime, rose, sandalwood, spearmint

Joy: lavender

Love: apricot, basil, chamomile, clove, copal, coriander, rose, geranium, jasmine, lavender, lemon, lime, neroli, peppermint, rose, rosemary, ylang-ylang, vetiver

Luck: orange, nutmeg, rose, vetiver

Peace: lavender

Prosperity: basil, clove, ginger, cedar, cinnamon, jasmine, nutmeg, orange, oak moss, patchouli, peppermint, pine, wood aloe

Protection: bay, basil, anise, black pepper, cedar, cinnamon, clove, copal, cypress, eucalyptus, frankincense, rose, geranium, lime, myrrh, juniper, lavender, patchouli, peppermint, pine, rose, sandalwood, vetiver

Sexuality: cardamom, cinnamon, clove, lemongrass, olive, patchouli, peppermint, rosemary

Cauldron

The cauldron represents the Goddess, its round basin symbolizing the womb. The cauldron can hold fire and represent rebirth—the phoenix rising from the ashes of the past. Usually, cauldrons stand on three legs for practicality and mobility. You can place a cauldron on your altar if there is room, or on the floor to the left of the altar. In spring, the cauldron can be used to hold earth or water. In winter, it can represent the rebirth of the sun and should hold fire. The form of the vessel may change. In the spring, the cauldron can be a rain-filled jar or flower-filled fountain. In the summer, it can be a cup, and at harvest, it can be a pumpkin or other hollowed-out gourd. You can play with this "vessel" concept in your own ceremonies. Cauldrons are very useful for mixing your herbs and essential oils, though you must be sure to clean them before and after each use. You can scry with a cauldron full of water to foresee the future by reading images on the surface of the water. You can use this magical tool to burn paper upon which you have written your intentions or spells. In doing this, you can send your wishes to the gods and goddesses through the flames. A cauldron is not the easiest magical tool to find, as they are not nearly as commonplace as one might think. I advise you to wish and wait patiently, and the cauldron of your dreams will arrive in the most enchanted manner.

Censer

A censer, or thurible, is an incense burner and represents the elements of air and fire. Place your incense at the center of your altar. Incense can be used to purify your other sacred tools and to cleanse your ritual space. The evocative scent and smoke can also transport you in a sensory way. Always test your incense prior to ritual, however, to discover how much smoke is produced by your incense stick or herbal mixture. The purpose of incense is to release energy into the ritual space, not to create billows of smoke that can cause respiratory problems in the circle. If you or someone else finds incense smoke irritating or worrisome, consider using another symbol of air instead, such as potpourri, fresh flowers, feathers, or a fan.

There exist an abundance of incense burners nowadays, so use your discretion and choose one that pleases you—perhaps a smoking dragon or a goddess to hold the fiery embers of your incense would add to the energy of your altar.

Incenses themselves contain inherent energies that you can use to further your intention and promote your purpose. I depend on *Wylundt's Book of Incense,* which I consider to be the ultimate reference for excellent information about essences and properties of incense. It contains an enormous amount of information in regard to loose, cone, stick, and cylinder incense. It also tells you how to work with herbs, which part of a plant to use, and how to gather, dry, and store the plants. The following is one of my recipes for an incense to use to cast a circle.

Circle Incense

2 parts myrrh

4 parts frankincense

2 parts benzoin

1 part sandalwood

1 part cinnamon

1 part rose petals

1 part vervain

1 part rosemary

1 part bay leaf

½ cup orange peel

This incense will significantly aid the formation of the sphere of energy that is the ritual circle. A fine grind of all the ingredients is the key to good incense, so you should add a mortar and pestle to your list of tools if you intend to make a lot of incense. A blender or food processor is a more modern approach that may save on time and elbow grease, especially if you are making a large batch of incense for a group.

Clearing Incense

1 part sandalwood

3 parts myrrh

3 parts copal

3 parts frankincense

This is an optimal mixture of essences to purify your home or sacred working space. Negative energies are vanquished and the path is cleared for ritual. Open windows and doors when you are burning this clearing incense so the "bad energy" can be released outside. It is also advisable to use this clearing incense if there have been any arguments or other energetic disruptions in your home. You can recreate a sanctuary with this incense.

Dream Incense

2 parts rose petals

2 parts cedar

1 part camphor

1 part lavender

6 drops tuberose oil

6 drops jasmine oil

This mixture will bring on psychic dreams. If you set up a bedroom altar, place this incense in your censer and allow the scented smoke to imbue your sleeping space with its unique energy before you drift off. Prophetic dreams may come to you and, even better, you will remember them!

Chalice

The chalice—another vessel symbolizing the feminine, the Goddess, and fertility—is a goblet dedicated specifically for use on your altar. Holding both physical fluid and the waters of our emotional body, it is connected to elemental water. Place your special chalice on the left side of your altar with all other representations of the energy of the female and the Goddess. A grail is also a chalice. Legend tells that the Holy Grail brought life back into the decaying kingdom of Camelot and restored Arthur and his people to health, giving rise to the rebirth of England itself. On your altar, your chalice can hold water, mead, wine, juice, or anything that has been blessed. It can contain holy water for consecrations and blessing rites. At the end of many ritual ceremonies and sabbats, it is customary to toast the deities with a hearty ale, cider, or wine and thank them for being present. After the circle has been opened, you can pour the contents of your chalice into the ground outdoors as an offering to benevolent entities.

Wand

A magical wand is a powerful tool used to cast the circle and invoke deities. Like an athame, a wand focuses, projects, and directs energy. Because it gathers and stores magical power, a wand is wonderful for healing and can also be the device with which you "draw" the shape when you cast the circle. If possible, find your wand in a serendipitous manner. Draw it to yourself through attraction. A wand makes a mighty gift. It may, however, be more practical and expedient just to purchase your wand. When you do this, purify it, cleansing off the energy of the shop, so it is truly yours. Before you race off to the nearest metaphysical five-and-dime, take a walk in the woods. You may very well find the wand of your dreams waiting there for you on the forest floor. Some folks favor "live wood," like cherry, willow, or oak branches that need to be cut off the tree. I prefer fallen wood that Nature has already harvested. Some folks like to ornament their wand with magical metals, such as copper, gold, or silver, and encrust it with gems and crystals. The most important determining factor for any wand is how it "feels" in your hand. You will know when you have found the right one.

Keep Your Muse Close

Any time an imaginative person feels her creativity is blocked, or if she feels uninspired, she can call upon a muse. Whether you're passionate about growing plants, painting, or writing music, you can stay in touch with your muse by using a special tool that will draw her to you with sweet-smelling smoke of sage.

Sage is hardy and sun-loving, so keep a pot of it on the windowsill. There are very simple steps to take to create a sage wand to use when you need inspiration. First, you will want to create a tight braid of materials. This braid will consist of a long fennel stalk, a twisted bundle of sage, long sticks of incense (I prefer cinnamon), and purple (for power) and gold (for money) string or thread. When you are about to embark on an artistic activity, simply light one end of your wand and gently wave it around your head to clear your environment. Your mind will be cleared in the process, freeing the way for creative ideas. A little sage smoke goes a long way, so you will not want to burn the entire wand at once. Keep a cup of water or a small bowl of earth on hand to extinguish your wand when you are done.

Making the Tools of the Magical Trade

Just as you can design your own rituals, you can create your own ritual accessories and tools. Your intentions and personal energy are the driving forces behind the enchantments you create, and the same is true of crafting magical tools.

Charm Boxes

Native Americans, Greeks, Celts, and Egyptians all used magical boxes during ceremonies and for storing sacred objects. Christian religions followed suit—the famous biblical Ark of the Covenant was, in fact, a magical box. Spell work during medieval times involved boxes for love, health, fertility and home and in the fields, prosperity, and changes of luck. In more modern times, a young woman's "hope chest" contained her wishes, intentions, and materials for a happy marriage.

You can make charm boxes, also known as spell boxes, very easily. A job spell box should contain aventurine or peridot stones, patchouli incense, green candles, and ferns. You can make a psychic spell box with cloves, rosemary, and amethyst and quartz crystals. A good love spell box contains a pink candle, rose petals, two pieces of rose quartz, and two copper pennies. These are just some of the examples; more suggestions are in the appendix in the back of this book.

Mirrors

Throughout time, people have been looking for answers in mirrors, gazing balls, pools, and even using bowls filled with ink to peer into another dimension. Primitive people used obsidian and other shiny rocks to communicate with spirits. Surfaces that are shiny, smooth, and reflective have always lent themselves well to scrying and other intuitive work. Because of their use in scrying, mirrors came to be seen as magical portals to promote psychic awareness to other worlds.

It is possible to create your own scrying mirror and empower it with energy and intention in a variety of ways. First, find a round mirror with a frame that will make it easy to apply crystals or other objects with glue (I like to use wood or plastic). The frame should have a lot of surface area on which you can affix your magical objects. There are many objects that are suitable for your mirror. If you collect sea glass or shells and pretty rocks, those will suffice. If you don't have any objects on hand, visit a rock shop or a New Age store. You can purchase seashells and fifty to a hundred small crystals. The crystals can be various quartzes and semiprecious stones of similar shape and small in size.

You can use a rainbow of colors or you can stick with just one kind of stone. I prefer to use all amethysts on my mirror; I feel more connected to this lovely purple gem because it is my birthstone.

Before applying the clear-drying glue to your frame, clean it with a soft, dry cloth. Take your crystals, shells, glass or other items and affix them one at a time, in any pattern you like. Some examples of mirrors I've come across featured concentric circles of color, following the spectrum from dark red garnet to clear quartz, and gorgeous spirals and paisley prints all across the frame.

Different kinds of questing and querying may call for several different magic mirrors.

Different Gems to Use for Your Mirror

Peridot—Issues relating to self-image and matters centered upon you

Rough Rubies—Matters relating to love

Jade—Money matters

Sea Glass and Seashells—Effective for Water signs (Cancer, Scorpio, and Pisces), especially if gathered during a walk on the beach while searching for answers

Anyone who feels drawn to the ocean will benefit from a seashell magic mirror. Many of us go for walks along the water to think. Using seashells on your mirror can help you be twice as effective in finding your answers.

Swords and Knives

Swords were used before gunpowder as the weapon of choice for warriors. The concept of a sword to us is that it is wielded within the spirit world to keep bad energy and negativity at bay. With sword in hand, you are the master or mistress of your domain, and you rule your circle of magic with your spiritual weapon. You can make your own sword, or athame. Purchase the metalwork from a New Age store or from a sword specialist. Find crystals that represent what you want your sword to do and affix them to the sword. If your athame already has crystals on it, you can charge them with your energy.

Cauldrons

Iron kettles typically serve as cauldrons. You can make your own symbolic cauldron out of any bowl-shaped object, including large stones or crystal geodes.

Magic Cord

A magic cord is a rope that binds you to magic. Ideally, your nine-foot-long magic cord should be made from strands of red (the color of life) wool, or ribbon, braided and tied into a loop at one end to signify feminine energy, and left loose at the other end to represent male energy. If you are braiding your own magic cord, start your braid with three strands that are fourteen feet long to achieve the nine-foot-long cord. To compound the magical quality of your cord, weave crystal beads into the strands. I recommend using clear quartz crystal beads because they are energy amplifiers. Other meaningful crystals you might want to include are citrine for grounding, amethyst for improved intuition and psychic ability, blue lapis for creativity, rose quartz for love, and jade for prosperity and success in work.

Magic Bottles

Spell bottles, or magic bottles, have been around since the 1600s and were often filled with hair, nails, urine, or blood. Now, they are used to empower us and they also serve a more decorative purpose. Though their popularity has waned since the Elizabethan age when they were known as "witch bottles," they are still used for a variety of intentions. You can customize your own spell bottle with crystal stoppers. Put one in the garden to help keep your plants healthy. A spell bottle on the mantel will protect your home. One next to your bed will bring love and happiness. A bottle in the kitchen will guard good health. Spell bottles are used for protection primarily, but you can also put symbols of your dreams and desires in them: cinnamon for the spirit of life, a rose petal for peace, or rosemary for remembrance. Make your own magic bottle by filling it with symbolic objects and inscribing the sigil of your choice into the lid or cork top.

For a peaceful and secure home, gather a teaspoon of soil from outside of your house and put it in a bottle with some smoky topaz or brown jasper. Put the bottle into a potted plant near the entrance of your home, and think about the sanctity of your home every time you water the plant. As your plant grows, so will the tranquility of your residence.

A bottle with a rosebud or rose petal, rose essential oil, and rose quartz next to your bedside will help with love. For six days, take oil from the bottle and burn it in a pink candle. On the seventh day your romantic prospects will brighten.

For luck with money, place three pennies and some pyrite or jade in a bottle and put it near your workplace. Whenever you think about your finances, shake the magic bottle and your fortune should improve in three days.

Purification Broom

A purification broom can be used to purify any space, usually a home space. You can use a home purification broom to clear away bad energy after a fight with a loved one, or if you are feeling blue and want to sweep away the sad feelings. Rid negative energy from your personal space with your broom. You can even sweep the "blahs" out every morning to freshen your surroundings. This makes room for good energy you want to bring into your life. You don't need to clean intensely—just symbolically sweep to maintain your home as a personal sanctuary.

You can make your own purification broom. A broom purchased from a craft fair or broom-maker will serve you fine, as long as you add energy to it. Or, you can bind straw to a fallen tree branch and create your own. Use copper wire to attach the straw to the stick. Copper is associated with Venus, and this will lend an aura of beauty as you brush away negativity. Attach crystals to the handle or to the wire for further energy.

Scrying Tools

Scrying, the art of divining by looking into a reflective surface and receiving visions, has been used by witches, magicians, and others since pre-biblical times. The word "scry" forms the root for the English word "descry," which means reveal or discover.

The ancients had special prophets and priestesses who engaged in foretelling the future, and it is certain they used scrying tools from various crystals. Perhaps a chunk of black obsidian was the first scrying mirror used by a Stone Age shaman. All these centuries later, we still use crystal balls made from quartz and obsidian.

It is known that Queen Elizabeth I employed Dr. John Dee, a mathematician and metaphysician, in all matters of the heavens and unseen. Dee's assistants used a mirror of polished black obsidian, which led the next generation of magicians and psychics to prefer black mirrors. Dee and his assistants used scrying to call upon certain angels and reported hearing knocking, and even voices that sounded like an owl screeching, during sessions. The legacy of alchemist and metaphysician John Dee lives on, and modern seers such as Edgar Cayce have built on his foundation.

In addition to divining the past, present, and future, you can use scrying to contact spirit guides or to improve your skills of creative visualization. Some practitioners of scrying even use it as a gateway to the astral plane.

Although scrying tools usually have shiny surfaces, you can scry with nearly anything. Water, a mirror on the wall, a crystal sphere, a slab of rock, flames of fire, ink in a bowl, or the bottom of a teacup all serve as scrying tools. You may find that smooth, neutral surfaces are less distracting and images will come through to you with less distortion. The ritual you follow when cleansing your scrying tools can be as elaborate or as simple as you like. My ritual involves cleansing my scrying tools before and after each use with rainwater that has sat through at least one day of sun and one night of moonlight. Just like with crystal balls and other sacred tools, you should polish any scrying mirrors or surfaces with a clean cotton cloth and store them in a special protective bag.

Crystal Balls

For thousands of years, highly polished, glasslike spheres of beryl and quartz crystals have been in use by healers, shamans, witch doctors, and medicine men for divination. Beryl, long reputed as a stone of power, was favored by the Druids. Crystals were used to see the future throughout the Middle Ages and the Renaissance. The mythical wizard Merlin kept his crystal ball with him at all times. At the height of the Renaissance, Paracelsus, a great philosopher and physician, claimed that conjuring crystals should be used in "observing everything rightly, earning and understanding what was." They still appear in fairy tales and Disney movies, too. This proves how ingrained the notion of a crystal ball is to our culture. From these examples, we can see that crystal balls have been an integral part of our folklore, myth, magic, and metaphysics for a long time. When even mainstream people are familiar with the power of crystal balls, you can be sure their popularity has not declined in the slightest! The reputation and the power of crystal balls have not dampened, either. We still use them today for the same purposes they were used ages ago.

When selecting a crystal ball, your choice should not be taken lightly. This is a very personal tool that will become instilled with your energy. Crystal balls have their own authority and they can strongly influence the development of our psychic abilities. You should think of the crystal as a container that houses your energy and make sure it feels right for you. The crystal should feel comfortable to hold—not too heavy and not too light. You should not allow anyone else to touch your crystal ball. If someone does touch it, place the ball in a bowl of sea salt overnight to cleanse it of outside energy and influence. Because quartz crystal balls have an inherent power, you have to practice working with them first. Pure quartz crystal balls can be quite expensive, but the price is worthwhile if you are serious about harnessing your intuition and using it for good. Don't expect your experiences to be like the movies. Most of the people I know who use crystal balls, including many healers and teachers, see cloudy and smoky images.

Work with a partner to sharpen your psychic skills. Sit directly across from your partner with the crystal ball between you. Close your eyes halfway and look *at* the ball and *into* the ball while harnessing your entire mind. Empty out all other thoughts and focus as hard as you can. You will sense your third eye, the traditional seat of psychic awareness, begin to open and project into the crystal ball. By practicing this way, you will train your mind. The patterns you see will become clearer and your impressions more definite. You should trust that what you are seeing is real and find a place of knowing, as I do with my stomach. Verbalize to your partner what you see, and then listen to your partner as she reveals her visions to you. After at least three rounds of individual reading and revealing, share visions at the same time to learn whether you are seeing the same things!

You should also do crystal ball meditations on your own. In a darkened room, sit and hold your crystal ball in the palms of both hands. Touch it to your heart and then gently touch it to the center of your forehead, where your third eye is located. Then hold the ball in front of your physical eyes and, sitting very still, gaze into it for at least three minutes. Envision pure white light in the ball and hold on to that image. Practice the white-light visualization for up to a half hour and then rest your mind, your eyes, and your crystal ball. If you do this every day, within a month you should start to become an adept at crystal ball gazing.

When we gaze into a crystal ball, it is possible to see into the fabric of time, both the past and the future. At first you may be able to see a flickering, wispy, suggestive image. Some of you may be able to see clearly defined visions on your first try. Most of us have to practice and hone our attunement with the energy of the ball. You must establish clearly your interpretation of what you see. Many psychics use a crystal ball in their readings, and some report seeing images of clients' auras in the ball. Projecting information about people's lives is a huge responsibility, so you need to feel sure about what you are reading. Learn to trust your body's center of intuition. For me and for many other people, it's a gut feeling—literally in my stomach. If I don't get a feeling of confidence, of knowing in my gut, I simply explain that I don't know what I'm reading or I'm not really "getting anything." Be wary: It is far better to say you don't know than to fake it.

Making Wonderful Wands

Most likely, you will use a wand in many of your daily activities. I recommend making your own wand, though you can find beautiful pre-made wands in metaphysical shops.

To make your own wand, you should find a tree branch that has fallen to the ground on its own (no pruned branches!). Sand and polish the rough edges of the stick. The smoke of burning sage will nicely smudge the wand if you pass the stick through the smoke. You'll need a variety of crystals to complete your wand. Affix large quartz near the handle. You should then find crystals with properties that will complement your magic to the wand. I recommend using citrine as the pointer for the wand, as it aligns your self-identity with your spirit. Refer to the table for more on stones you can use to harness various powers.

Stones for Your Wand

Amber—Grounding

Amethyst—Balance and Intuition

Aventurine—Creative Visualization

Bloodstone—Abundance and Prosperity

Calcite—Warding Off Negativity

Fluorite—Communicating with Fairies and other Unseen Beings

Garnet—Protection From Gossip

Geode—Getting Through Periods of Extreme Difficulty

Hematite—Strength and Courage

Jade—Wisdom to Interpret or Realize Powerful Dreams

Jasper—Stability

Lodestone—Bringing a Lover Back into Your Life

Mahogany Obsidian—Feeling Sexy and Emanating Sensuality

Moss Agate—Powers of Persuasion and Healing

Quartz Crystal—Divining Your Dreams

Rhodochrosite—Staying On Course With Your Life's True Purpose

Rose Quartz—Love

Turquoise—Safety When Traveling

Watermelon Tourmaline—Help with Planning Your Best Possible Future

Consecrating Your Ritual Tools

You should design a personal consecration ritual for your magical tools. Use the following ritual as a simple "temple template" to build on. In essence, in this ritual you are dedicating yourself and your tools for the betterment of all and setting a foundational intention for your good works. Every time you acquire a new tool or treasure, perform this rite. As you grow in experience, you can embellish the ritual. Refer to your Book of Shadows. Is there a certain phase of the moon that brings you more clarity? Should you use corresponding colors, crystals, essential oils, incenses, and herbs for your own astrological sun and moon sign? Is there a specific deity with whom you feel an affinity? Use these correspondences to begin designing the rituals of your dreams. The more associations you learn and use, the more effective your power will grow. Keep good notes of your ritual work in your BOS, and soon you will become a "maestro of magic."

Ritual Tools That Need Charging

You will need a symbol of each of the four elements—air, earth, fire, and water—such as: a candle for fire, incense for air, a cup of water, a bowl of salt.

One way to design your own ritual is to look at Chapter 8, which explains the four elements. Choose a symbol from the information there or from the appendices. Also let your instinct guide you to choose as you wish or what you are inspired by.

Take the new ritual tool and pass it through the scented smoke of the incense and say:

Now inspired with the breath of air.

Then pass the tool swiftly through the flame of the candle and say:

> *Burnished by fire.*

Sprinkle the tool with water and say:

> *Purified by water.*

Dip the tool into the bowl of salt and say:

> *Empowered by the earth.*

Hold the tool before you with both hands and imagine an enveloping, warm white light purifying the tool. Now say:

> *Steeped in spirit and bright with light.*

Place the cleansed tool upon your altar and say:

> *By craft made and by craft charged and changed, this tool [fill in the actual name, bolline, Book of Shadows, etc.] I will use for the purpose of good in this world and in the realm of the gods and goddesses. I hereby consecrate this tool _____.*

Other tools you will use in ritual are more intangible. These include your breath, your intuition, your psychic powers, and your ability to focus your mental powers and spiritual intentions. Because they are intangible, only your intention can purify them. From time to time, you will use colors, herbs, oils, crystals, and numbers. Many of these ritual correspondences and associations have been passed down through the centuries, whereas many of them were invented by modern authors. Information on them can be found in the appendices in this book.

Crystals can also be charged. But tools that come from nature and are not "manmade," but are of divine design, such as flowers, feathers, and herbs, already contain an intrinsic magic of their own and can be used as you find them.

Your tools will collect and hold the magic that lives inside you. They will become instilled with your energy and stored at your altar or in your sacred space. They will become your power source and will magnify the strength of your ritual work. Your altar should be a place of peace and meditation where your spirit can soar. Adorned with your treasured objects and the tools of your practice, it is a place of focus where you can enrich your life through ritual. You can create a wellspring of spirit so you can live an enchanted life every single day.

You can also perform rituals and make magic without any tools or implements at all. Your intention alone is extremely powerful. This simple approach could be called "Zen magic." When you perform ritual in this way, you are one step closer to the methods by which early men and women created ceremonies.

Chapter Three

ESTABLISHING A POWER SOURCE: CREATING A PERSONAL ALTAR

Before there were temples and churches, the primary place of reverence was the altar. The word *altar* comes from a Latin word that means "high place." With a personal altar, you can reach the heights of your spirituality and grow higher in wisdom. You construct an altar when you assemble symbolic items in a meaningful manner and focus both your attention and intention. When you work with the combined energies of these items, you are performing ritual. Your rituals can arise from your needs, imagination, or the seasonal and traditional ceremonies that you find in this book and in others. In her marvelous collection, *A Book of Women's Altars*, Nancy Brady Cunningham recommends "bowing" or placing your hands on the ground in front of your altar as you end the ritual. "Grounding symbolizes the end of the ritual and signals the mind to return to an ordinary state of awareness as you re-enter your daily life."

An altar is a physical point of focus for the ritual, containing items considered sacred and essential to ritual work and spirituality. An altar can be anything from a rock in the forest to an exquisite antique table. Even portable of temporary altars can suffice—a board suspended between two chairs, for example, can become sacred space if it's consecrated. You can also create more than one altar if you have the room or have multiple, specific needs, such as attracting work, creativity, love, or healing. You can also have altars dedicated to various deities, if you desire to go deep into the energies of those gods or goddesses. You can also create shrines to honor a deity. A shrine is a place devoted to a divinity that becomes hallowed by that association. A shrine can be any size that suits your circumstance, such as a corner in a room, an entire building, or even a small shelf or windowsill that receives the light of the moon and sun. You can also use a large space or create a home temple space that accommodates highly complicated and intricate rituals for regular use with a large group.

Tradition usually places the feminine Goddess space on the left-hand side of the altar and the masculine God space on the right. Once you are comfortable and experienced with ritual work, you can begin to customize the altar.

Tripods: Mobile Altars

Outdoor altars are usually of a temporary nature—the beach is a wonderful place to set up a one-day altar on driftwood with seaweed and shells. There, unless the beach is too crowded, you can commune with the water deities and seek your deepest reaches of spirit. Forest, farm, and meadow offer earth and sky and the sanctity of nature in which to build your altar.

In Athens during the classical period, the lane leading to the temple dedicated to the god Dionysus was called the Avenue of Tripods because it was lined with small tripod altars; this was a holy road indeed. *Tripod* originates in the Greek word meaning "three footed," and these altars functioned as the sites of offerings. A three-footed altar is more practical for outdoor use than a regular four-legged table because it is stable on uneven ground. For your outdoor rituals, therefore, it's best to acquire a tripod that will provide a steady surface for your ritual work performed out in the holy realm of Nature.

At Delphi, the revered oracular center, the Pythoness and her sisters prophesied from the sacred seat of power, a tripod.

Fireplace Altars

Vesta is the Roman cognate of the revered Greek goddess, Hestia, "first of all divinities to be invoked" in classical rituals. In Greece, they had public hearths called *prytaneums* that came under the domain of the most revered Hestia, protector of "all innermost things," according to the great philosopher Pythagoras, who also claimed that her altar fire was the center of the earth. The altar of Vesta in classical Rome was tended by the Vestal Virgins and was also believed to be the very center of the earth. The insignia for the goddess Vesta was an altar table with flames at both ends, forming the Greek letter "pi," which is the numerological symbol for the Pythagorean sect.

The Vestal Virgins were the keepers of Rome's eternal flame. It was believed that if the fire of Vesta's altar went out, the Roman Empire would fall. In the fourth century, CE, Christians extinguished the vestal fire and began the process of erasing pagan religions and symbols.

The oldest lore of Hestia and Vesta comes down to us from Cicero's *De Natura Deorum* and stems from ancient forms of worship performed by people for whom the hearth and clan fires were under the province of the clan mother. During the ages when people were hunters and gatherers, one dominant woman took care of the clan by keeping the fire burning at all times. She fed her clan and became the presence at the very heart and center of the tribe. She held the tribal wisdom and stories, healed wounded hunters, acted as midwife, and took on the role of key caretaker of the people. These most basic needs of life—food and warmth provided by fire—created the solid center of life for clans and tribes and soon became holy. This sacred center of fire has continued to evolve through the millennia to our modern altars, shrines, and churches with their candles.

Fireplace altars today hearken back to this earliest custom. Home and hearth have primal appeal to the comfort of both body and soul. If you have a fireplace, it can become the very heart of your home. The fireplace is also one of the safest places of the ritual work of fire keeping. Sanctify your fireplace with a sprinkling of salt, and then set it up as an altar to the four seasons. Like the Vestal Virgins of old, you can keep a fire burning in a votive glass holder in the back of your fireplace and have an eternal flame. The fireplace can be your simplest altar and a reflection of the work of nature. If you don't have a real fire in your fireplace, you can place in it beautiful sacred objects—pretty rocks, feathers, seashells, glistening crystals, beautiful leaves, and anything representing the holiest aspects of the world around you. Let nature be your guide.

In ancient times, altars were blessed by blood. In fact, the word "blessing" is derived from the Old English *bletsain*, derived from the older form *bleodswean*, which means "to purify thought the application of blood." Indeed, altars were blessed in earliest times by the blood of animals or even captives from tribal wars. Now we bless altars by sprinkling them with salt, a magical substitute for blood.

Seasonal Altars

There are many reasons to create personal altars, and four of those reasons are the seasons of the year. You altar helps you to maintain balance in your life and deepens your spiritual connection to the world around you. A seasonal altar is your tool for ceremonies to honor Mother Nature and connect with the deeper wisdom of the earth. A seasonal altar enshrines the natural world and blends the energies of flowers, stones, shells, leaves, and any and all gifts of the season. I think of my seasonal altar as the middle ground between earth and sky, the meeting point of the four elements: earth, air, fire, and water. Creating a seasonal altar is a life-affirming act. It is my way of honoring our ecology and our planet.

Spring

You can create a wonderful outdoor altar for spring by planning two seasons ahead and planting tulip or hyacinth bulbs in a circle. When the flowers begin to bud, place an image or statue in the center. It could be a bust of the Greek youth, Hyacinth, immortalized in myth and in the gorgeous flower itself. Throughout the spring, you can stand inside your circle and pray or chant for the rebirth of the world all around you.

Summer

During this season of sun and heat, th fullness of life and growth can be celebrated with colors of yellow, green, and red. As you travel on vacation, bring back shells and stones and create an altar devoted to this season of joy.

Fall

The leaves are now falling and the harvest is here, calling for a gratitude altar that reflects the bounty and continuance of live. An arrangement of pumpkins, acorns, multicolored branches, and a handsome bouquet of leaves will honor the natural changes that characterize autumn.

Winter

White and blue represent snow and sky. Star-shaped candles and a bare branch on your altar symbolize this time to go within, explore the inner reaches of self, and draw forth the deepest wisdom for the coming spring. In *The Blessed Bee*, a Pagan family magazine, Selene Silverwind writes on the subject of setting up a candle-free children's altar. She emphasizes the importance of changing the altar for every season and holy day, specifically for Samhain, our modern-day Halloween, and Yule, the precursor to our Christmas. In so doing, Silverwind points out that you are "teaching children to connect with faith at a deep level," helping them participate in their religion in a physical way instead of trying to stand quietly at a ritual. You are also teaching them the meaning of the seasons and how they affect us.

Healing Altar: Crafting Well-Being

Creating a healing altar will safeguard your physical health and that of your loved ones. Your altar is your sacred workspace. It is charged with your personal power. Set up your healing altar facing north, the direction associated with the energy of manifestation. North is also the direction of the hour of midnight, the "witching hour," and an altar set up facing north at midnight promises potent magic.

To ensure healthful beginnings, find a pure white square of fabric to drape over your altar to make a *tabula rasa,* or altar equivalent to a blank slate. Take two green candles and place them in green glass holders or votive glasses and position them in the two farthest corners of the altar. Place your incense burner in the center between the two candles and light the incense. Sandalwood, cinnamon, camphor, and frankincense are all powerful purification incenses that are perfect for the creation of a healing altar. Burn one or all of these purification essences to consecrate the space. Adorn your altar with objects that symbolize healing energy to you. You may perhaps choose a candleholder carved from a chunk of amethyst crystal, which contains healing properties; an abalone shell with the iridescent magic of the oceans; a sweet-smelling bundle of sage; a small citrus plant bursting with the restorative power of vitamins; or a bowl of curative salts from the sea.

These symbolic items, and any others that you select, will energize your altar with the magic that lives inside you. It is also important that the altar be pleasing to your eye and makes you feel good when you look at it so that you want to spend time there each and every day. After you have been performing rituals there for a while, a positive healing energy field will radiate from your altar.

Altar Herbs

Refer to this list whenever you are setting up your altar and setting your intention for ritual work. It is a concise guide to the enchanted realm of herbs, essences, plants and plant properties.

- ✦ Benzoin can be used for purification, prosperity, work success, mental acuity, and memory.

- ✦ Camphor can be used for healing, divining the future, curbing excess, especially romantic obsessions, and a surfeit of sexuality.

- ✦ Cinnamon refreshes and directs spirituality. It is also a protection herb and handy for healing, money, love, lust, personal power, and success with work and creative projects.

- ✦ Clove is good for bringing money to you, for protection, for your love life, and for helping evade and deter negative energies.

- ✦ Copal should be used for love and purification.

- ✦ Frankincense is another spiritual essence that purifies and protects.

- ✦ Lavender is a plant for happiness, peace, true love, long life, chastity, and is an excellent purifier that aids with sleep.

- ✦ Myrrh has been considered since ancient times to be deeply sacred. It aids personal spirituality, heals and protects, and can help ward off negative spirits and energies.

- ✦ Nutmeg is a lucky herb that promotes good health and prosperity and encourages fidelity.

- ✦ Patchouli stimulates and grounds while engendering both sensuality and fertility. It also supports personal wealth and security.

- Peppermint is an herb of purification, healing, and love. It supports relaxation and sleep as it helps to increase psychic powers.

- Rosemary is good for purification, protection, healing, relaxation, and intelligence. It attracts love and sensuality, helps with memory, and can keep you youthful.

- Sage brings wisdom, purification, protection, health, and a long life. It can help make your wishes come true.

- Sandalwood is a mystical, healing, protecting essence that helps attract the objects of your hopes and desires and dispenses negative energies and spirits.

- Star Anise is a lucky herb that aids divination and psychism.

- Tonka Bean brings courage and draws love and money.

- Vanilla brings love and enriches your mental capacity.

- Wood Aloe is good for dressing or anointing talismans and amulets you want to use for protection.

Prosperity Altar: Using the Laws of Attraction

Your altar is the nexus of your magical powers; it is also your medium through which you give gifts to the Roman god of abundance, Jupiter, also known as Jove. Jupiter is a rain and thunder deity who also controls fertility. He will rain abundance down upon you if you gain his favor through ritual observance. His "jovial" qualities include leadership, jollity, generosity, expansiveness, and a royal manner. Your middle finger is your Jupiter finger and you can also increase your fortunes by leaving a ring on your altar overnight and then place it upon the middle finger of either hand. Ideally, for the best result, it will be a green or gold stone such as peridot, tourmaline, or citrine. If you can find a statue or bust of Jove, you should place this symbol on the right side of the altar, accompanied by the image of an eagle, which is the ideal prosperity altar emblem, as the eagle is Jupiter's bird totem. The eagles of Rome and America are this royal bird of the king of gods. Lapis lazuli, the beautiful blue stone beloved of the Egyptians, is also sacred to Jupiter. The alchemical symbol for this stone is the astrological sign of Jupiter in reverse, and the blue of the lapis stone is associated with the blue of the sky god. You can increase your prosperity by remembering one of the most basic principles of prosperity: *By giving, so shall you receive.*

To create a prosperity altar, consecrate the area with sea salt. Cover a low table with green and gold altar cloths or scarves and place matching candles on it. Each day, "recharge" your altar with an altar gift such as flowers, jade or other green crystals, golden flowers, scented amber resin, and coin-shaped pebbles. On any Thursday or new moon, light your candle at midnight and burn frankincense and myrrh incense. Make an offering of a golden fruit such as apples or peaches to Jupiter, and anoint your third eye with a corresponding essential oil such as myrrh, frankincense, apple, or peach. Pray aloud:

This offering I make as my blessing to all.
Greatest of gods, Lord Jove of the sky.
From you, all heavenly gifts do fall.
Most generous of all, you never deny.
To you, I am grateful, and so mote it be!
Put the candle in a safe, fireproof place and let it
burn all night. You will dream of your loved ones,
including yourself, receiving a bounty of material and
spiritual wealth.

Pot of Gold: An Abundance Altar Blessing

Cauldron magic is more about the act of brewing something new than it is about purification by water. To attract money, fill a big pot with fresh water and place it on your altar during the waxing moon. Pour into it an offering of a cup of milk mixed with honey. Toss handfuls of chamomile, woodruff, moss, and vervain into the cauldron. With your hands raised, say aloud:

I call upon you, gods and goddesses of old, to fill my purse with gold. In return, I offer your honey's gold and mother's milk. With harm to none and blessings to thee, I honor you for bringing me health and prosperity.

Place the offering bowl on your altar and leave the aromatic mixture there to imbue your space with the energy of abundance. When the magic has been fulfilled (or before the milk and herbs begin to spoil, pour it outside your home into the ground and bow in appreciation of the kindness of the gods and goddesses.

The Bounty of Nature

The following list of herbs can be used in ritual work whose intention is prosperity. Try these alone of in mixtures, tinctures, or incense. You can also plant a prosperity garden and refresh your abundance altar with herbs and flowers grown by your own hand.

Prosperity herbs include: allspice, almond, basil, bergamot mint, cedar, cinnamon, cinquefoil, clove, clover, dill, ginger, heliotrope, honeysuckle, hyssop, jasmine, myrtle, nutmeg, oak moss, orange, peppermint, pine sage, sassafras, vervain, and woodruff.

Peace of Mind: A Happy Home Altar

On a low table or chest of your choosing, place a forest green scarf and a brown candle to represent your family. Add lovely objects that you have found around your home and garden: a special fallen leaf, ocean-carved driftwood, lacey dried lichen, smooth stones, or whatever your heart desires. It is of utmost importance to add a bouquet of wildflowers native to your area that you have gathered close to your home or purchased locally. This bouquet will help integrate your home into your neighborhood and the geographic area in which you live. If possible, add a sweetly scented sachet of potpourri made from your home kitchen garden. Add personal mementos like photos or a locket with a photo of your spouse and children. Burn your favorite essential oils, the ones that create an aura of instant comfort for you, such as vanilla, cinnamon, or sweet orange neroli in an oil lamp. Finally, anoint the brown candle while concentrating on peace and bliss surrounding your home. Chant:

> *Here burns happiness about me.*
> *Peace and harmony are in abundance,*
> *And here true bliss surrounds.*
> *From now on, disharmony is gone.*
> *This is a home of peace and blessings.*
> *Here sheer joy lives.*

This consecrated space will ease your spirits at any time. Your altar connects you to the earth of which you are a part.

Home Protection Potpourri

Simmer this mixture whenever you feel the need to infuse your home and heart with the energies of protection. This will safeguard you and your loved ones from outside influences that could be negative or disruptive. Set your intention and gather together the following herbs:

¼ cup rosemary

4 bay laurel leaves

1 tablespoon basil

⅛ cup sage

1 teaspoon dill weed

⅛ cup cedar

1 teaspoon juniper berries

Mix the herbs together by hand. While you are doing this, close your eyes and visualize your home as a sacred place protected by a boundary of glowing white light. Imagine that the light runs through you to the herbs in your hand and charges them with the energy of safety, sanctity, and protection. Add the herbs to a pan filled with simmering water. When the aromatic steam rises, intone:

By my own hand, I have made this balm;
This divine essence contains my calm.
By my own will, I make this charm;
This precious potpourri protects all from harm.
With harm to none and health to all,
Blessed be!

Astrological Herbology

You can also choose the herbs for your altar based on your sun or moon sign. Explore making tinctures, incense, oils, potpourri, and other magical potions for your rituals using celestial correspondences. For example, if the new moon is in Aries when you are performing an attraction ritual, try using peppermint or fennel, two herbs sacred to the sign of the Ram. If you are creating a special altar for the time during which the sun is in the sign of Cancer, use incense oils, teas, and herbs corresponding to that astrological energy, including jasmine and lemon. These correspondences create a synthesis of energies that adds to the effectiveness of your magical work.

Sanctuary and Serenity Magical Potpourri

Potpourri was a medieval product revived by the Victorians, who used the symbolic meanings and powers of flowers. Grow these flowers in your kitchen garden or buy cut flowers. Dry them; then pace them in a pretty container. Choose flowers that connect with your astrological sign and personal energy from the following list:

Aries, ruled by Mars: carnation, cedar, clove, cumin, fennel, juniper, peppermint, and pine

Taurus, ruled by Venus: apple, daisy, lilac, magnolia, oak moss, orchid, plumeria, rose, thyme, tonka bean, vanilla, violet

Gemini, ruled by Mercury: almond, bergamot, mint, clover, dill, lavender, lemongrass, lily, parsley

Cancer, ruled by the Moon: eucalyptus, gardenia, jasmine, lemon, lotus, rose, myrrh, sandalwood

Leo, ruled by the Sun: acacia, cinnamon, heliotrope, nutmeg, orange, rosemary

Virgo, ruled by Mercury: almond, cypress, bergamot, mint, mace, moss, patchouli

Libra, ruled by Venus: catnip, marjoram, mugwort, spearmint, sweet pea, thyme, vanilla

Scorpio, ruled by Pluto: allspice, basil, cumin, galangal, ginger

Sagittarius, ruled by Jupiter: anise, cedar wood, sassafras, star anise, honeysuckle

Capricorn, ruled by Saturn: mimosa, vervain, vetiver

Aquarius, ruled by Uranus: gum, almond, acacia, citron, cypress, lavender, mimosa, peppermint, pine

Pisces, ruled by Neptune: anise, catnip, clove, gardenia, lemon, orris, sarsaparilla, sweet pea

New Moon Herbal Potpourri

This flower-infused potpourri is wonderful for clearing the way for the new in your life and planting "seeds" for new moon beginnings. You can also create a wreath with garlic bulbs for self-protection and insurance that your newly laid plans won't go awry.

Flower ingredients:

- ✦ Rose, Marigold, Cyclamen, Snapdragon, Carnation

Place the flowers in a bowl and then sprinkle them with a few drops of geranium, clove, and cinnamon oil. Place the mixture on the south point of your altar for the duration of a full lunar cycle, from new moon to new moon. A wreath of these same flowers with garlic cloves woven in will protect you from harm and illness. If you want to remain calm at your place of work, place a small, sweet-smelling bowl of your sanctuary incense on your desk for constant comfort.

Inspiration Altar: Unleash Your Creative Powers

Your personal altar is the ideal environment to incubate your ideas and can be a touchstone for daily conjuring and contemplation. By preparing your home and sparking your inner flames, you can clear away personal blocks and invite in friendly spirits who will aid you in personal pursuits, no matter what your line of work is.

On a low table or chest, place an orange or gold scarf and the following elements: yellow, orange, and gold candles for stimulating intelligence and clarity; bergamot oil for energy; and vanilla incense for mental power.

In an amber or clear glass bowl on the altar, place cloves and sage leaves or bundles. Next, add items that symbolize your personal creativity—perhaps a poem you wrote, a figure you sculpted, or a photograph you took of the altar.

Place benzoin, an herb for all-around mental strength and clarity, in your incense burner; it will bring inspiration from the psychic realm. Add any gifts from nature that inspire you—luminous shells, chunks of quartz, or feathers. Arrange your altar in a way that pleases you and stimulates your senses. Now, anoint the candle with bergamot essential oil while you meditate to clear your mind of any distractions. This is an essential step in opening the mental and spiritual space necessary to create, whether your intention is to create a ritual of your own design or an art project. Once you feel focused, light a sage leaf and wave it gently around so the cleansing smoke permeates your altar space. Light the anointed candles and the incense with a candle. Now set and speak your intention:

By my hand,
And by the blessing of the spirits,
The fire of my creativity
Burns bright,
Burns long,
Burns eternal.
Blessings to me and all who create!

Banishing Creative Blocks: Nature as Altar

To overcome any blocks of fear obstructing your creative output, you can dispel the negative energy by going for a walk in the nearest park. Find a round, flat rock, six to ten inches wide. This will become an altar supplied directly to you by Mother Nature, and it will have the purest energy. Begin by charging this stone on the full moon at your home altar. Light a white candle for purification, and then place your hand on the stone and chant three times:

> *Goddess of Night, moon of tonight,*
> *Fill this stone with your light,*
> *Imbue it with all your magic and might,*
> *Surround it with your protective sight.*
> *So mote it be.*

Ideally, you'll want to perform this spell three times on three consecutive full moons before you begin drawing upon its energy. Like your altar, your stone will be a reservoir you can turn to any time you feel stuck or uninspired. Make a pilgrimage to it when you require creative rejuvenation.

Aphrodisiacal Altar: Sacred Space for Love

To prepare for new relationships and deepen the expression of feeling and intensity to your lovemaking, create a center from which to renew your erotic spirit. Here you can concentrate your energy, clarify your intentions, and make wishes come true. If you already have an altar, incorporate some special elements, such as red candles or red crystals, or anything associated with Venus, like copper or a seashell to enhance your sex life. Your altar can sit on a low table, a big box, or any flat surface dedicated to magic. One friend of mine has her sex altar at the head or her bed. Begin by purifying the space with a sage smudge stick—a bundle of sage that you burn as your pass it through the space. Then cover your altar with a large red silk or silk-like fabric. Place two red candles at the center of your altar and place a soul mate crystal—two crystals naturally fused together—at the far right corner of the altar. These are available at metaphysical stores. Anoint your candles with jasmine and neroli oil. Also keep the incense you think is sexiest on your altar. Your sex altar is also a place where you can keep sex toys that you want to imbue with magic. Place fresh Casablanca lilies in a vase and change them the minute they begin to fade. Lilies are heralded as exotic and erotic flowers prized for their seductive scent.

Love Altar Dedication

Light candles and incense and dab the jasmine and essential oils above your heart. Speak aloud:

> *I light the flame,*
> *I fan the flame,*
> *Each candle I burn is a wish.*
> *My lust will never wane.*
> *I desire and I will be desired.*
> *Harm to none, so mote it be.*

Sacred Aztec Animal Altar: Become Conscious of Your Nagual

In Central Mexico, the Nahuatl Indians believe we all have at least one "animal soul." Like your natal chart, the animal soul, or *nagual*, is born exactly when you are. It is tied to your destiny. Legend tells us that our soul animals are kept and cared for in the underworld by the Aztec Lord of Animals. If you care for your *nagual*, you will also be under the safekeeping of the Lord of the Underworld. One excellent way to take care of your *nagual* is to create and altar to honor and work with it. Place photos and mementos of living loved ones and pets on an altar table in a circle to represent the world in which you live. Hang symbols or illustrations of protective presences on the wall behind your *nagual* altar—gods, goddesses, saints, orishas, or whoever you feel is benevolent. These deities connect you to the realm of the sky. Beneath your altar, place a treasure box of photos, gifts, or keepsakes in honor of your ancestors to please the spirits of the underworld and their realm, known as *Talocan*.

Place fresh flowers upon your altar every day and "feed" your soul animal, the Lord of the Underworld, and his throng. They will feel well served if each day you share with them water, food that you have cooked for yourself, freshly baked bread, and sweets. While it might seem surprising, the spirits of the nether realm like the earthly pleasures of tobacco and alcohol, so provide them with these offerings as well. Light a candle on your altar each and every day as homage. Obtain a feather, a horn, a bone, and another animal relic to place on your altar; it is important that you get this sacred object without harming any beasts. Your altar is a blessing to the animals of this world and the next.

You now have a way to discover your personal soul animal. The dream world is where we can encounter such spirits. Sleep in front of your Aztec altar, and pray to the Lord of the Underworld to care for you and reveal your *nagual* to you. Keep a dream journal and pay close attention to any animals that show up in your life. As you go about your day, take time to pet and commune with these animals if it is safe or possible to do so. Taking care of animals is our sacred duty and is pleasing to the spirits of Talocan.

Magical Animal Correspondences

- ✦ **Canary:** harmony, joy, love, luck
- ✦ **Chameleon:** mutability, color, invisibility, protection, and power over weather
- ✦ **Fish:** wealth, family, children, divination, finding your spouse
- ✦ **Frog:** initiation, transformation, regeneration, annihilation of the negative and psychic blocks
- ✦ **Bird:** travel, amplified mind and memory, divination
- ✦ **Cat:** independence, protection, uncovering secrets, spirits
- ✦ **Dog:** loyalty, sustained effort, hearing, friendship, guardian
- ✦ **Lizard:** dreams and dream divination, powers of the imagination
- ✦ **Lovebirds:** love and marriage, partnership and companionship
- ✦ **Parrot:** impersonation, mindless chatter, repetition
- ✦ **Snakes:** creativity, wisdom, psychism, rebirth and regeneration, relation to spirits
- ✦ **Spider:** insight, originality, new start
- ✦ **Turtle:** patience, perspicacity, longevity

Stone Shrines: Creating a Crystal Altar

By building a stone shrine, altar, or power center in your home, you can create a place for daily conjuring, rituals, and thinking. This will set the stage for you to focus your ideas and make them grow. Having a shrine in your home allows you to rid yourself of personal obstacles and invite friendly spirits. Your shrine will spark your inner flame and bring daily renewal. The more use an altar gets, the more energy it builds, making your spells even more effective.

Create your shrine on a low table covered in a white scarf. Set rainbow candles in an arc and then add black and white candles. Place a heatproof bowl containing amber incense (good for creativity and healing), and place it in the center of the rainbow, surrounded by quartz. You should also keep a stick of sage or a seashell on your altar for cleansing the space every day.

Prosperity stones should be to the far left on the altar, in the money corner. Romance crystals should sit to the far right on the altar.

The rest of your altar should consist of meaningful, personal symbols. They should reflect your spiritual aspirations. I keep fresh wildflowers in a vase, a statue of a goddess, abalone shells, a magnetite obelisk, and a rock-crystal ball on my altar. An obelisk or pyramid on your altar can be used for writing out desires and wishes. You can use just about anything—photos of loved ones, religious images, and so forth.

With your altar, you can create a bridge between your outer and inner worlds. It can even be a place where you commune with the deepest and most hidden parts of yourself. An altar is where you can honor the rhythms of the season and the rhythms of your own life. An altar is a touchstone, a place to see the sacred and incorporate it into your life each and every day. It can be your special corner of the world where you can rest and connect with your spiritual center. Creating and augmenting your altar every day is one of the most soul-nourishing acts you can do.

Following it a table of different crystals and what their presence on your altar will mean:

Altar Crystal: amazonite, aventurine, carnelian, chrysolite, chrysoprase, citrine, green tourmaline, malachite, yellow fluorite
What They Mean: Creativity

Altar Crystal: amethyst, azurite, celestite, lapis lazuli, moonstone, selenite, smoky quartz, sodalite, star sapphire, yellow calcite
What They Mean: Intuition

Altar Crystal: amethyst, magnetite, rhodochrosite, rose quartz, twinned rock crystals
What They Mean: Love

Altar Crystal: bloodstone, carnelian, citrine, dendritic agate, diamond, garnet, hawk's-eye, moss agate, peridot, ruby, tiger's -eye, topaz, yellow sapphire
What They Mean: Prosperity

Altar Crystal: amber, apache tear, chalcedony, citrine, green calcite, jade, jet, smoky quartz
What They Mean: Protection

Altar Crystal: azurite, chalcedony, chrysocolla, green tourmaline, hematite, rutilated quartz, tiger's-eye
What They Mean: Self-Assurance

Altar Crystal: amber, aventurine, blue jade, dioptase, Herkimer diamond, jasper, kunzite, moonstone, onyx, peridot, quartz, rhodonite
What They Mean: Serenity

Altar Crystal: carnelian, obsidian, quartz, selenite, sodalite, topaz

What They Mean: Success

Altar Crystal: agate, aventurine, bloodstone, calcite, chalcedony, citrine, dioptase, emerald, garnet, orange calcite, ruby, topaz

What They Mean: Vigor

Altar Crystal: emerald, fluorite, Herkimer diamond, moldavite, serpentine, yellow calcite

What They Mean: Wisdom

Chapter Four

THE FACES OF THE GOD AND GODDESS: MYTHOLOGY FOR MODERN TIMES

In designing your own rituals, you can pull from the wealth of the world's mythologies and create original rites based on the merging of your intention and the deity's sphere of influence. When selecting deities to call upon in your circles and ceremonies, you will need to have an understanding of gods and goddesses and their domains or powers. It is also helpful to have an affinity for the deity. You should feel drawn to whomever you invoke. If you feel inclined toward a specific deity, however, you must do your homework and find out everything you can about it. Good research can often reveal the reason for your intuitive affinity. Discretion and caution should be exercised with any god or goddess. Some divinities can have a major impact on your life and create chaos and disturbance. Kali, for example, is a dark and destructive goddess to be approached very carefully. Always be careful about invoking more than one deity at once, as there are often fundamental incompatibilities. Choose the deities you invite into your ritual carefully. For example, if you want to create a ritual of peace, you do not want to invoke Mars, who is a warlike divinity.

A few years ago, a group of female coworkers were experiencing great difficulties and harassment from their male boss. We created a ritual in which we called upon the Amazons to come to our aid. We created a circle and a ceremony for a situation none of us had experienced before. The energy of Penthesilea, the Amazon who stood against Achilles at the gates of Troy, was exactly the kind of defensive power we needed.

You can use the energy of the gods and goddesses in practical and helpful ways. A recently unemployed friend is researching the rites of Lakshmi, the Hindu goddess of prosperity, to invoke her generosity. An infertile couple can call upon Tara, the "Mother of all Buddhas," and a man looking for physical love could invoke the lusty Arcadian god, Pan.

Whatever your spiritual aspirations, there is surely a god or goddess to appeal to for help in your ritual work. With practice, experimentation, and time, you will begin to develop special relationships with deities that you can refine in the days and years to come. I strongly advise caution, common sense, and good manners in any dealings with the deities and denizens of the mythical realms. The friendship of fairies, for example, can be a blessing or a curse. If you call upon the fairy folk and then don't thank them and wish them well on their way, they may play pranks on you. Unless you work with consideration and cautiousness, The Good Neighbors will give you not-so-subtle reminders. They can make mischief in many ways. If your car keys suddenly go missing after you have invoked the fairies, you know you have been insufficiently courteous.

The Lord and Lady of Magic

Wiccan traditions frequently address twin deities and energetic dualities. The early Celtic goddess Danu, matriarch or the Tuatha de Danaan, or People of the Goddess Danu, is one of the goddesses venerated through this modern earth religion. Wicca is based on "the old ways" that hold a sacred connection to earth and to spirit—secrets, legends, and lore from European fertility cults that survived in various forms through the ages. Similar influences can be traced farther back in history to Paleolithic peoples who worshipped a hunter god and a fertility goddess. They represent the twofold principles of feminine and masculine energy inherent in nature. Wicca is enormously popular today, in part because it gives us freedom to create our own way of worshipping. Understanding the primal aspect of nature and the world as revealed in the gendered mysteries and myths, you can begin to plan rituals customized to fit your truest nature.

The God represents the sun. He is born on December 21, the winter solstice, and grows steadily until June 21, the summer solstice, when his power reaches its fullest. After Midsummer, his power wanes and he expires with the shortening daylight hours. On the longest night of the year, he is reborn again. The God is seen and represented in the physical and tangible. He can be seen in the hunt, in harvest, and it vitality, strength, sexuality, and passion.

> *The Goddess is creator of all; the Horned God is her consort. The Great Mother is the keeper of the cycles of birth, life, death and rebirth that are reflected in nature and the seasons. In some modern traditions, the God rules the physical world while the Goddess governs intuition, dreams, and the mind.*

The Triple Goddess is a combination of the Maiden, the young, sweet girl; the Mother birthing us all; and the Crone, the wise older woman. The three faces of the Triple Goddess are reflected by the waxing, full, and waning phases of the moon.

Invoking the Gods

Here is a selection of male deities to choose from in your ritual work. Included are some of the more commonly invoked gods and also some rare and obscure powers to consider for ceremonies and incantations. There are many rich resources for further study, such as mythology, which is a real tapestry of humankind's deepest truths, eternal struggles, and victories. I have learned many stories that have inspired and enriched my spiritual practices from books such as *Bullfinch's Mythology*, Robert Graves's *The White Goddess,* and James G. Frazer's *The Golden Bough*. Reading more about the history and folklore of deities will give you ideas and inspiration for rituals of your own creation.

Adonis

He is the god of love, and partner of the goddess of love, Aphrodite. Adonis is also an herbal deity with domain over certain plants and flowers, representing earth, fertility, and health. He is often invoked for love rites and spells. Ask Adonis for help with your gardens and for healing.

Apollo

He is the god of music and the arts and brother to Artemis, the Greek goddess of the moon and the hunt. If you are an artist of musician, ask Apollo to help you with the creative process or invoke him to banish writer's block.

Cernunnos

He is the Horned God of the Celts, sometimes also called Herne the Hunter. Cerunnos is a virile figure and represents man's sexual power. He is the one to call on for animal magic, for fertility, and any earth or environmental ceremonies you want to create and represent the wild man's spirit.

Dagon

He is the fishtail god of the Phoenicians who symbolizes the sea and rebirth. Originally a corn god, Dagon protects against famine and is also a god for oracles. He can be called on in water, gardening, and food rituals, and the celebration of life. Pisceans should familiarize themselves with this half man-half fish god when creating original rituals and should ask for Dagon's aid in divination.

Ganesha

This elephant-headed Hindu god of good fortune is the "remover of obstacles." Ganesha's domain is literature and he dispenses much wisdom. Summon him for any new business and for rituals of prosperity. Many people keep Ganesha figures and images in their offices and on altars to ensure that he keeps obstacles at bay. Money spells and work-related rites are greatly abetted by the presence of this agreeable divinity.

Hermes

He is associated with the Roman god Mercury and the Egyptian scribe god, Thoth. Hermes is an important deity for astrologers and metaphysicians as he is credited with the invention of alchemy, astrology and several other occult sciences. "Thrice Great Hermes" is revered by ceremonial magicians and is believed to be the wisest of all. He is the psychopomp who conducts the newly dead to the Underworld. Early Christians and Gnostics saw Hermes as a precursor to Christ, a divine prophet, the revealer of mysteries, and the giver of enlightenment. The Hermetic Cross is an adaptation of the insignia of Hermes. Hermes should be invoked if you are fashioning any rituals using the signs of the zodiac, foretelling the future, or acquiring the deepest wisdom.

Horus

He is the Egyptian god of light and healing, the "all-seeing eye," and child of Isis and Osiris. Horus is often depicted with the head of a falcon and the body of a man. You can turn to him in meditation and prayer when you are looking for his beacon of "enlightenment." Horus is also a healing power to invoke in healing rituals.

Janus

He is the gatekeeper from whom the word "janitor" comes. Janus has two faces and was at one time identified with Jupiter. He is the gatekeeper of the year, as the divinity of the first month of the year, January.

Lugh

His name comes from the Celtic languages, translating to "Shining One." He is a warrior sun god and also guardian of the crops. Lugh has his own festival, Lughnasadh, which takes place every year on August 1 to celebrate harvest time. A ritual of gratitude for life, luck, and prosperity will keep the bounty flowing. If you need a guardian or help with interpersonal problems at work, turn to Lugh as your defensive deity.

Mithra

He is the "Bringer of Light," a Persian god of the sun and protector of warriors. Mithra corresponds with the element of air and comes from a deep mystery tradition of Mesopotamian magic and fertility rites. If you have a loved one in a war far away from home, you should create a special altar for your beloved with Mithra, who is the "soldier's god."

Odin

He is the Norse equivalent of Zeus and Jupiter and is King of the Aesir. Odin rules wisdom, language, war, and poetry. You can appeal to him by carving runes or writing poetry. Odin can help you with any kind of writing, giving you the energy to forge ahead with purpose and passion. He can even help you write your own rituals and poetic magical chants.

Osiris

He is the Egyptian god of death and rebirth who also takes care of the crops, the mind, the afterlife, and manners. Husband to Isis and father of Horus, Osiris is a green god who is deeply connected to the cycles of growing and changing seasons. Turn to this god for rites of remembrance and for help with grief and mourning.

Pan

He is the goat-like god of the pastoral world as well as of lust and fertility. Pan represents the earth element and can be invoked for any erotic spells or ceremonies of a sexual nature. Call on Pan any time you want to have fun. As a minor love god, he is an essential guest for Beltane, a modern Pagan version of Valentine's Day.

Talieisin

Although not technically a god, this monumental figure is said to live in the land or "summer stars" and is invoked in higher degrees of initiation in some esoteric orders. Talieisin is the harper poet from Welsh tradition, steeped in magic and mystery. He is associated with the magic of poetry, and embodies wisdom and clairvoyance. Talieisin is a helpmate to musicians and creative folks. If you are a solo practitioner and want to create a ceremony of self-initiation, Taliesin is a potent power to engage.

Thor

The Norse sky and thunder god of justice and battle uses his thunderbolt to exact his will. Medieval Scandinavians believed the crack of lightning and thunder was Thor's chariot rolling through the heavens. Turn to Thor when you need spirituality to solve a legal matter. He is also a powerful protection deity to use in ritual.

Invoking the Goddesses

Below is a group of goddesses you can invoke and honor in your ritual work. I strongly advise placing images of a goddess on your altar when you need her aid, her strength, or her special qualities. Please refer to the chart on page in the back for a quick breakdown.

Aradia

She is the Italian "Queen of the Witches" who descends to earth to preserve the magic of the goddess, Diana, her mother. Through Aradia's lineage, she is also a lunar deity. She is affiliated specifically with Dianic Wicca. Aradia is an excellent goddess to invoke for protection of for any moon rituals you perform or create.

Artemis

She is the Greek goddess of the moon. In her Roman form, Diana, she is the deity to whom Dianic witches and priestesses are devoted. She is a bringer of luck, the goddess of the hunt, and a powerful deity for magic and spell work. As the huntress, she can help you search out anything you are looking for, whether it is tangible or intangible. As a lunar deity, she can illuminate you. Invoke Artemis when you want to practice moon magic, and study her mythology further to design original lunar ceremonies. Enshrine her to bring good luck.

Athena

She is a goddess who rules both wisdom and war. Athena is a deity to invoke if you are doing ceremonies for peace, learning, protection, or any work-related issues. She can help you overcome any conflict with friends, families, or foes.

Bast

She is the cat goddess and the Egyptians' great protector. Her domain includes cats, childbirth, healing, passion, pleasure, joy, and happiness. Bast is associated with the element of fire. Call upon her to watch over you when you travel. If any of your feline friends are taken ill, pray to Bast and create a healing altar and ritual for your cat with a statue of her on the left side. Bast is a wonderful deity to develop a relationship with, and she can come into your life in the form of a stray cat. Remain open-minded about unexpected new animal friends. They could be Bast on a mission!

Brigid

She was a Celtic solar goddess of poetry, smithcraft, and healing before the Catholic Church canonized her as a saint. Brigid is dually connected to the elements of water and fire. One way to bless water for ceremonies, your altar, and home is to pray to Brigid to sanctify the water. She is a guardian for all animals and children, taking care of all matter related to child rearing. Brigid is also a goddess of inspiration. You can create creativity rituals or purification rites that include Brigid.

Ceres

She is the great Roman grain goddess. Think of her every time you have some cereal, which is named after her. The early summer festival, the Cerealia, honors Ceres for supplying the harvest and an abundance of crops. Any ceremony for planting, growing, and cooking could involve this bounty-bringer. If you are going to plant a magical garden, craft a ritual with Ceres and make and outdoor altar to this grain goddess.

The Eye Goddess

She is an extremely ancient Mediterranean deity depicted as an all-seeing eye. She was a goddess of justice in the form of a pair of huge, unblinking eyes, and no transgression could be concealed from her. The Eye Goddess's first appearance was around 3500 BCE. You can conjure the Eye Goddess's powers of justice with the depiction of eyes and invoke her assistance any time you need the truth brought to light. You can also practice simple protection magic for the home and for your car with eyes watching out for you. Her symbol is sometimes mistaken for the evil eye, which makes workers of mischief nervous and causes thieves to think twice before committing a crime.

Hathor

She is the "cow goddess" who represents life, beloved in ancient Egypt for her ability to bring fertility. Hathor was also associated with royalty, and her priests were artists, singers, dancers, trained midwives, and seers. As the celestial cow, she held the golden disk of the sun in between her horns. Hathor's other sacred animals include the lion, cobra, falcon, and the hippopotamus. The sacred sistrum, a rattle used in ritual, was used to summon her. Mirrors were also her sacred tool. During spring rains and floods, you can stage a ritual dance for her to sanctify the joy of life. Invite your friends and let your imagination run wild with headdresses, costumes, and masks. Rattle, drum, and sway into the great dance of life.

Hecate

She is a crone goddess who shows her face in the dark moon. Hecate is the goddess of where three paths meet and the banisher of evil, which serves us well in rites of closure, "letting go," and getting rid of any negatively charged aspect of your life. Any time you want to bring something to an end, invoke Hecate for help. Funeral rites or ceremonies of remembrance, especially those for older women, are appropriate occasions for summoning Hecate. As the personification of the dark moon, she is also the goddess of divination and prophecy. Try creating a dark moon prophecy circle and invite her for deep and wise insight. Design a ritual during the dark moon with Hecate for ultimate feminine wisdom and a fresh new beginning.

Hestia

She is the goddess of home and hearth whom the Romans knew as Vesta. Hestia is associated with the element of fire and is concerned with the safety and security of the individual as well as families. As goddess of the hearth, she rules the kitchen, making it possible to perform magical baking recipes with your mixing bowl serving as a cauldron, enchanting it with spices such as cinnamon and cloves. Hestia is the perfect deity to help design a new house. She is a blessing there to help you with cleaning and purification rituals in your living space and sacred space.

Hokmah

She is the holy spirit, an ancient Hebrew goddess of wisdom, the Gnostic Sophia. Hokmah is also related to Egypt's Ma'at, mother of creative works of power from which the universe was formed. It was believed by scholars that *bereshith*, the very first word of Genesis, really refers to this goddess of wisdom. The book *Targum of Jerusalem* discusses the first words of Genesis and the goddess of wisdom at length. *Bereshith* is traditionally translated as "in the beginning." Hokmah appears often in pre-Christian and early Christian writings, and Philo of Alexandria described her as the spouse of Jehovah. King Solomon himself decreed that Hokmah must be obeyed in "The Wisdom of Solomon," a chapter not included in the biblical canon and established as apocryphal. Hokmah's symbol, like that of Venus, is the dove.

You can summon the eternal wisdom of Hokmah with an image of a dove on your altar. Ignored and redacted from history, she holds vast beneficial power. You can design a women's mystery rite by meditating on this ancient spirit. Allow inspiration to come and be literally filled with the holy spirit. Her wisdom will enlighten you and reveal how the rite should be designed.

Isis

Isis is the only goddess who could guarantee the immortality of the Egyptian pharaohs, resurrecting them as she did Osiris. Her worship spread and became an enormous cult that appealed to the entire Roman Empire. She has great appeal as a divine mother. Isis is the daughter of Nuit, the goddess of the sky, and of Seb, the god of earth. The ancients worshipped her as the Queen of Heaven, and she is often depicted with wings.

Isis is the link between birth and death and can be invoked in rituals designed to celebrate existence under our banner of stars.

Juno

She watches over the daughters of the earth, and as such attends nearly every female need and function. The Latin word for a female soul is *juno*, and as the mother of all women she can be invoked in any woman's mystery of birth, menses, croning, and death. Some of her aspects include a goddess of fate, Juno Fortuna; of war, Juno Martialis; of marriage, Juno Domiduca; of bones, Juno Ossipage; of mother's milk, Juno Rumino. Because Juno is a special protector of brides, you can invent a Juno-centered ceremony to celebrate your own nuptials or those of a friend who espouses women's spirituality.

Kali

She is the Hindu goddess of the ever-cycling nature of creation and destruction. Kali can be called on to protect and defend women of any age. If you are afraid for yourself, pray aloud to Kali in her destroyer aspect, which wears a necklace of skulls that will scare off any attacker. If someone is recovering from an abusive relationship, Kali can be called on to help with healing and renewing courage and self-esteem. Kali is not to be feared, but respected and admired. One of Kali's aspects is the Indian goddess, Vac. This incarnation of Kali is the "Mother of All Creation" who spoke the first word, *OM*, which gave birth to the universe. She also invented the Sanskrit alphabet.

An image of Kali in your office or cubicle will keep trouble at bay and keep you strong and active and fully in your power. Give offerings to her occasionally with your girlfriends in your life with "womanpower" rituals.

Persephone

She is the Greek goddess of the underworld. She spends half of the year, fall and winter, with her husband, Hades, in the underworld, and the other half, spring and summer, above with her mother, Demeter. Persephone is a wonderful deity to invoke once winter has ended, since her return from below marks the beginning of spring. Also, if a dear friend is moving, you can create a pomegranate ritual to ensure regular visits. Persephone is also associated with the element of earth. During equinoxes, you can design rituals with plants, flowers, trees, and fruits of the seasons and acknowledge Persephone's transition to the other world. This goddess represents the balance between light and dark.

Selene

She is the full moon, another Greek aspect of the lunation cycle. She sheds light on the world and on all of us, inside and out. Her mythology is that as a teacher of magic and all things supernatural, she passed her special knowledge on to her students. She is also a mentor, and her light illuminates our intelligence and ability to think clearly with logic.

Shekina

She is the female deity who is "God's glory" and the spouse of an ancient Hebrew god. Older rabbinical texts describe her as the "splendor that feeds angels." She was the only one to get away with being angry with the Hebrew god. She is associated with Sophia and Mari-Anna. Having been redacted from all biblical texts, Shekina was veiled in obscurity until some medieval cabbalists rediscovered her. Glimmerings of Shekina show up in passages of the Talmud telling the story of the exiled Israelis wandering into the wilderness with Joseph's bones and a second ossuary, or "bone box," containing "the Shekina" in the form of a pair of stone tablets. Be very creative in designing rituals, altars, offerings, and ceremonies honoring this deity, since you are rebuilding a lost part of goddess history. One daring ritual could include calling a women's circle and rewriting the tablets of wisdom. Call upon your inner Sophia and inner knowledge for guidance in this highly original approach to ritual.

Sige

This Gnostic goddess charges us to be silent. In Roman mythology she stands for the secret name of Rome, which could not be spoken aloud, and thus she is depicted as a hooded woman with a finger to her lips. Gnostic texts speak of Sige's origins as the mother of Sophia. She is the primordial female creator: out of silence came the *logos,* or the word. The cult, rituals, and folklore regarding Sige were held so strictly secret that we know nothing about them now. But, since creation comes out of silence, there is complete creative freedom for you to recreate new myths, stories, and celebrations for this obscure deity. Silent celebrations, quiet meditations, and secret spells no doubt have the approval of Sige.

Sunna

She is the ancient Germanic goddess of the sun, proof that our big star is not always deified as male. The Teutons also referred to this very important divine entity as "Glory of Elves." In the great Northern European saga, the *Poetic Edda*, Sunna was said to have a daughter who sheds light on a brand-new world. Other sun goddesses include the Arabian Attar, the Japanese Amarterasu, and the British Sulis, "the sun's eye."

Venus

The Roman goddess of love, Venus is associated with ultimate femininity, ultimate sexuality, ultimate fertility, and all that is beautiful. The word *veneration* means to worship Venus, and she should be venerated in all the love spells of your own design as well as celebrations and circles taking place on her day—Friday. The lore and mythology of Venus is well known, as she has been imprinted on our consciousness as the beautiful naked nymph on a half shell rising out of the foamy wave of the ocean. Honor her by creating venerable dances on the beach, and write love prayers and poems inspired by the love in your own heart.

Summary: Gods and Goddesses of the Ancients

Supreme God: Woden, Frigg (Germanic); Jupiter, Juno (Roman); Zeus, Hera (Greek); Ra (Egyptian); Marduk (Babylonian)

Creator: Ptah (Egyptian); Anu (Babylonian)

Sky: Frigg (Germanic); Jupiter (Roman); Uranus, Zeus (Greek); Nut (Egyptian); Anu (Babylonian)

Sun: Apollo (Roman); Helios (Greek); Ra (Egyptian); Anu, Anshar (Babylonian)

Moon: Diana (Roman); Artemis (Greek); Thoth (Egyptian); Sin (Babylonian)

Earth: Sif (Germanic); Tellus (Roman); Gaia (Greek); Geb (Egyptian); Enlil (Babylonian)

Air: Enlil (Babylonian)

Fire: Hoenir (Germanic); Vulcan (Roman); Hephaestus (Greek); Girru (Babylonian)

Sea: Niord (Germanic); Neptune (Roman); Poseidon (Greek)

Chapter Five

MOTHER MOON: CELESTIAL GUIDANCE AND RITES OF THE NIGHT

Since prehistory, we have looked into the night sky with wonder. The moon is both magical and majestic and she rules the ocean tides, the crops in our fields, and our moods and emotions. The moon is mysterious and reflective. Aside from the sun, our brightest star and the source of life, the moon is the single-most important light in our sky. Every culture in the world, both past and present, has moon lore, myths, rites, and a great respect for our favorite "night light." The early Babylonians called the moon "the boat of life," while the Taoist Chinese believed the moon was a white dragon. A most unusual perspective came from the usually reasonable Plutarch, who theorized that girls grew into women as a result of a female essence that came down from the moon. The very name of our galaxy, the Milky Way, comes from the mythical white cow that jumped over the moon. It may well be that no other celestial object is as revered as the moon. A common and beloved ritual, baking, decorating, and eating a birthday cake, is descended from the Greek custom of celebrating the monthly birthday of the moon goddess Artemis with full-moon cakes. To this day, modern Pagans "draw down the moon" in some rituals. In Asia, it is said that the moon is the mirror that reflects everything in the world. Some cultures consider the moon to be male and the sun female: for example, the Japanese honor the sun goddess Amaterasu and her brother the moon god Tsukiyomi. In this chapter we will explore some of the myths and lore of the moon, and supply you with many approaches to ritual from the treasury of our human history. We will begin by exploring each phase of the moon and suggest a sample ritual. Let Luna be your guide as you design and develop your own moon ceremonies and rites of the night.

Phases of the Moon

Performing a ritual at the optimal time of the lunar cycle will maximize your power. As you read, keep this basic magical guideline in mind: Each lunar cycle begins with the new moon phase, when the moon lies between the sun and the earth so its illuminated side cannot be seen from the earth. During the next two weeks, the moon gradually waxes until it has moved to the opposite side of the earth. When the moon has reached the far side of the earth, its lit side faces us as the full moon. Now it begins to wane until it apparently vanishes. Then it cycles again.

The entire cycle takes approximately a month, during which the moon orbits the earth. To determine the sun sign governing the moon on any given day, you will need a celestial guide or almanac. My favorite is Llewellyn's *Daily Planetary Guide.* The moon moves into a new sign every two to three days.

The New Moon

The new moon is sometimes called Diana's Bow, a reference to the Roman goddess of the hunt. The Maiden phase arrives when the moon comes out of the shadows and begins to show its first glimmering crescent of light. The new moon is the time to begin new projects and bring new energy into your life. It is an auspicious time for blessing rituals. I save new ventures to begin them on the new moon. Now is the perfect time to plant a garden, reorganize your office, start a new business, begin an art project, or embark on a new relationship—anything that requires the energy of developing and growing. Budding and building are the key words for the new moon.

New Moon, New Beginnings

This new moon time is a wonderful opportunity to involve yourself in personal improvement and transformation, whether spiritual or health-related, like practicing yoga or following a new diet. The new moon has great advantages for healing. This phase is also marvelous for rituals that draw something to you. Rituals and charms commenced in the new moon can have tangible results by the next new moon. Divinatory rituals performed during the new moon can also bring great clarity.

Here is a new moon ritual to ignite new energy for new projects and new beginnings.

The Eternal Flame

When the first narrow crescent of the waxing moon appears in the twilight sky, place a green candle beside a white lily, freesia, or a spicy smelling stalk of stock (a plant in the mustard family). Make sure the flower you choose has a scent that you really love, as the floral essence is key to stirring your emotions, dramas, and visions. White flowers have the most intense aromas. For me, the best flower is a white gardenia floating in a clear bowl of water.

Anoint the candle with tuberose or rose oil. Take a handful of seeds such as sunflower, walnuts, or pistachios, still in their shells, and place them in front of the candle. Close your eyes and recite this aloud:

> *Under this newest of moons,*
> *In Eden fair, I walk through flowers*
> *In the garden of my desires,*
> *I light the flame of my mind,*
> *I plant the seeds of things to come.*

Now speak out what you want in the coming time. By speaking your desires and intentions aloud, you are planting seeds for your future.

When the candle has burned down, take the little bit of leftover wax, the nuts and seeds, and your flower of the new moon and bury them in your yard or in the soil around your houseplants. Wonderful new energy and new ideas will begin to bloom immediately in your life. As the moon grows, you should continue to build upon what you began with the new moon. Projects and rituals you initiated will continue and you will begin to see changes. This is an active, creative time. You should use it to the fullest in your personal rites and ceremonies.

Waxing Moon

As the moon grows to full, rituals for bringing about positive change are the order. Ceremonies for luck, growth, and love will succeed during the waxing moon. The moon is in full

Maiden aspect for the fourteen days of the typical waxing period. Invocations for personal and positive change in your environment and the people around you will burgeon during this phase.

Invoking the Blessing of Nikadama

In China and Tibet, the mountain holds a special place in mythology and religions because they are so close to the sky. Tibetan Buddhists bring down the blessings of one of their most benevolent deities, Nikadama, the female protection deity who lives high in the Himalaya Mountains. To get her attention, tie strings of Tibetan prayer flags or white silk scarves to the trees and bushes near your home or in your yard. If you live in the city, you can hang them at your door to fly in the breeze. Every time the flags and offering scarves flutter in the wind, Nikadama is blessing you! Here is a very simple ritual you can perform alone or with loved ones to bring luck and blessings during the waxing moon. Spring is the best time to do this, but any waxing moon will bring fortune and providence.

Tibetan Prayer Flag 101

The color symbology of a string of Tibetan prayer flags comes from hundreds of years of tradition. Monks always fly the blue flag highest and it should be at the top of the string of flags, as it symbolizes the closest you can get to higher consciousness. Other colors that represent aspects of nature are as follows:

Blue: Sky
White: Cloud
Red: Fire
Green: Water
Yellow: Earth

Full Moon

When the moon is full, that means Mother Moon is at her zenith, parading in all her glory across the night sky. Rituals that transform and call forth your personal power and psychic awareness are called for at this time. The full moon is powerful and promotes strength and supremacy. Her luminous glow surrounds us, and now is the time to clean our ritual tools, scrying mirrors, tarot decks, and crystals. Take time to honor the moon goddess during this phase. Wiccans have a tradition of "drawing down the moon," which is a way of invoking the moon's power into your body, thereby embodying the lunar goddess.

Lunar Eclipse Ritual: Hunting the Sun

In Norse mythology, the sun and moon were created by benevolent gods to bring light to a dark world. The Norse gods placed the sun and the moon in chariots that flew across the sky, shedding light on the entire world. However, the hungry Fenris Wolf chased the sun and, every once in a while, caught up with it and devoured it, which darkened the sky. When the sun began to burn the insides of the wolf, he would cough it back into the sky. This, according to Nordic folklore, is how eclipses happen.

Eclipses are celestial events that still fascinate us, and you can easily gather a group together for a ritual. Invite enough people to form two circles. Twenty is ideal so you have ten in each circle. Ask half of the people to wear all gold and the other half to wear all black. Those in black are the Fenris Wolves who will eat the sun, represented by those in gold. For safety, everyone needs to wear their best UV protection sunglasses (in gray, brown, or green) to safeguard their eyes.

Well in advance of the eclipse, form the circles and tell the story of the Fenris Wolf. Ask other people if they have any experiences of past eclipses that they can share with the group. Ten minutes before the eclipse begins, have the gold group form a circle around the black group. Direct the two circles to walk, dance, or move in opposite directions. Five minutes before the eclipse begins, have the black group move outside the gold circle and have the gold circle sit down.

When I was at a retreat in Mendocino, California, I witnessed people barking, howling, and moaning to express their roles and the immense power of this imminent heavenly happening. During the actual event, however, everyone will grow silent and experience the extraordinary power of this rare and sacred heavenly moment. As always, people should only look at the sun through special filters. The best way to experience this ritual is to sit with eyes closed and *feel* its immensity.

In about ten minutes, as the eclipse is occurring, the black-garbed folks should walk away one by one at least ten feet and sit in a circle. When the gold circle is the only group left, the symbolism is the full reappearance of the sun.

When people begin to stir and want to talk, ask everyone to share what came to mind. People often have amazing insights and visions during eclipses. Document these "eclipse epiphanies," if possible, and remember to include them in your storytelling for the next solar eclipse ritual.

One Moon for All the World

Although many cultures around the world have had ceremonies to celebrate the full moon, only a few are still practiced today. The Balinese have received wide interest for their full moon ritual, and Bali has become a popular destination for people on a pilgrimage or for tourists who want to be in touch with the sacred. A growing number of nature-worshiping people gather in magical circles to do the same in North America and Europe.

In Peru there is a sacred site, the Quenko-Labyrinth of the Serpent, where full moon ceremonies are held. It is believed that on this site you can experience your true connection with the earth, the feminine, and life, for this sacred site embodies the Goddess. Rites of passage and sacred ritual offerings have been performed here for centuries. Shamans teach this as an important way for humankind to connect with and balance nature and community.

Balinese Full Moon Ceremony

Nearly every temple and Bali celebrates this monthly event.

Essential elements for this ritual are incense, offerings of fruit and lots of flowers, rice, and holy or blessed water.

Gather a group of like-minded folks and head to the nearest body of water—a lake, pond, creek, river, or the ocean. Nature will be your temple.

Begin by sitting in a circle and making garlands of flowers. You should talk, laugh, or be silent as you wish, but most important, be comfortable. When everyone is settled with a garland of flowers, place the garland around the neck of another person. Light the incense and set the rice and holy water in the middle of the circle.

Go around the circle and offer the water to people, sprinkling it on them gently with your fingertips in the Balinese fashion, and offer everyone a cupful of the holy water to rinse their mouths with so the words they speak will be holier. Each person should make a fruit or flower offering to the gods, and lay it near the cleansing smoke of incense. After the offerings are made, everyone should anoint their neighbor's forehead with grains of rice and speak blessings aloud for each person. If a body of water is accessible, get wet, even if it is just to dip your hands or walk in the water.

Silently acknowledge the blessings in your life through prayer and meditation, and, again, give quiet thanks to the gods for the gift of your life. Unlike most Western-based rituals, there is not much talking during the Balinese Full Moon Ritual. Bask in the tranquility and listen to your thoughts.

Pung-Mul Norj

Pung-Mul Nori is a full moon ritual that has been performed for about two thousand years and continues to this day. Korean traditional folklore combines ritual, acrobatics, dance, and music. *Toyo Ongaku*, music for this ritual, has remained popular since ancient times when it was performed day and night to protect the crops and dispel evil spirits.

Developed by and for Korean farmers, this ritual was devised to help them keep up their strength and their spirits during the exhausting labor of planting and harvesting season. Many years ago, it was especially important for everyone in the community to participate in this expression of thanksgiving. Every man, woman, and child who was physically able to do so had to sing, dance, drum, play instruments, and perform acrobatics. The word *Nori* in Pung Mul Nori means to play and, indeed, this is one of the most playful of all the world's moon rituals.

Lunar Lore: A Thirteen-Moon Guide to Rituals Throughout the Year

Thanks to the way the earth orbits the sun and the way the moon orbits the earth, our calendar year contains thirteen full moons and moon cycles. Here are some traditional correspondences from astrology and folklore:

January is known as the Cold Moon or Wolf Moon. This is the time for new beginnings, for planning for and conceiving a child, as well as making other goals for yourself, your working life, your health goals, and any other aspirations. You should look deep inside yourself and take this time during the Wolf Moon to think about and contemplate what is most important to you, and how you can have what is truly meaningful in your life. The Cold Moon is also when you should perform protection spells for yourself and your loved ones and rituals of safekeeping for your home and the people and things you really care about.

February is the time of the Wild Moon or Snow Moon, Now you can begin growing the seeds you panted in your soul during last month's Wolf Moon. The Wild Moon is an excellent time for purification rituals and for cleansing old "bad" energy out of your life, your home, your psyche, and your office. The Wild Moon can be a time of great healing, especially after a ceremony for energy cleansing. One of the best cleansing rites you can perform is true acceptance of yourself, letting go of all self-loathing and saying goodbye to your inner critic. A ritual of self-love and recognition would be a wonderful observance of the Wild Moon of February.

March is Crow Moon or Seed Moon and is a time to balance your life energies. After the cleansing and goal-setting of the past two moons, now you can begin to activate your plans.

This March full moon is also an excellent time to concentrate on prosperity. Crow Moon is a wonderful time for an abundance ceremony.

April is the Hare Moon or Pink Moon, one of the most creative times of the year. This is the moon when you can act on what you have been dreaming of during the earlier moons. You can begin to manifest your deepest desires during both in terms of your aspirations and your amorous side, since Hare Moon is made for love spells and other rites of romance. Pursue your passions with confidence and optimism.

May is the Merry Moon, the Flower Moon, the Green Month in terms of green magic and the time of the fairies. Nature has now burst into a glorious full spring. In May, your inner wisdom is at its height. Now is the time to connect with nature and explore the beauty of our beautiful and sacred planet. Rites of spring are a wonderful way to commune with spirit.

June is the Mead or Strawberry Moon, the Lover's Moon. Now we can taste the sweetness of life and celebrate our strength and fruitfulness. It is a time of security and protection. Assess the results of all that you have planned and seeded in the past months.

July is the Thunder Moon or Blessing Moon, a time for divining meaning and focusing on spirituality. Now we can expand our consciousness and listen to the messages of our dreams. The Thunder Moon is when we receive the blessings of the rain and feel the charged energy of the thunderstorms. The Thunder Moon is an auspicious time for a dream ritual or a divinatory rite.

August is known as the Corn Moon or Red Moon. This time of years is bursting with health, vitality, and ardor. This is an optimal time to gather friends and family together and celebrate the brightest side of life. Feasting, dancing, and delight are the order of the day.

September is the Harvest Moon and Singing Moon. Now we see completion of plans and ideas and the harvesting of our crops. Now we reap what we have sown earlier in the year—our thoughts, actions, words, and projects. The Singing Moon is a wonderful time to organize our lives and let go of anything that is no longer working. If something is worn out, broken, or simply does not suit your life anymore, including emotions, patterns, beliefs, and even people, this is the perfect time to let go. Declutter and simplify your life.

October is the Hunter's Moon or the Falling Leaf Moon. Great transitions are taking place all around you now and change is also taking place within. Take time to observe and feel these transformations in your life and in the world around you. Notice how the temperature changes, how the trees shed their brightly colored leaves, how the geese and other birds fly south. The Hunter's Moon should honor the very human need for physical nourishment, warmth, and rest. Seek inner peace now after the hurly-burly of summer. This is the season for relaxation and release. This is a karmic time during which you can seek karmic completion. You should acknowledge the changing of the seasons with ceremony.

November is the Beaver Moon or Mourning Moon. At this time you should get in touch with your spirit through introspection. Many countries observe November 1 as an Ancestors' Day and remember the dead through ritual and feasting.

December is Winter Moon or Long Nights Moon. This is when we experience a metaphorical death and rebirth. We can also light the flame of our hearts and souls through journeys of the spirit.

The "extra" or thirteenth full moon of the year is the blue moon of the expression, "once in a blue moon," which refers to rare and special occasions. How do we know when the blue moon occurs? It is on that rare occasion when two full moons occur in one calendar month. The blue moon is to be used wisely. Take this opportunity to look at your long-term plans and goals and to give thanks for what you have accomplished. As you take stock, be grateful for what you have and for the people in your life. Bear in mind that "what you have" should not make you think about your fat stock portfolio but rather about good health, children, a job you enjoy, good friends, a comfortable home, and opportunities.

The blue moon is also a time for prophecy. Each blue moon ritual you create should contain an aspect expressing thanks to the gods and goddesses and to Mother Nature, who gave you life.

The Gift of the Full Moon: A Native American Ritual

Many Native American tribes saw the moon as a teacher, for the bright light of the full moon was truly illuminating. While I advise caution with using aspects of indigenous culture, I think that learning the lessons offered while always honoring the source and ascribing references can be life-enriching. My motto is "appreciation without appropriation."

Accept the wisdom that is offered and respect the resource. Here is a full moon teaching from my friend Liz, who is of Native American descent and whose many happy clients attest that she is a very wise woman. The full moon ceremony should be led by a woman, an elder, who chooses a young man to be the warrior. His job is to serve the circle and serve the community by tending the fire as the Keeper of the Flame. The warrior is to be pure of heart. Selection by the elder is the greatest honor because she sees into the pure heart and perceives the good this man brings to the community. Once the fire is built, other women can approach the fire circle crying out, "Ho! Ho! Ho!" When everyone else has arrived, the young man leaves and returns only when the fire is dying down to rekindle the flames. Whenever he approaches, he should announce, "I am the Keeper of the Flame."

The elder leads the women in discussion of whatever she feel is important, such as the welfare of an individual or the village, or she tells a story. Ultimately, this is a woman's council fire and the well-being of the community is served in this monthly ceremony.

The elder is the leader of the full moon teaching and it lasts as long as she sees fit; only the elder can excuse women from the circle. Many full moon teachings, the council fires have grown shorter, the elder must know things are going well for the community!

Astrological Almanac: Moon Signs of the Times

The astrological signs of the moon are of great significance. Each moon sign has special meaning set down through the centuries. Ancient and medieval folks paid strict attention to moon phases and moon signs for planting and harvesting. Here is a guide to each sign with tried and true lore from olden days along with applications for today's rituals.

Aries is a barren and dry sign that is perfect for planting, weeding, haying, and harvesting. Moon in Aries is the optimum time for rituals pertaining to leadership, pioneering, ambition, and authority, as well as rebirth. Any healing regarding the face and head is more successful during Aries.

Taurus is an earthy and moist sign that is excellent for planting root crops like potatoes and peanuts. Love, money, and luxury are the watchwords for moon in Taurus. If you are buying real estate, moon in Taurus is an excellent time for that. Because the throat and neck are ruled by Taurus, this is a prime time both for singing and speaking.

Gemini is another dry sign that is best time for mowing, cutting, and getting rid of plants or pests. Communication is improved during moon in Gemini. Healing or the arms and hands and pulmonary system is well advised during a Gemini moon.

Cancer is a fruitful watery sign conductive to planting; in fact, it is the most productive sign of all. Hearth and home are the focus now and lunar rituals are well timed during moon in Cancer. Healing rituals for the stomach are done best at this time.

Leo is the driest and least fertile of all moon signs, good only for cutting and mowing. Leo moon is good for bravery, striking out in a new direction, like performing on stage or taking a position of authority. Matters of the heart and literal healing or the organ are advisable now.

Virgo is both damp and barren, but is a great time for cultivation. Virgo moon is good for working hard and seeking employment, tending to all aspects of health, nutrition, and healing the nervous system and bowel.

Libra is both wet and fruitful and is wonderful for grains, vines, root crops, and flowers. Now is the time for artistic endeavors, romantic liaisons, and balancing your life. The lower back and kidneys can be restored to health during moon in Libra.

Scorpio is humid and bountiful and is good for all types of planting. Make your moves during moon in Scorpio. This sign is also conducive to plumbing the depths of the spirit and achieving psychic growth. Sex rituals are at their most potent during moon in Scorpio. Healing of the sensitive reproductive organs can happen during this moon time.

Sagittarius is another fire sign that is a poor time for planting and is best spent harvesting and storing. Rites of passage and travel and rituals relating to higher truths and philosophical matters succeed during moon in Sagittarius. Sports and horses are also in the spotlight during this time. Healing for the legs can be undertaken during this time.

Capricorn is an earth sign that is also wet and is excellent for grafting, pruning, and planting trees and shrubs. Rituals relating to work, goals, and organizing can be commenced at this time. Political careers, dreams, and aspirations should be launched during moon in Capricorn. Skeletal wellness is advisable during this cycle, as well.

Aquarius is an infertile and parched moon time that is best for harvesting, weeding, and dispelling pests. The Aquarian moon is appropriate for rites regarding personal freedom. Friendship, the intellect, and starting a new phase of life all come into play now. Rituals of a more radical nature are best during this sign. Shin and ankle health goes better now, too.

Pisces is fecund and fruitful and is good for all kinds of planting. It is remarkable for fruits of all kinds. The highly sensitive moon in Pisces is good for spells and charms for creativity, intuition, divination, dream work, and music. Care and healing for the feet is most favorable during this sign of moon in Pisces.

Everyday Sacred: A Ritual Guide to the Days of the Week

Each day of the week has specific correspondences and meanings. Here is an at-a-glance guide to the days of the week, gleaned from the mythologies of centuries put to practice for different types of ritual. I do a money-enhancing ritual every Thursday, or "Thor's Day," which is the day for prosperity. Perhaps you want new love in your life; if so, try a "Freya's Day" ritual on a Friday night.

Sunday is the day for healing and vitality, as well as creativity and new hope. It is a day of confidence and success. This is the day ruled by the Sun, so it corresponds to fire and the sun sign, Leo. The colors for this day are gold, orange, and yellow, and the sacred stones for this day are also in those colors, amber, citrine, carnelian, and topaz. Sunday's herbs and incense are cloves, cedar, chamomile, frankincense, amber, sunflower, and heliotrope.

Monday or "Moon Day," is a dreamy day for intuition, beauty, women's rituals, and your home. Monday is associated with the element of water and the sign of Cancer. The clouds are shiny silvers, pearl, pale rose, white, and lavender, which are reflective like the moon. The gems and stones are similarly shaded moonstone, pearl, quartz crystal, fluorite, and aquamarine. The herbs and incense are night blooming jasmine, myrtle, moonwort, vervain, white rose, poppy, and camphor.

Tuesday is the day for action, as mighty Mars rules it. Now you can seek your passion, surge toward your goals, find your destiny, and be strong and courageous. "Mars's Day" is the time for high energy in your career, for physical activity and sports, for aggression in meetings and negotiations, and for strong sexuality. Both fire and water come into play and the astrological assignations are Aries and Scorpio. Red is the day's color, and the corresponding gems and crystals are ruby, garnet, carnelian, bloodstone, and pink tourmaline. Incense and herbs for Mars's Day are red roses, pine, carnation, nettle, patchouli, pepper, and garlic.

Wednesday, or "Odin's Day," is when the planets of communication, Mercury and Chiron, rule. This is the optimum time for writing, public speaking, intellectual pursuits, memory, and all other forms of communication. It is also a day to recognize your karmic duties through astrology and your Chiron sign, an important asteroid placement in your chart. Through introspection, try to find your "sacred wound" and heal it so it does not hold you back in life, trapping you in old patterns and relationships. The element for Wednesday is earth and the sun sign is Virgo. Colors for this mercurial day are light blue, gray, green, orange, and yellow. The crystals are sodalite, moss agate, opal, and aventurine. The herbs and incense are cinnamon, periwinkle, dill, sweet pea, cinquefoil, and ferns.

Thursday is the day for business, politics, legalities, bargaining, good fortune, and material and fiscal wealth. In other words, it is money day! The elements that come into play are water and fire, and Jupiter, the planet of abundance is the ruler. Pisces and Sagittarius share this planet as ruler. The colors are blue, purple, and turquoise. As you might suspect, the crystals are turquoise, sapphire, amethyst, and lapis lazuli, so favored by the Egyptians. The herbs and incense for the day are saffron, cedar, nutmeg, pine, oak, and cinnamon.

Friday is doubtless everybody's favorite day of the week, as it is ruled by Freya, the Nordic Venus, goddess of love. Friday is all about beauty, love, sex, fertility, friendships, and partnerships, the arts, harmony, and music, and bringing the new into your life—new energy, new people, new projects. Haven't you met a lot of people on a Friday night out? Air and earth are the elements and the signs of Libra and Taurus are the astrological signs. Pale green and deep green, robin's-egg blue, pink, and violet are the colors, and the crystals are emerald, pink tourmaline, rose quartz, as well as jade, malachite, and peridot. The herbs are incense for Fridays are apple, lily, birch, pink rose, verbena, ivy, rose, and sage.

Saturday is ruled by Saturn and connects the elements of air, fire, water, and earth. It is a time for protection, discipline, duty, binding, family, manifestation, and completion. The sun signs are Capricorn and Aquarius, with their colors of black, brown, and deepest blue, Saturday's crystals are amethyst, smoky quartz, jet, black onyx, obsidian, and darkest garnet. The incense, plants, and herbs for this day are ivy, oak, rue, moss, myrrh, deadly nightshade, mandrake, hemlock, and wolfsbane. (Many Saturn herbs are poisonous; please exercise caution when using them.) How do we use these magical correspondences in ritual? You can create your own ritual simply by choosing candle colors, crystals, and incense from the list that matches your intent and go from there. I have included some sample rituals that draw from these magical correspondences.

Thursday's Prosperity Incantation

This ritual is excellent for getting a new or better-paying job. You will get the best results on a new moon or full moon Thursday night, but any "Thor's day" will do.

To prepare yourself, take a money bath by pouring a few drops of green apple or lemon verbena essential oil into hot running water, and bathe by the light of a single green candle. As you close your eyes, meditate on your true desires. What does personal prosperity mean to you? What do you really *need*, and what do you really *want*?

When you are clear about your answers, focus on the candle flame while whispering:

Here and now, my intention is set.
New luck will be mine and all needs will be met.
With harm to none and plenty for all.
Blessed be.

After your sacred bath, perform this tried and true prosperity ritual that can help get a job and bring fiscal abundance your way.

Light a gold candle, although red will also do.

Repeat this incantation eight times while envisioning yourself with perfect abundance or at the perfect job:

I see the perfect place for me; I see the place of plenty.
Upon my heart's desire I am set.
Prosperity will come to me now.

Festive Friday Frolic

Venus rules this most popular day of the week. Small wonder that this is the night for a tryst! To prepare yourself for a night out flirting, you should take a goddess bath with the following potion in a special cup or bowl. I call mine the Venus Vial. Combine:

1 cup sesame oil

6 drops orange blossom oil

4 drops gardenia oil

Stir with your finger six times, silently repeating three times:

> *I am a daughter of Venus; I embody love.*
> *My body is a temple of pleasure, and I am all that*
> *is beautiful.*
> *Tonight I will drink fully from the cup of love.*

Pour this potion into a steaming bath and meditate on your evening plans. As you finish, repeat the Venus spell once more. Don't use a towel, but allow your skin to dry naturally. Dress up in your finest Friday Night Out garb and dab a bit of the mixture on your pulse points. When you are out and about, you will most definitely meet lovely new people who will be drawn to you. You will receive compliments, and indeed, you will be at your sexiest. The rest is up to you.

Chapter Six

RITES OF PASSAGE AND MARKING TIME

People have a psychological need to observe rites of passage, from birth to the coming of age, graduation, marriage, and death. There are numerous rites of passage that are less acknowledged by our society, such as divorce and retirement, as well as other occasions. It is important to recognize the big firsts, such as a first job, adoption or birth of a child, and first home. These are special times in your life and deserve to be acknowledged publicly and privately. You can go a long way toward fulfilling this deep psychological need for yourself and the people in your life by creating rituals involving loved ones in them. By marking the special moments of your life, you can ensure better mental and spiritual health, and you can also build closeness to your family, your friends, and your "tribe."

In my spiritual community, we create individual rites and ceremonies to observe life passages such as the first Saturn return, which occurs for every person around age twenty-eight, when the planet Saturn returns to the exact natal placement where it was when he or she was born. Astrologically, this event marks a true initiation into adulthood since we are confronted with the major issues—career, relationships, and destiny—of adulthood. Often at this point in life people move long distance, lose a job, or experience a major breakup or other personal upheaval.

We also acknowledge a woman's passage from Maiden to Queen or Mother and to Crone. To the contemporary aging population, croning rituals are becoming important and are wonderful opportunities for you to design special rituals for the special people in your life. As people grow older, they often become more isolated, which is a great loss for everyone. Older people have so much wisdom to share, and one way to honor this wisdom is through the medium of ritual.

Society does observe some rites of passage, such as birthdays, anniversaries, graduations, marriages, and funerals, but they have become gift-giving opportunities, mostly devoid of spiritual sophistication. Still, they are usually occasions for bonding and feasting and represent the last vestige of ritual for the masses outside of religion. Confirmation, baptism, and initiations conducted by secret fraternal organizations are also examples of ritual that have continued to the day. The *bris* practiced by those of the Jewish faith is a wonderful name giving ritual for babies, and circumcision is still practiced although it is now largely thought of as "hygienic" and has lost its ritual aspect. *Bar mitzvahs* and *bat mitzvahs* are jubilant community celebrations for young Jewish men and women to mark their passage to adulthood. This wonderful tradition ensures the greater community remains involved in people's lives in much the same way tribes of older days did.

Early peoples would begin their rites at birth with magic, purification rituals and taboos, such as what foods could or could not be consumed and what length of time a baby and new mother were to be isolated for spiritual safety. Among indigenous peoples such as Congolese tribes, a youth was initiated as "a new person" with circumcision, headdress, tattoos, and special clothing in light of maturation.

In the Dark Ages, May Day was an occasion for ritual combat with jousting, races, and all manner of courtly exercise. Springtime combat between the Queen of May and the King of May in the fields recalled older fertility rituals, where the king of the land would make love with a representative of the Goddess in the fields to ensure health and fertility of the crops for the medieval Europeans.

Dance has long been an important aspect of ritual. Movement and rhythm are vital to many of the traditional ceremonies in this book and should also be included in those you design for yourself and your community.

Rituals of Engagement

Using ritual to create sacred space in your life puts you between the worlds. You are on the threshold where all things are possible. The magic circles is a boundary, separating the sacred and the magical from the mundane. Out of all the rituals marking the passage of life, engagement is unique in that it is a threshold between stages in life. You are no longer single, but you are not quite married, either. As courtship turns into engagement, the relationship has deepened, yet the foundation is not quite solid. You are still in the process of building, exploring, and discovering. Engagement is the marker, the boundary, separating your old life from the new path you will walk with your betrothed.

Rituals of engagement are quite common. Most married people who would never see themselves as any sort of ritualist have performed engagement rituals. Asking for someone's hand in marriage, accepting the offer, and trading rings are rituals that involve special words and ritualized actions, such as getting down on one knee, that carry life-changing significance.

Unlike marriage, which usually requires an official minister, engagement rituals are private, personal, and often spontaneous. They are simple and heartfelt. They can involve anything your imagination creates. Sometimes the individual who proposes hides a ring in a special place, creating a romantic treasure hunt, or has it as part of the presentation in a romantic dinner. Each ritual can suit the couple's personality and style.

In a magical context, there are two kind of modern engagement rituals. The first is the question and answer. One person—traditionally the male in heterosexual couples—"pops the question" and presents a ring. The second can be a more magical acceptance of the engagement, where both people are clear, conscious, and purposeful in their magical intent in order to formalize their engagement and walk toward the path of marriage together. This is an approach to getting married through deep discussion and agreement.

The ring is the most important tool in this ritual. Some people get hung up on the size and quality of the ring and its stone, and jewelry companies have come up with creative marketing plans based on your monthly pay to determine the money you should spend on this ring. Obviously, they have their own interests at heart, not yours. To the magically inclined, the price and size of the diamond aren't as important as the love and magic put into the ritual of choosing and offering it.

Diamond rings are most often used in engagement. The ring is a circle, a wheel, forever turning, an unbroken line. Gold is the metal of the sun and conjures a bright future. Magically, it symbolizes good fortune, success, health, creativity, and immortality. A gold ring is a symbol of a union that will last forever, shining brightly. The sun also rules the diamond. It is a most beloved gem and spiritually is one of the most powerful, for it represents the powers of light and transformation. In a diamond, the blackness of coal has been transformed into purest light and the color spectrum.

To bring out these blessings, consecrate the ring before offering it to your beloved. Wash it in pure water, envisioning all unwanted energies dissolving away. Hold the ring up to the sun and feel the rays of light catalyzing the powers of the gem and the precious metal. Feel it fill with light, and then hold it to your heart. Feel the love you have for your future spouse. Charge the ring with your love, your hopes, dreams, and magical wises. Enchant the ring's energy to grow as the two of you grow as a couple, increasing your live and blessings. Then put it back into its box, or whatever container you will present it in, and close it. Don't let anybody else see or touch the ring until you hand it to your love. As you present it, feel the love you have invested in it radiate outward. Let it inspire your heart and mind as you ask, "Will you marry me?"

The Myth, Mystery, and Meaning of Rings

Rings have been a meaningful adornment from the times of the ancient Egyptians, through the age of the Greeks, and continuing into today. Throughout time, rings have served as mere decoration, they have indicated rank, and rings have also symbolized deeper meanings such as eternity, reincarnation, energy, unity, power, and, safety. If a sing is set with a stone, it can bind you with the energy of that stone. Some Native Americans wear turquoise, and that power doubles when the stone is set in a ring. Some even interpret the presence of a ring in a dream as representing a desire for reconciliation of the different parts of your personality. The use of amber in a ring can help deepen a friendship if two amber rings are exchanged between friends.

The way you wear a ring—on which hand and on which finger—affects your energy. The bottom of the ring setting should be open, allowing the stone to be closer to your skin. Thumb rings have become a popular trend, but they block the energy of the thumb, awakening egoism and selfishness.

Wearing the correct gem on your index finger can help you achieve your goals. Lapis lazuli can help you gain wisdom. Pearl, moonstone, or garnet will help you better to love yourself and others. Carnelian is for those who want success. Sodalite chrysocolla, or turquoise can help quiet and calm the mind.

Idea, insight, and intuition are associated with your middle finger, and you should only wear stones of it if you want to receive psychic input from the world around you. Sapphire or quartz crystal will help you access your higher good and understand your life purpose. Amethyst will help increase sensitivity and creativity. Rubies awaken inner and outer beauty.

Obviously, the ring finger on the left hand symbolizes a direct connection to your heart and serves as the love center. The ring finger also symbolizes creativity, and wearing an emerald will inspire ingenuity. Wearing tiger's-eye or cat's-eye will also help you meet creative goals. Wearing turquoise on this finger helps with practicality in your work and art. Traditionally, diamonds are worn on the left ring finger for deep and loyal love ties. A moonstone will also express your love. An opal shows service to your community and to the world. A ruby helps with serenity—both within and without.

Last, and certainly not least, the right gem on your little finger can help you change the direction of your whole life! Wearing aventurine can bring new energy and prospects into your life. Turquoise can help you unwind and simplify. Pearls will help you achieve better organizational habits.

Because the left hand is the receptive hand, gems to awaken and release emotions should be worn on it. Career-related and lift-goal gems should be worn on the right, or projective hand.

Engagement Blessing Ritual

The important thing to remember in the engagement process is to make sure you share similar ideas about the path of life. Being engaged is a time to make sure you are compatible on many levels as you enjoy the romance. You will need to have frank discussions on career, home, health, children, sex, and the expectations you have for yourself and your partner in all these areas. Sometimes when we are in love, we expect people to simply "know" what we want. Magical people expect that even more, feeling that their partner is so intuitive that they should be able to anticipate each other's actions and opinions on these aspects of life. Though it would be ideal, that's not realistic thinking. Sometimes it can be hardest to read the person we are closest to. A good relationship requires good communication. This formalized engagement ritual involves dream sharing, and should only be done after such frank discussions so that nothing comes as a shock. Wanting to perform this ritual is a good way to initiate such talks. It can be done right after the acceptance or at any point later in the engagement process. Just make sure you are both aware of each other's ideas of the future before you begin your life together.

When you are ready to move forward and begin the ritual, first go someplace comfortable where you will not be disturbed. This ritual can be done in your home or even at a quiet restaurant or coffee shop. Perhaps you'll want to take your love to the place where you first dated.

Start with your favorite drinks. I like a good wine or champagne, but it doesn't have to be alcoholic, just something you both enjoy and can share. Have three glasses ready.

Light three candles: one of your favorite color, one of your betrothed's favorite color, and the third of a color you both like. Unless you choose the same color for all three candles, the third candle should be different from the first two, so that neither of you dominates in the energy of the relationship. When in doubt, three white candles work well. Each of you light your candle, and together light the flame of the third with your two candles.

Pour the drink into two of the three glasses, making each about half full. Hold the two glasses near the fire. Don't get too close—you don't want to shatter your glasses. The light, not the heat, is the important part. Speak close to the mouth of the glass, and whisper into the wine your hopes, dreams, and blessings for the marriage. What do you feel? What do you want to do? What do you want to create together? Envisioning a long, healthy, happy life together, you can talk about home, family, and careers. See yourselves supporting each other in separate goals and working together for your joint dreams. You each should speak your words into the liquid. Then pour both drinks into the third empty glass, combining your hopes and dreams. Share that one glass, savoring its flavor and reflecting on your future. Do not speak until you have both finished the combined drink. Look into each other's eyes, and kiss. The ritual is complete.

Two Come Together as One: Marriage Rites

Nowadays, weddings are a big business and can be huge productions that take no less than a year of planning. This is one of our most beloved rituals, and while weddings often cost a pretty penny they are usually deeply meaningful for every person in attendance. My friend, the esteemed author Daphne Rose Kingma, wrote a lovely collection of ceremonies called *Weddings from the Heart* that run the gamut from traditional to highly alternative. This book is a great resource for engaged couples celebrating the journey of love.

I have had the good fortune to officiate at two weddings and have created a variation of the classic handfasting, which I will share with you here. These are two very happy couples, so it seems that this particular variation of this ritual is effective.

Handfasting Ritual

Weddings are usually planned at least a year ahead. If at all possible, choose a day during the new moon phase, as a marriage is a very important new beginning. Create a bower of beautiful, scented flowers and burn lightly scented candles. Traditional flowers recommended for the bower include roses, cherry and apple blossoms, and gardenias. As a gift at one handfasting, I gave the happy couple long-burning Votivo candles in mint-pomegranate scent, which lasts for days. On their anniversary, I always give them the same candles, so that they can rekindle the moment of their wedding, since smell and memory have powerful ties.

In Western culture it is customary for the bride to wear a veil and some red and blue in her wedding finery. Giving gifts is also an important part of the convention of weddings. The bride and groom should wrap small, symbolic presents for each other and set them on the altar, which is placed in the eastern part of the room or space. Altar decorations are simple and symbolic: just two white candles and a willow wand. The wedding rings are affixed to the willow wand. At this handfasting, I also gave the bride and groom symbolic gifts of small rings and ribbons of blue to represent the energies of the air, red incense to be lit from the candles to represent the energies of fire, and a gardenia to represent the earth. Wine, which represents water, should be in a chalice on the altar. Wine for all, along with sweet cakes, should also be ready for the celebration and sharing with the guests and witnesses. Wiccan tradition calls for both a priest and a priestess to perform the handfasting, but in this case, and according to the wishes of the bride and groom, I officiated alone.

Since most of this couple's family members were Methodist and Catholic, we wanted to make everyone as comfortable as possible with the concept of a highly ritualistic Pagan marriage. We created little cards explaining the origin of the handfasting and also provided the text and instructions for audience participation. The cards were tied to little bells to be rung at the end of the ritual to signal through sound that the marriage ceremony had been completed. Not only were the wedding guests comfortable with the ritual, they loved it. The bride wore a scarlet wedding dress, a lovely red veil, and a willow wand headdress. The groom wore an elegant tuxedo, which set off her fiery gown perfectly.

The text of the handfasting is as follows:

The priest or priestess speaks:

> *May the place of this marriage be consecrated,*
> *For we gather here in the ritual of love and bliss*
> *With two who would be wedded*
> *[Bride's name] and [Groom's name], please step forward*
> *and stand here before your friends and family and before*
> *the gods and goddesses of the world.*
> *Be with us here, O spirits of the air.*
> *And with your swift fingers, tie the bonds between*
> *these two who would be married and tie them closely*
> *and securely.*
> *Be with us here.*

At this point, tie the two symbolic gift rings together with blue ribbon, then loop them over the willow wand and replace it on the altar.

> *Be with us here, O spirits of fire,*
> *And light their love and passion*
> *With your fiery ardor.*

Light the incense from the candles and place it on the altar, then say aloud:

> *Be with us here, O sprits of the earth*
> *And ground deep the roots of their love.*

Pick up the willow wand and tie the gardenia to it. Then say:

> *Be with us here, O spirits of water,*
> *And let joy flow forever for [Groom's name] and*
> *[Bride's name],*

For as long as they are married,
Blessed goddess and merry god.
Give to [Groom's name] and [Bride's name], who stand
before us in the light of their love, your love and protection.
Blessed be!

Here the audience responds:

Blessed be.

Hold the willow wand with the rings and gardenia tied to it out to the bride and groom, instructing them:

Place your right hand over this wand and the rings of this
rite of marriage.
Above you are the stars,
Below you the stones.
As time passes, think upon this:
Like the eastern star, your love shall remain constant.
Like a rock, your love will stand firm,
Possess one another, but always be understanding.
Have patience at all times,
For stormy times come and go, but they leave upon
the wind.
Give each other love as often as possible
Of the body, the mind, and the spirit.
Be not afraid and do not let the ways of others dissuade
you from your path.
The gods and goddesses are always with you,
Now and forever.

After a short pause, ask the bride:

[Name], is it your wish to become one with this man?

She answers.

Ask the groom:

[Name], *is it your wish to become one with this woman?*

He responds.

Does anyone here today say nay?

Say to the bride and groom:

Place the rings on each other now, [bride] and [groom].
Before the gods, goddesses, and everyone here as witness,
I now proclaim you husband and wife!

Now the bride and groom kiss. Next they speak any words
they have prepared for each other. Finally, it's time for them to
exchange their symbolic gifts. At the end, say:

Now we ring the bells and it is proclaimed—this ritual
is done!

Divorce Ritual: Graceful Goodbyes

Performing a ritual to acknowledge the end of a relationship
is an important part of the healing process. Whether it is a
breakup of a love affair or the dissolution of the legal bonds
of marriage, approaching this change with ritual will help and
heal. I have also known those who performed this same rite
with the ending of a friendship. This ceremony is intended
to resolve issues, tie up loose ends, and move on. It is very
important psychologically, psychically, and emotionally
to recognize that a divorce is a very big deal. This ritual is
best done privately, although you may want the support

of a carefully chosen friend. I have outlined some carefully considered questions for you to ask yourself when trying to figure out if a divorce ritual is what you want to do. As with all rituals, I strongly suggest that this one be given a lot of thought. With this divorce ritual, I recommend going to an even deeper level of introspection, as you will be bidding farewell to an important part of your life that, doubtless, brought you as much joy as it did sorrow. Many emotions are going to rise up and you can, gently and with love, put these feelings to rest and assign them a place in your life: the past.

Questions for Yourself

Thinking about and writing down concerns, worries, and questions you may have about your divorce and new solo life will help you begin this new passage of life.

- ✤ Do I want to have any ties in the future to my former spouse? Or do I wish to cut off all ties completely?
- ✤ If any kind of relationship continues with the individual whom I wish to divorce (and if there are issues involving the custody of children, these issues will remain), what are the safe and peaceful ways to remain connected?
- ✤ What are the aspects of the relationship I wish to be divorced from (i.e. fighting about money, unfaithfulness, dishonesty, and stress)?
- ✤ What are the positive memories I want to keep?
- ✤ What fears do I have?

Today, divorce seems to be no more important than signing a piece of paper and sending it off in the mail. I have many friends who have said, "Is this all there is?" This ritual is an answer to that question.

Go to a place in nature where you went together—a lakeshore, a special beach, a path in the woods, or a park. Take a photocopy of your divorce papers and a copy of a photo of you both, and place them together in an envelope. Write on the envelope:

> *On this date* _____, *I divorce myself of* [write the aspect you are divorcing, not the name of the person].

Say aloud:

> *Now I am free to pursue my happiness, a new love, and new people in my life. Good memories I will treasure and independence is my pleasure. I say goodbye to this part of my life and release all pain and sorrow.*
> *I welcome the new and the good into my life*
> *I am clear.*
> *I am free.*
> *I am me.*

Take the envelope and bury it where it will decompose undisturbed—no need to burn or throw it in the water. Allow it to return to the elements, as is Nature's way. There is no doubt that you will feel sad and by all means, allow yourself to cry and mourn. Each tear releases toxins from your system. As you return to your home, you will feel lighter. Your conscience is clear and your future is bright!

Celebration of Pregnancy: A Home for the New Soul

When a new member of the tribe is on the way, it is cause for true jubilation among the family and community. I recommend waiting until the second or third trimester and then having a tribal stomp. This is a whole different take on baby showers.

While it provides for the baby's needs, it also addresses the real, practical needs of the expectant mother and father.

Begin by asking the new mother what is her preferred day for a time of feasting and fixing. Ask her also to provide a blank book for guests to write in so that the parents can look back in the years to come and remember who attended this special gathering.

This ritual is rather like a barn raising. Each guest brings something or creates something for the new family. Artists can bring paint and paint a mural on the wall of the baby's room. I have seen beautiful clouds and castles to keep a pair of brand new eyes busy. Handymen and carpenters can bring baby-proofing supplies, such as expandable gates; craftsmen can make a crib or rocker; cooks can prepare and freeze meals for when the new mother and father are too tired to think straight and make nourishing meals for themselves.

My tribe, which is how I like to think of my group of friends, is a very practical bunch. We pass on baby clothes we no longer need, as well as toys, high chairs, and the like. A big part of our ethos is to avoid the mass consumption and materialism that we fall into because we are surrounded by consumer culture. We recycle or share as much as possible, passing on books, clothing, cookware, and furnishings to the next person entering a phase of life where special equipment will be needed. For a new baby, this includes bassinet, baby monitor, infant health books, storybooks, and mobiles. Books and materials that will serve as guides for the first-time expectant parents are also ideal.

On this celebratory day, the new mother and father should be treated like a king and queen. Shawls, slippers, and special healthful teas and juices are wonderful personal, supportive items to give them.

The new about-to-be mom and dad should enjoy this day and relax, as they are about to embark on the busiest time of their lives! They should be given special seats at the feast, where they can sit back and simply "receive." Receiving is not as easy as it seems in our culture, but it is important to accept and appreciate the help and advice from those who love us.

One way to commemorate this day and remember it in the years to come is to create a "Book of Blessings" that is filled with advice from the tribe. This can be accomplished easily, despite the hubbub of this special day, by leaving the blank book chosen by the expectant mother at the door or on the dinner table, so that each member of the tribe can add his or her advice and blessings during the day. At the feast, the expectant parents can read from it. The Book of Blessings will be a free-form compilation with a great variety of entries, ranging from "Put the baby's room near the laundry room and the sound of the dryer will help the baby sleep" to "I offer to baby-sit at least once a month so you can have a night out" to "Our family welcomes you to the neighborhood."

It will be a day remembered for many years to come.

Baby Naming Ceremony

Often, there is a name given at birth based on an ancestor or family member. Later, when a child has come of age, another name is given to acknowledge maturation. This tradition needs to be revived, and I believe it is a wonderful rite of passage to institute in the lives of young people today who are so desperately in need of community support and inclusion. Of all the wonderful customs of the world, my favorite baby naming custom comes from joining the names of the parents. For example, if the father's name is Robert and the mother is named Carolyn, you could name the baby Roblyn. Christina and Toby's child could be Christoby, or if you needed a more conventional version, Cristobel. Anna and Justin's child could be named Justina. The possibilities are endless, as you can see. They don't always work well, however, so Filipino families sometimes end up using the names of grandparents, godparents, and the revered "aunties," women who are not actually related but are very special friends of the family. Sometimes they choose to overlook the custom entirely and opt for outside names, but naming is alive and well in this modern age.

Here is a ceremony for a baby naming as performed by the wonderful Viray family, a joyous and generous "tribe" of Filipinos that stretches from Indiana to California to many of the Philippine Islands.

Baby Naming Ritual

An essential element for this ceremony is holy water.

Select a day when as many family members and friends can come, ideally a fair Sunday at the parents' or grandparents' house. Ask the guests to bring their very best and most dazzling dish to share—your prize-winning pie or a casserole that always gets second and third helpings—and to write down their favorite lullabies and sleepy-time stories to share.

Begin the ceremony with a family blessing for the new parents and the baby. Grandparents and other family elders should take turns holding the baby and touching a drop or two of holy water to the forehead of the baby. This common blessing of water is similar to baptism. A grandmother or other elder should lead the group in a song, but if that is not possible, common and well-known lullabies should be sung.

Now the parents present the infant with his or her new name and tell the story behind the naming. After the name is given, every guest and family member should come up to the baby and welcome the new baby by name. Now is the time to also present the stories and lullabies to the parents with good wishes and other gifts. Ideally, this should not be an overly materialistic event, but I have observed that most people simply can't resist giving presents to new babies and parents out of sheer happiness.

Finally, the food is shared and the bonds of the family expand to include the new baby.

Mask-Making: Finding the Sacred Self

The elements needed for this ritual include:

- Posterboard, newspaper, water, and white flour to make a plaster-like paste, paint, glitter, feathers, sequins, colored markers, sticks
- Music—harem music, women's opera choruses
- Butcher paper (also tape butcher paper to the wall)
- Scarves

Whatever room you're in, create sacred space there. Light incense, lamps, and candles, and put on belly dancing or other women's music.

Lay out the mask-making supplies on tables covered with butcher paper. Build a little cardboard wall between mask-making stations to create privacy so each participant feels completely comfortable in disclosing the heretofore hidden side of her sacred self. Before stating to make her mask, each woman should take a turn and step up to the paper on the wall, state aloud the positive qualities she sees in herself. She should proclaim her affirming, esteem-boosting aspects. This should be as free-form and upbeat as possible.

After the personal statements, other women should chime in with encouraging words. It is amazing to hear the unexpected perceptions of others, and this part of the experience can be life changing. Write everything down.

Each woman should then take her affirmations to her workstation. These words are the source of inspiration for masks of power and beauty. Next, draw a large version of the mask you envision and cut it out, making sure you have eyes, nose, and mouth holes. Mix the white flour and water into a thin glue. Take your newspaper and tear it into strips and glue it onto your mask shape. Remember to create the features for your mask face, such as a long nose, a beak; use your imagination to the fullest. After it has dried a bit, you can begin shaping the mask into a curve to fit over your face, and then glue on the decorations and adornments.

Now, turn up the women's music, and with paint, glue, and glitter, create an expression of your inner and outer beauty on paper. Listen to the throbbing drums and the hypnotic beats; listen to your own inner rhythms. Eventually, each woman will finish one or more masks. Glue a stick to the base of each mask so that they can be held over the face like Venetian masquerade masks. As these masks dry, dance to the music. When everyone's masks are dry, each woman should reveal her "secret" self. She can take a turn and step out into the middle of the room, wearing a veil or scarf over her mask. Before casting off the protective veil, each woman should announce her revelatory self. An example might be: I am the Fire Goddess" or "I am the Selkie of the Irish Coast." I did a self-portrait mask of "Peacock Girl" that profoundly affected my life. Every time I see it, I feel reaffirmed.

All of the beautiful masked women should dance together to the music and raise the energy in the room. While this is taking place, the level of self-esteem in the room will skyrocket.

Our masks should be kept as totems to be worn in the event of poor self-image. Hang your mask on the wall in your bedroom or office as a constant reminder of your true and beautiful self.

Croning Rituals

Our modern society has taken an unfortunate attitude toward aging, characterized by denial and shame. Rather than embracing the realization of their own highest wisdom, aging women are socialized into unhealthy regimens such as Botox and plastic surgery in vain attempts to turn back the clock.

Women should feel good about aging. They should celebrate long, full lives. Women should be respected and honored for the wisdom they bring to the community. One of the roles ritual plays in the world is to change the dynamic between a person and her community. Therefore, croning rituals are the signal to the group that a woman has ascended into a new role of service and leadership to the family, the tribe, the village, and the sisterhood.

Theories vary as to when a woman becomes a crone. Z. Budapest in her *Holy Book of Women's Mysteries* says it happens to every woman at age fifty-six. Others say it is at age fifty-four, and Diana Paxson says it's a range from sixty to seventy-one for the evolution from Queen to Crone. Often cronehood is confirmed at fourteen months past a woman's last period, and when she has come to her second Saturn return. A woman should decide for herself when she feels she has reached the age of "cronehood," however; if she is not prepared to take on the title, then by all means she should wait until she is ready. Discussing it with other women will help authenticate what you know and feel inside. Support from the sisterhood is essential, and in many circles of friends and family, women who are of similar ages should sustain each other in life's passages and honor each other as they wish to be honored.

The Crown of Cronehood: A Ritual of Honoring

The essential elements for this ritual are enough candles to represent every year of the crone's life, flowers, silver wire, crystals, water, flowering branches, silver moon-shaped paper cutouts, and potluck food. The potluck food served at the party after the ritual will be even more special and good for all if they are "women's food," such as estrogen-filled yams, calcium-rich broccoli, and yogurt. Soy is recommended as well.

The first part of the ritual takes place before the honored guest, the new crone, arrives. Working together, women should take the silver wire and form a round crown. Glue semiprecious crystals to this crown, attach charms and amulets, and affix the silver crescent moons. Make it beautiful and meaningful. The silver moon is a sign of the Goddess, and the new crone is a representative of the Goddess's third aspect. The crystals, which are the stones and bones of Mother Earth, add power and the beauty of Gaia. Charms and amulets are for health, protection, good luck, and good life. As you make it and place the jewels and charms on the crown, state your intentions and hopes for the new crone.

When the crown is complete, place it on a beautiful purple pillow or the altar.

Upon the arrival of the soon-to-be-crowned crone, the eldest woman present should take a flowering branch and dip it in water and sprinkle it on her head, just a few drops, and speak a blessing, such as:

I bless you in the name of the Goddess.
I bless you in the name of Mother Earth.
I bless you in the name of every woman.
Sister, do you accept the role of teacher and leader
as crone?

The crone responds. If she accepts the title, then the eldest woman says:

She is crowned.

Now the elder places the Crown of Cronehood upon the new crone's head. Go around the circle and have each woman speak of the gift she added to the crown.

I give you amethyst to represent the healing power of
the planet.
I give you silver, sacred to the moon.
I give you roses, the flower of desire.
I give you a sacred heart charm to represent the mysteries
of love.
I give you a blue star because you are a star.
I give you an abalone shell because you are powerful like
the ocean.
I give you moonstone because you are wise and reflective.
I give you an angel pendant because you are so beautiful
in body and in soul.

Now everyone should speak together:

> *We gather together to celebrate that* [new crone's name] *is entering the Wise Age.*

Now the eldest woman lights one candle, and each woman present takes turn lighting a candle until all fifty-six (or the appropriate number equaling this crone's age) are lit.

Singing and chanting now take place with the circle holding hands:

> [Crone's name], *Lady Mine,*
> *We now honor you; we will never forsake you.*
> [Crone's name], *we listen to your wisdom with the love of our hearts.*
> *We accept your teachings with ears and hands.*
> *Blessed be the new crone! Long life and good health! Happiness and joy!*

After everyone has spoken her tribute to the crone, she can speak her thanks. At this point, the crone assumes her leadership role. Leadership is best handled with great gravity and lightness at the same time. "Benevolence" and "wisdom" are the watchwords. The crone should speak anything she is holding in her heart. Doubtless, she will want to speak her gratitude toward the support of the sisterhood, but she should also speak forth any concerns she has. The concerns can be specific to her world, which is now her domain—her family, her group of friends, her spiritual circle, her community, or even the planet. The crone can choose to ask a pair of disputing friends to make up and work it out. She can request that a healing garden be made for her people. Whatever comes to her mind that will be helpful and essential to the group and the greater good is what she should speak. I know a crone who has asked people to help her build a community center, and it is happening. I know another crone who quit her high-powered corporate job to study the medicine wheel and become a shaman. Still another elder friend has taken up the brush and is painting beautiful art after years of working for the defense department. This is my mother, Helen, who is a wonderful example of the power of cronehood.

When the crone has spoken from the wisdom of her heart, everyone should again hold hands. The eldest woman who inducted the new crone again holds out the flowering branch and hands it to the new crone. The crone speaks her blessing to everyone present, touching everyone's heads with a few drops of blessing water and reciting words from her heart to each person. When she is done, she says:

This circle is now open. Blessed be to all.

Now the food is served, and it should be a birthday party to remember for the rest of the crone's life.

Stones with Purpose: What to Wear and What it Does

Agate—Ensures you speak the truth when worn on an amulet; attracts favors from powerful people

Black Agate—Ensures success in business and in athletic competition if worn on a short chain or in a ring

Amazonite—Brings luck when worn while gambling

Amber—Brings love into your life; increases sexual pleasure

Amethyst—If worn by a man, will bring a good woman into his life

Bloodstone—Brings court victory in legal matters

Carnelian—Protects from lightening

Cat's-Eye—Helps retain beauty and life, depressing when worn as a ring

Coral earrings—Attracts men to your life

Dark Peridot Ring—Raises your spirits; brings you money

Diamond with a Six-Sided Cut—Protects; ensures victory in conflict if worn in platinum

Diamond Set in Onyx—Incites loyalty in partner; overcomes sexual temptation

Frog-Shaped Jewelry—Protection while traveling, especially travel across water; potent if includes aquamarine gem

Geode Worn as Jewelry—Attracts love; helps women avoid miscarriage

Jade—Attracts love to your life if shaped like a butterfly

Lapis Lazuli—Offers health, growth, protection if in the form of beads on gold wire

Moss Agate—Healthy harvest if worn while gardening

Opal Earrings—Awakens psychic powers

Rite Before Surgery

There are certain occasions in life that, although extremely difficult, offer enormous opportunities for learning. One of these occasions is illness. I am a breast cancer survivor and had several surgeries and lengthy recoveries. I will be forever grateful for my beloved friends who came together to support me before the surgeries to offer healing and love. My doctors were amazed at how well I healed; one female surgeon told me I was healing faster than any patient she had ever worked with. I told her I believed it was because of the healing ritual we had performed. She was fascinated and wanted to know more about this alternative approach to wellness.

A Gathering of Angels: A Ritual of Preparation for Surgery

Call your friends together before the surgery. It can be at your home or any place that feels safe and secure. I highly recommend healing energy at the home of the person who is to undergo the surgery, as it will create an aura of restoration. Ask each person to bring something to comfort, reassure, and cure the celebrant: soup, fixings, a soothing eye pillow, sleep balm, a hand-knitted scarf for warmth, body lotion, herbal teas, books, or lavender-infused slippers are all wonderful gifts.

Form a circle of care around the celebrant and light candles. Unscented soy candles are probably best for health reasons. As you go around the circle, ask each person to give his or her gift of caring to the celebrant and say what it represents.

> *I give you this herbal tea mix so you can sip tea and draw from it healing and heat.*
> *I give you all my love and healing energy and I know you will come back from the hospital healthier than ever before.*

The ritual continues until everyone has had a turn to speak and healing gifts and loving energy surround the celebrant. I suggest giving the celebrant hankies beforehand, as I know I could not stop my tears of joy. It is completely up to the celebrant to say or do whatever he or she feels during the ritual. In many cases, they may say nothing due to the intensity of this event.

Personal Rituals for Renewal

Every day, you can renew your own health and wellness in many small ways. A cup of green tea with a morning prayer can be a simple ritual that gives you calmness and builds bodily strength. Create and incorporate some personal ritual for your own renewal.

Body Healing Blessing

As I mentioned, I have undergone several surgeries and, although support and positive "vibes" surrounded me, I was also very scared and had to overcome the possibility of viewing my body as a battleground. In my case, I had to look at my body, and instead of feeling horrified, betrayed, or angry, I had to work hard to feel love for it. I could feel the change in my attitude, and it has helped enormously in the long run. I frequently performed self-healing rituals such as the Body Purification Ritual Rub, which is a real boost to body and soul.

Body Purification Ritual Rub

Since the time of the ancients in the Mediterranean and in Mesopotamia, salts from the sea combined with soothing oils have been used to purify the body by way of gentle ritual rubs. From Bathsheba to Cleopatra, these natural salts have been used to smooth the skin and enhance circulation, which is vital to overall body health as the skin is the single largest organ. Salts from the Dead Sea have long been a popular export and are readily available at most health food stores. You can make your own salts, however, and not only control the quality and customize the scent, but save money, too. The definitive benefits that is far and above cost saving is that you can imbue the concoction with your intention, which is absolutely imperative when you are performing rites of self-healing. Cook up your own "kitchen cupboard cure."

Shekinah's Salts

Shekinah translates as "She who dwells within" and is the Hebrew name for the female aspect of God. Legend has it that she co-created the world side by side with Yahweh, the god of Israel. The simple recipe for salts calls up the scents and primal memories of what the Edenic paradise must have been like. A real plus to this recipe is that you can change the essential oils to suit your needs and mood.

The ingredients for the recipe are as follows:

3 cups Epsom salts

½ cup sweet almond oil

1 tablespoon glycerin

4 drops ylang-ylang essential oil

1 drop jasmine essential oil

1 drop clary sage essential oil

Mix well and store in a colored and well-capped glass bottle. You can use these special Shekinah salts in your ritual rub. Prepare for what I call the body glow session by lighting citrus and rose-scented candles. Step out of your clothes and hold the salts in the palms of your hands and pray aloud:

Shekinah, your wisdom helps me reflect your image.
My body is a temple to you.
Here I worship today with heart and hands,
Body and soul.
I call on you for healing.
Shekinah, bring me breath and life.
Ancient One, I thank you
With heart and hands,

Body and soul.

Use these salts with a damp, clean washcloth or a new sponge and gently scrub your body during a waning moon at midnight. Rinse with warm water. (Women with sensitive skin should avoid this salt rub. Instead, blend the essential oils into a quarter cup of almond oil and massage the blend into your skin with the damp washcloth or sponge; then rinse. Use the salt scrub only on your body, never on your face.)

The Sukhavti: Buddhist Ritual for Death

A few years ago, I attended a memorial service for my dear friend Duncan's mother, Maggie. Maggie was an amazing woman. Born into a middle-class Jewish family, she thrived in the hippie years, traveling the world and experimenting with many different religions. Eventually the road took her to Buddhist shrines and ashrams, places of study and meditation. Maggie attended the esteemed Naropa Institute in Boulder, Colorado, and delved deeply into her practice, meditating for hours on end. While in an ashram in Nova Scotia, keeping a vow of silence, she became very ill and died. The occasion of her death was observed by the Buddhist ritual, *Sukhavti*.

Courtesy of the late Maggie's son, Duncan McCloud, here is a portion of the prayer from the funeral ritual. It is taken from sacred Tibetan texts and was translated by Maggie herself.

Prayer for Reincarnation

Whose outstanding deeds give endless glory to beings
Whose mere remembrance banishes Death
With love, we speak this prayer for reincarnation
and rebirth
May I be free of sadness and misery
May I still feel the love of those I have left behind
May I pass by the demons

May I remember well my faith and consolation
May I see for myself Amitabha, the Greatest Teacher of
us all,
Supreme Being Highest and Lord of All
May I see the greatness and the glory.
At the moment of my death, may I receive enlightenment
May I be reborn.

The *Sukhavti* is a series of little vignettes, stories, and collected memories of the dead. The Buddhists believe in reincarnation, that death is a step in the soul's continuing journey. The purpose of the *Sukhavti* is to help talk the newly dead spirit through the *bardos*, which are a sort of continuum through which the spirit must pass. Safe passage is not guaranteed, for the deceased must get past Tibetan demons of terrible aspect.

At Maggie's service, to help her through the *bardos*, people said sweet things, sad things, funny things, and extremely honest things about her. In fact, it is of the utmost importance to be very frank and tell the truth, as the honesty will help the spirit through the *bardos*.

Steps for a Successful Sukhavti

1. Gather Tibetan temple incense and flowers, and invite people to a room set up for meditation with floor mats and pillows. If possible, invite the newly dead person's spiritual teacher or someone well acquainted with both Tibetan Buddhism and the subject of the service.

2. Begin with a statement of the purpose of the *Sukhavti* for those who have never attended one, followed by a ten-minute silent meditation.

3. Light incense and place it together with flowers in front of a photo or image of the newly dead person.

4. Invite anyone who has anything to say about the person to speak, explaining the helpfulness of truth and honesty in aiding the spirit through the *bardos*. The serene nature of this Buddhist ceremony allows for silence and reflection; speaking should not be forced.

Again, although this method of honoring the dead was unusual to my Western mind, Maggie's ritual was one of the most meaningful ceremonies I have ever experienced.

In this look at life's passages, we have made the journey from birth to death and many phases in between. The more rituals you create and perform to acknowledge these phases of human life, the richer your life will be.

Chapter Seven

A COVEN OF ONE: RITUALS FOR THE SOLITARY PRACTITIONER

Ritual can take many forms, from a huge number of people participating in a community celebration to one person seeking deeper understanding of himself or herself. Our lives are basically a search for meaning. When you hold a memory dear, it is because the original event meant something to you. It was relevant, shedding light upon your soul and touching your heart in a special way. Creating and performing rituals on your own will help you define and strengthen your own identity and customize your desired outcome according to your individual will and intention. Performing rituals by yourself means you are your own priest or priestess, a solo seeker progressing along the spiritual path at your own pace. Ideally, you will also participate in rites involving groups of people. In this way, you can get all the benefits of staying in touch with your community by continuing to learn from others and receive the stimulation of being with like-minded people. If you are a loner, it is even more important for you to stay tied to a special community.

However, for many folks, doing ritual alone is incredibly powerful and enhances their personal evolution. While group ritual is about service, connection, and change, individual rites are powerful inner workings that kindle soul development and spiritual expansion. Group rituals are frequently tied to events, such as holidays, or a community crisis, such as an illness. Solitary ritual comes from your deepest inner rhythms. It comes from your own needs, your own questing, and your own psyche. With solitary rituals, you can also addresses more private matters that you would rather not share with others or broadcast to the community.

Personal rituals can be a major force in your personal development. I have known many people who are going through a rough time for whom ritual was a touchstone and an aid. Ritual will help you not just get through something but also learn from it and come out the other side transformed. As the author of *Women's Rituals,* Barbara Walker, says, "Meaning develops out of doing."

The human spirit loves ritual and needs it. Observe your own children or those of your neighborhood and notice how they create their own spontaneous rituals. Ritual seems to be an important part of human development. The inclusion of ritual and celebration in our lives not only enriches us, but can also make us healthier and happier people.

Here is your opportunity to explore yourself through ritual. Ultimately, there will come a time when you need to design your own ritual as it springs up from the depths of your soul. Use the tools described for rituals of examination of your deepest inner self.

Constructing Your Inner Temple

Call forth your powers within to make magic with ritual. Your mind and will are potent magical tools, and ritual is the practice of exercising your will. In order for your solitary rituals to be successful and a positive force in your life, you need to think a few things through:

- ✦ Identify your intention
- ✦ Plan your ritual
- ✦ Prepare for your ritual

Once you have gathered your essential ingredients and tools together, you should prepare everything and once it is in place, you should:

- ✦ Relax completely
- ✦ Enact the ritual
- ✦ Clean and clear the space with everything in its place

Setting Your Intention

A well-defined and focused intention is the key to success in a life-enhancing ritual. Good results depend upon clarity. If your intention is not crystal clear, you are likely to fail. You must approach your ritual with a definite concentration. If a nagging worry is hovering in the back of your mind, you are not properly focused. You may even want to perfect an image of your intention and desire with creative visualization.

Part of your preparation should also include using ritual correspondences—the phase of the moon, the day of the week, the color of the candles you use, and much more. These things add to the depth and meaning of your ritual.

Do you need to clear the energy and refresh your altar with some housecleaning and smudge? Do so and continue to focus on your intention as you create the foundation for a successful ceremony.

While you are clearing energy in your space, you must also clear out the clutter in your mind. If you are in a state of inner chaos, the outcome will simply not measure up to your expectations. Perhaps it will help you relax if you play CDs of instrumental music or sacred chants. Conscious breathing or stretching will also help you make yourself ready for ritual.

Constructing your inner temple is a marvelous process that can aid in your journey deep inside yourself. Sit or lie down in a position that is comfortable enough to relax you, but not so comfortable as to allow you to drift off to sleep. As you breathe slowly and rhythmically, imagine a peaceful, beautiful place specific to your desires. It could be a white marble temple in a lovely sculpture garden under a still blue sky. It could be a mirror pool by a sacred grove. It must be pleasing to you, a place you can visit frequently in visualization. It can be any size or shape but should have certain aspects:

- **The Center:** Your inner temple should have a single center from which you can access all areas of the temple. This center is a representation of your personal power center.

- **Reflective Surface:** Here is where you can take a look at yourself spiritually. The reflective surface can be a scrying mirror, a crystal ball, or even a pool of water. You can also use it to look at the past, present, and future.

- **Water:** Your inner temple can have any number of water sources, such as a waterfall, a well, a stream, or an ocean. Water represents our deepest levels of consciousness. Commune with your deepest self here.

✦ **Earth:** Here is where you ground yourself, and create manifestation. Take stock of your deepest desires and goals here in a garden, forest, meadow, or wherever your imagination guides you.

Ideally, your inner temple has four doorways or gates, one each for the four directions and elements. Once you have created your ideal inner temple, you can now use it to perform ritual, as you have created permanent sacred space inside and outside this temple through visualization.

Intention Candle Spell

Essential elements for this ritual are one candle of your favorite color, a candle holder, copal or cinnamon essential oil to represent spirituality, paper and pen, a ritual knife, and any visual aids you may require, such as photos, tarot cards, or a drawing of a deity you have made or found specifically for this ritual. Carefully select a representation of a deity with whom you feel a connection or who you believe will be benevolent toward your intention.

The "body" of the ritual refers to the act itself. It will further your intention if you carve related symbols and power words into your candle with the tip of your knife. Anoint the candle with the essential oil you have chosen. Dressing the candle from top to bottom adds the influence of attraction to your spell. Conversely, dressing the oil in the opposite direction, bottom to top, adds banishing power to your spell.

Write your intention on the paper and then speak aloud:

> *Thus I consecrate this candle in the name of* [insert name of the deity here],
> *So this flame will burn brightly and light my way.*

Place the anointed candle in the candleholder, light it, and say:

Blessed candle, light of the Goddess,
I burn this light of [deity's name].
Hear my prayer, O [name the deity], *hear my need.*
Do so with all your grace,
And magical speed.

Now read your intention as you wrote it on the paper. Roll the paper into a scroll and, using a few drops of the warm wax from your intention candle, seal your sacred statement. Place the paper on your altar or in a special place where it can be safe until your intention is realized.

Allow the candle to burn down completely in order to truly raise and release energy. It can be useful to use small candles or tea lights for spells that require candles to burn out completely so you're not left sitting there for several hours. Once you have seen your spell come to culmination, burn the written intention in a metal dish or in your fireplace in gratitude to the god or goddess who helped you. While other faiths may pray to God for help and favors, this differs in that you are helping yourself: you are taking action and setting your intention, not simply turning over all responsibility to a higher power.

Ritual Knotting

You can add an additional aspect of manifestation to empower your statement of intention with a knotting spell. All you need is your paper scroll and a length of red thread or cord. The color red signifies life and active energy.

As you read your statement of intention, picture the end result in your mind and pour all your powers of concentration onto the paper. After you feel you have fully focused your energy into the scroll, roll it up. Now, proceed to tie knots in the order of the following traditional chant:

> *By knot of one, this ritual is begun.*
> *By knot of two, my wish comes true.*
> *By knot of three, so mote it be.*
> *By knot of four, the magic is even more.*
> *By knot of five, the gods are alive.*
> *By knot of six, my intention is fixed.*
> *By knot of seven, under the influence of heaven.*
> *By knot of eight, I change my fate.*
> *By knot of nine, all powers are divine.*

When you have completed the knots, tie the cord around your scroll.

Centering: Getting Grounded in Yourself

The best way to prepare for personal ritual is to center yourself. I call this "doing a readjustment," and I believe this is especially important in our overscheduled and busy world. Doing a readjustment helps pull you back into yourself and gets your priorities back on track. Only when you are truly centered can you do the true inner work of self-development that is at the core of ritual.

Centering takes many forms. Experiment on your own to find out what works best for you. My friend Kat Sanborn, for example, does a quick meditation that she calls "the chakra check-in." The chakra system comprises energy points in the astral body associated with various endocrine glands in the physical body. My friend closes her eyes and sits lotus-fashion (if possible, but if you are on a bus or in a meeting you can do this centering exercise just sitting down, feel on the floor) and visualizes the light and color of each chakra. She visualizes each chakra and mentally runs energy up and down her spine, from bottom to top, pausing at each chakra point. After she does this a few times, a soothing calm surrounds her. I have seen her perform her "chakra check-in" at trade shows and in hotel lobbies, surrounded by the hubbub of many people. She is an ocean of calm at the center of a storm. By working with your chakras, you can become much more in touch with your body and soul.

The root chakra is at the base of your spine and is associated with passion, survival and security and the color red. Above it is the sacral chakra in the abdominal region, which corresponds to such physical urges as hunger and sex and the color is orange. The solar plexus chakra is yellow and is associated with personal power. The throat chakra is blue and is considered the center of communication. The third eye chakra is located in the center of your forehead and is associated with intuition and the color indigo. The crown chakra at the very top of your head is your connection to the universe and is violet in color.

Prior to performing a ritual, try this centering exercise. Take a comfortable sitting position and find your pulse. Keep your fingers on your pulse until you feel the steady rhythm of your own heart.

Now begin slowly breathing in rhythm with your heartbeat. Inhale for four beats, hold for four beats, and then exhale for five beats. Repeat this pattern for six cycles. People have reported that although it seems hard to match up with the heartbeat at first, with a little bit of practice, your breath and heartbeat will synchronize. Your entire body will relax and all physical functions will seem slower and more natural than ever before.

Candle Centering

Another excellent way to center is to light a candle and meditate on it. By focusing on the flame, you bring your being and awareness into focus. You can take this a step further with this spell for new insight into your life.

1. Place one candle on your altar or "centering station." Light your favorite meditation incense. For me, *nag champa* immediately sanctifies any space and creates a sacred aura.

2. Scratch your name into the candle with the tip of your knife. Next, scratch your hope onto the candle.

3. Light your candle and recite:

> *This candle burns for me.*
> *Here burns my hope for [say what you are hoping for].*
> *Here burns the flame of insight,*
> *May I see clearly in this new light.*

4. Sit with your eyes closed for a few minutes and picture yourself enacting your hopes and desires. You are setting your intention. Picture yourself in the company of people who inspire and teach you, those who bring insight and new light into your life. Let the candle burn down completely.

New Year, New You: Metamorphosis and Transmutation

Here is a personal ritual I recommend for the New Year, whether it is Samhain (October 31, All Hallow's Eve) or

Saturnalia (December 17–24). It can also be performed any time you feel the need for renewal or personal reinvention.

Like a caterpillar, we can burst out of our old form and shed old skin. Old habits that no longer serve should be released. If drinking alcohol, for example, has become a problem for you, let go, find a Twelve-Step program, and let miracles happen in your life as you release the old and welcome the new. We must let go of the past in order to look to the future.

A well-timed ritual can be the process by which you let go of that past. It formalizes the act and marks the time of entry into a new present and new future.

Start with a ritual bath, or this Inspirational Immersion, to cleanse yourself.

Immersion

At the day's last light, pour a bath. As your run the water, pour drops of bergamot, rosemary, vetiver, and eucalyptus oils into the steaming waters. Bathe in the gathering dark. As darkness begins to fill the room, meditate and pray for positive change in your life. Know that this is the day your life will surely change forever.

Metamorphosis Ritual

Choose a place in your home or wherever you feel secure to do this deeply personal ritual. Allow it to be dark. You are in the dark cocoon and about to burst out into the light. Cast your circle of change by moving clockwise around the room three times. Notice as you walk that you can feel the darkness increasing. You are creating a magical space in which you will work for your desired change.

Stand in the middle of the circle and speak aloud what you want to get rid of in your life. Speak the truth from the safe center of your sanctuary. Close your eyes and turn to the east. Now, using creative visualization, call up the element of air. Picture a piece of the day sky filled with clouds and the night filled with stars. This is the element of air. Wait until you feel its presence fully entered in the circle and speak aloud:

> *I face the east; I am air. I call upon the powers of the sky and the stars to aid me now.*

Now turn to the south and visualize a flaming red ball of sun, which is fire, heat, and life. You will know the element of fire is present by the heat you feel in your circle. Speak aloud:

> *I face south; I am fire. I call upon the powers of flame and heat, the passion of fire to help me through. Burn away the old, my former self.*

Now turn to the west and visualize the waters of the world— oceans, rivers, creeks, and lakes— all merging into a single drop of the holiest water. Speak aloud:

> *I face the west. I am made of water. I call upon the powers of water, more powerful than any stone. I ask the waters of life to cleanse me and purify me, ready me for total change.*

Now face the north and visualize the green of the earth, the soil and seeds of change. Speak aloud:

> *I face the north. I am grounded in this earth. I call upon the powers of earth, our planet, to give me the strength to change.*

Stand still in the center of your circle and feel the energies of the elements, the powers of the four directions, and the strength of nature's helpers. Relax into this energy and allow visions, ideas, and inspiration to arise. Welcome new feelings and sensations. You should be open to experiencing new patterns of thought. Thinking in a new way is one way to shed your old skin. Now begin to move and stretch in your circle of magic. Reach up as high as you can, and bend and bow as you emerge from the cocoon of your old self. Breathe deeply, inhaling and exhaling slowly and fully. After ten breaths, you should begin to feel a buzzing sensation at the top of your head. This is the signal that you have arrived at a new level of consciousness. You have shed your old limits; your transmutation is complete.

Walking counterclockwise, retrace the steps of your circle. As you walk, speak your gratitude to the elements and the directions, taking care to give thanks for all the help you have received during this circle of change. Your circle is now open.

As you go through the next few days, reflect on your new feelings and impressions. New people will come into your life. New opportunities will arise. You have given yourself the gift of new life. Enjoy this new post-metamorphic phase of change and treasure it.

The Vision Quest

While the term "vision quest" comes from Native American teachings, it is really the passage of the personal journey. No matter what your spiritual orientation is, for true personal development, it is essential to do the inner work. You must explore yourself deeply and discover what is important to you, sense where you need to go, and set your spiritual goals. At the end of the day and at the end of your life, it will not matter how many houses or cars you have; what really matters is what kind of person you were and how you treated others. Was the work of your life soul work? Did you express yourself creatively? Did you take care of your family? Did you help others?

Look inside; face these questions. Can you answer them satisfactorily? By doing so you will be able to determine and change the future course of events. A vision quest is an essential step in a life well lived, a life full of soul work, a life hard but ultimately joyful.

This ritual, performed in keeping with the Native American tradition, is a rite of passage requiring courage and fortitude. At the end, you will most certainly know who you are! Going into the wilderness by yourself with no food, water, or other creature comforts to do nothing but pray certainly forces you to face your inner self. The purpose of the vision quest is to receive a vision. Not everyone succeeds. Some people are too frightened, hungry, and cold to continue. Others experience an altered reality or deep visions due to sensory deprivation and the extreme physicality of the vision quest.

Personal Vision Quest

Carve out at least twelve hours for this day-long journey to your inner self. Ideally, it should begin at first light of dawn and end past twilight. Traditional Native American vision quests lasted up to four days, but this one-day version is still an effective path to self-discovery. Another aspect of this vision quest is that it is safe and easily practiced by urban spiritual seekers who only have the weekends for mystical pursuits and who lack access to mountainous regions.

To ready yourself for your inner work, you should fast with juice, weak tea, and plenty of water. If you have access to a sauna, you can perform a purification to ready your spirit. Pack a bag with a sage smudge stick, matches, water, juice, a blanket, a cell phone, and anything you feel you need for safety of in case of an emergency, such as an energy or granola bar, apples, energy drinks, and so forth. Let someone know what you plan to do, and where you plan to do it, and ask them to meet you at a specified time to bring you home; the last thing you'll want to do is trek to the bus or drive a car. While Native shamans traditionally sent people out into the wild, it is better to be safe. Select a garden or nearby park. Ideally, your place will be outdoors but if that is not possible, you can choose someplace different to contemplate. Do some research on the place you have selected so there are no surprises that can interfere with your plans.

Draw a circle in the dirt, sand, or grass with a fallen branch or with your feet. Bless the circle with sage smoke and choose rocks to mark the four directions. Now settle into being alone, utterly alone. Pray, meditate, and contemplate for as long as you can without interruption: no food, no books, no cell phone, and no distractions. Pay attention to nature around you and be prepared to receive a visit from your totem animal in the form of a vision. Think about who you are and where you are going, your origins, and your spirit. I recommend taking a journal and making notes, as you feel inspired. Chanting and singing is a good way to open your spirit. No two vision quests will be alike. I cannot predict what will happen to you, whether you will have epiphanies, breakthroughs, visions, or how insight will come to you. What I do know, however, is that you will undoubtedly know yourself better at the end of your vision quest.

If at any time you feel endangered or unwell, end your vision quest. The pursuit of spiritual enlightenment should not come at the cost of your safety.

Animal Spirits

Oftentimes, messages come with animals, either live or in spirit vision. If this happens to you, you should study the meaning of this animal, as it may well become your personal totem or power animal. Bear in mind, too, that your animal totem might be a real surprise. You may be a 300-pound linebacker, and your totem might be a mouse. Remember, the totem picks you; you don't pick the totem.

I was surprised when my spirit animal totem first came to me. For whatever reason, I thought I was not a nature girl. I did a personal vision quest, and while a trip to an exotic place such as the Amazon jungle was not in my immediate plans, I felt I could definitely journey to the shore and make it a spiritual trek. Between Santa Cruz and San Francisco, there is a wonderful national park by the Pacific Ocean called Big Basin. Big Basin features a waterfall with a very large creek that flows down a mountain directly into the ocean. For sheer physical beauty and drama, Big Basin is nearly unmatched. The waterfall is a "word of mouth" phenomenon that only occurs after the rainy season. If you go at any other time, the waterfall is dry and, for all intents and purposes, simply does not exist. I decided that, for my purposes, I could experience a little magic.

So I set off on the seven-mile journey up the mountain to find Berry Creek Falls. Because I was hit by a drunk driver some years back and suffered physical trauma, I am not a hiker. But I was extremely motivated to try, and the beauty of the spring day I had selected for my vision quest was sheer joy to behold. Through flowering spring trees, the singing brook, and a lush green landscape, I felt like I had rediscovered Eden all by myself. After about five miles, my ankle, which had been smashed in the accident, was begging me for a respite. I moved down the bank of the big creek and dipped my throbbing leg into the cool water. It felt so good, and I was so hot and hungry, that it seemed absolutely essential that I plunge into the creek. I think I lay in the water for at least two hours, and I felt an enormous sense of release there. I wept, letting go of deep emotions as the water flowed around me. Lichen, moss, leaves, and some small sticks caught in my hair, but these only added to my sense that I was getting closer to nature. I was in my element and very glad of it.

Eventually, I became aware of the world outside my mossy mermaid creek bed. It was getting late and, lacking flashlight or fire, I could either wash out to sea or return to the world and my life. Refreshed, a little more lucid, and a lot hungrier, but with no distinct vision, it seemed that it was going to take another trip for me to get any real enlightenment.

I started the journey of several miles down the incline, deep in thought. After a few minutes I noticed that I was not the only one walking in the woods. I stopped, and the other footsteps stopped, too. I started and the other footsteps started again. The steps were very close. It seemed that someone or something was walking just off to my left, practically beside me. I started to get frightened; being followed was not in my vision quest plans!

Carefully and quietly, I turned to look in the dimming light. To my utter amazement, there was a young female deer walking beside me. We looked at each other, and I am not sure who was more frightened. We walked together and soon grew fairly comfortable with each other's presence. I touched her and she didn't flinch or run away. This was miraculous. I marveled that she remained at my side. I grew up in West Virginia, where deer simply don't "hang out" with humans. I came to realize that this doe was my animal totem. She picked me, and definitely let me know that she was there for me, escorting me down the mountain from my vision quest. At the end of the grassy hill, before it became sand and beach, she turned, and with a long gaze gave me her goodbye. I was practically shaking with excitement and an indescribable bursting feeling inside.

All those Native American teachings I had heard were completely real and true. Never again did I doubt the veracity of vision and spirit from the elders.

The realm of the spirit is there. It's just waiting for you to walk in.

Animal Totem Symbology

Native American tribes have given us the great gift of animal wisdom. This wonderful lore and legacy handed down to us can act as a daily oracle. When you see an animal or a representation of one, consider these meanings.

- **Bear**—emerging consciousness
- **Beaver**—building, manifesting hopes and dreams
- **Bobcat**—mystery and secrets, stealth and silence
- **Buffalo**—abundance and right livelihood
- **Bull**—fertility
- **Cat**—magic, the unknowable, autonomy
- **Coyote**—wisdom, recklessness

- ✦ **Deer**—kindness and tenderness, adventure and incorruptibility
- ✦ **Dog**—faithful guardianship
- ✦ **Whale**—song and music, inner intensity, creation
- ✦ **Wolf**—ritual and spirit, allegiance and custodianship

Song of Myself—A Ritual for Self-Expression

This is definitely one of the more entertaining solo rituals. It requires you to look hard at yourself, but it's also fun. Essential elements that are necessary for this ritual include:

- ✦ Big sheets of butcher paper
- ✦ Color markers, glitter, beads, shells, cloth, ribbon, yarn—whatever colorful materials you respond well to
- ✦ Sewing kit and craft boxes with random scraps, buttons, and/or shiny objects

It is good to undertake this ritual on a Sunday, but whenever you need support, reserve half an hour of quiet time and brew up some willpower to help you with your self-expression. Light a white candle anointed with peppermint oil and light spicy incense such as cinnamon. Prepare for your Song of Myself by sipping this warm drink for encouragement: Take a sprig of mint (homegrown is best), a cup of warm milk, and cinnamon sticks and stir together clockwise in a white mug. Recite:

Herb of menthe and spicy mead,
Today is the day I will succeed.
In every word and every deed.
Today I sing the song of me.

Drink the brew while it is still warm and "sit for a spell." You will know when you are ready.

Now take the paper and markers and begin your song of yourself. Write with any marker you pick up and finish this sentence at least twenty-four times: *I am* _____.

Be as wild and free and true as you can. You are so many things. Express them here and now, once and for all. I will share some wonderful "Songs of Self" that I have seen and heard:

I am a wild woman.
I am beautiful.
I am wide.
I am a secret.
I am sexy.
I am brilliant.
I am a blue sky.
I am all possibility.
I am a dream come to life.
I am truth.
I am the Goddess.
I am the living incarnation of wisdom.
I am life.
I am a living blessing.
I am the road.
I am perfect.
I am a tiger.
I am yesterday and today.
I am hope.
I am angry.
I am art.
I am a crone.
I am a sister to the sun.

> *I am a poem.*
> *I am creative.*
> *I am me!*

This can go on as long as you want it to. Only when you feel you have expressed every aspect of yourself should you put down your marker and begin to decorate the paper. Paint on it, glue mirror shards to it, do one or many self-portraits. Scrawl symbols on it. Write more words and allow yourself total and absolute creative freedom. There is no wrong or right; there is only you and all your myriad aspects. Celebrate yourself and reveal yourself completely. By the end, you should have a one-of-a-kind self-portrait that tells your real story.

Hang your self-song portrait in a sacred place, perhaps near your altar or shrine area. Its energy will permeate the place with your personal essence in a wonderful way.

Summoning the Muses

Whenever you embark on a new life phase, a creative project, or personal ritual, you are further awakening to your destiny. The nine muses, daughters of Memory and rulers of creative endeavors, can help you find your true path. Here is a "field guide" to the muses to help you determine which one you should invoke for aid.

Calliope, "The Fair Voiced," is the eldest of the muses and presides over epic poetry.

Clio, "The Proclaimer," is the muse of history. She carries a scroll of knowledge.

Erato, "The Lovely," has domain over the poetics of love and mimicry. She carries a lyre.

Euterpe, "The Giver of Pleasure," plays a flute. Her sphere of influence is music.

Melpomene, "The Songstress," wears the mask of tragedy, over which she presides.

Polyhymnia, "She of Many Hymns," is the muse of sacred poetry. She wears a veil.

Terpsichore, "The Whirler," had dominion over dance.

Thalia, "The Festive," wears the mask of comedy.

Urania, "The Heavenly," presides over both astronomy and astrology.

In truth, you can call upon any god or goddess with whom you feel a deep connection, but the muses can guide you to personal inventiveness. They will help you sing the song of you and express yourself through poetry, art, dance, theater, academia, music, communication—any way in which you need to reveal unseen and unknown sides of yourself.

Place an offering to your chosen muse on your altar or shrine— perhaps a verse of poetry or a drawing—that shows your gratitude and appreciation for all you have received and will continue to receive as inspiration from your muse.

The Goddess, in all her glorious incarnations, is the supreme creative force and brings all into being. Long before the birth of Christianity, people worshipped the Goddess who represents fertility, rebirth, wisdom, and life. Decide which muse you want to work with and chant aloud:

O [name of muse], wise and true,
I will walk with thee in the Elysian Fields and back.
Anoint me here and now.
Thanks to you, inspiration I will never lack.

Walking the Labyrinth—A Path of Grace to the Inner Self

At the Grace Cathedral on California Street in San Francisco, scholar Lauren Artress oversaw the installation of not one but two labyrinths. Sue Patton Thoele, author of *The Woman's Book of Soul*, invited me to go there one fine day a few years ago. I remember squeezing it into my schedule, feeling hurried, and hoping it would not take more than half an hour or so. I am a bit embarrassed to admit this, but I know I am not the only busy life-juggler who has found herself surprised by the Sacred.

When we got there, a magnificent stillness presided over the entire cathedral. We chose the indoor labyrinth instead of the outdoor one, as there was a distinct chill in the foggy air that day. We read the simple instructions and, as told, removed our shoes to tread the path in bare or stocking feet. For my part, I had already begun to calm down, thanks to the peaceful atmosphere. As I walked in the light of the stained glass shadows, my schedule started to seem petty. Suddenly it seemed as if I could give this just a little more time.

Sue, an experienced labyrinth walker, had gone ahead and seemed to be in a reverie, as did the tourists, students, and random folks who populated the nave. I checked the instructions again just to make sure I performed my barefoot ritual "correctly."

As I began, thoughts skittered through my head, and I had to struggle to focus and be in the now. With no small amount of effort, I was able to have an authentic experience. As I walked the winding path, a replica of the labyrinth on the floor of Chartres Cathedral, I felt a growing excitement. This was meaningful; perhaps there was hope even for me and my over-busy "monkey mind." My breathing relaxed and I had a growing sense that I was going somewhere. When I reached the center of the labyrinth, I looked up at the soaring high ceiling of Grace Cathedral. At that exact moment, the sun struck a stained glass window and a golden shaft of light shone directly upon me. I was mystified, and a beaming Sue, having completed her walk, noticed what was happening to me. I studied the window to see if there was any kind of symbol from which to draw further meaning. To my astonishment, the sun had lit up a window that contained the medieval tableau of a sword in a rock. As a lapsed medieval scholar, I immediately recognized Excalibur of the famous Arthurian legend. Tears came into my eyes, and I realized this was a message. I had often felt a bit guilty for not completing my master's degree in medieval studies. At that moment, I knew I had to complete that quest. One of my specializations was the Arthurian saga, and here, in no uncertain terms, Arthur's sword had spoken to me as I stood in the center of the labyrinth. Exhilarated, I retraced my steps, and returned as I entered, brimming with joy. Now, I truly understand what it means to be "illuminated."

Walking Meditation—How to Walk the Labyrinth

The labyrinth represented wholeness to the ancients, combining the circle and the spiral in one archetypal image. The labyrinth is unicursal, meaning there is only one path, both in and out. Put simply, it is a journey into the self, into your own center, and back into the world again. As a prayer and meditation tool, labyrinths are peerless; they awaken intuition.

Do your best to relax before you enter. Deep breaths will help a great deal. If you have a specific question in mind, think it or whisper it to yourself. You will meet others on the pilgrim's path as you are walking; simply step aside and let them continue on their journey as you do the same. The three stages of the labyrinth walk are as follows:

Purgation: Here is where you free your mind of all worldly concerns. It is a release, a letting go. Still your mind and open your heart. Shed worries and emotion as you step out on the path.

Illumination: When you have come to the center, you are in the place of illumination. Here, you should stay as long as you feel the need to pray and meditate. In this quiet center, the heart of the labyrinth, you will receive messages from the Divine or from your own higher power. Illumination can also come from deep inside yourself.

Union: This last phase is where you will experience union with the divine. Lauren Artress says that as you "walk the labyrinth you become more empowered to find and do the work you feel your soul requires."

Use the rituals in this chapter to become one with yourself and find peace within. May you use this learned tranquility to better participate in other rituals that focus on important aspects of your life.

Chapter Eight

NORTH, SOUTH, EAST, AND WEST: THE FOUR DIRECTIONS AND THE FOUR ELEMENTS IN RITUAL

There are many layers of meaning to add to ritual that are based on centuries of mystical and spiritual source material that still influence us today. These sources are called "magical correspondences," and the transformative process that is ritual calls for as many correspondences as possible to add to the overall effect, creating a synthesis of energies to work these changes in your life and in the world. Just as there are the specific astrological influences of the stars and planets, such as the rhythmic phases of the moon, and a range of powers in stones, there are particular powers in the elements you can call upon in your ritual work.

Earth, air, fire, and water are the four elements of the ancients. The pre-Socratic Greek philosopher, Empedocles of Sicily, taught the theory of the four elements about 2,500 years ago. Modern metaphysicians and magicians no longer believe literally in four elements but find them useful tools for magic.

Earth

Earth is the manifestation of the "solid." It is matter made tangible. Earth represents intransigence, constancy, and durability. We are made of earth, and so we are part of our own planet. Upon our death, we once again return to the earth. Earth is the stable material and the stable element. You can place salt in a ceramic bowl or soil in a small vial upon your altar to represent this element. You can call upon the element of earth to become more grounded or to build a new aspect into your life. Earth signs Taurus, Virgo, and Capricorn should perform earth ritual on a regular basis to stay centered.

Water

Water is the fluid state of matter, the nurturer of all life and essential for all continued existence. The blood that flows through the veins of animals is mostly water with trace minerals flowing within it. Water cleanses, nourishes crops, and washes away what no longer serves a purpose. Water is the opposite of earth in that it flows: it lacks stability. Even ice, water in a stable form, can melt. Water in our rivers, lakes, and oceans is ever-changing. Water is a very important cleansing and blessing element to bring into play in your ritual. A fountain or bowl of water in your home represents the all-important water of life. You can use water for any kind of releasing ritual. Water signs Cancer, Scorpio, and Pisces should stay in tune with their sensitive, creative natures with water rituals.

Air

Air is an ever-changing element, matter in its gaseous form. Air has ultimate mobility and dynamism. The oxygen in the air we breathe is essential to the continuation of our life. Air is unseen and is, in and of itself, formless. Wind is the power of air to move and stimulate change. Air signs Gemini, Libra, and Aquarius can maintain their brilliance and superior communication skills with rituals invoking their native element of air.

Fire

Fire is sheer transformational power, capable of changing the other elements. The most visible form of energy, fire is also heat. Watch the flicker of your candle flame, the ember of your incense, and the blaze of your council fire, and you will see a constant transmutation of matter. Fire has the ability to both excite and incite us and is used to bring about active change. Fire signs Aires, Leo, and Sagittarius will stay strong and vibrant when they employ their personal element, fire.

How the Four Directions Relate to the Four Elements

The four directions we invoke in modern magical circles and ceremonies correspond to the four elements. Calling out to the four directions creates the sacred space of the circle, the center of ritual work. In doing this, you are also calling forth elemental entities and energies. Here are some general modern associations for the directions. Be aware that these associations are not universal. They can vary from culture to culture, as well as among traditions and from practitioner to practitioner within a spiritual path.

North

The north corresponds to earth and wintertime. Brown and green are the traditional colors and the totem animals are elk, wolf, and the mighty bear. The tarot suit of pentacles is associated with both earth and the north.

South

The south corresponds to fire and summertime. Gold and red are the traditional colors and the totem animals are lizard, snake, and the lion. The tarot suit of wands is associated with both fire and south.

East

The east corresponds to air and springtime. Yellow and pink are the traditional colors and the totem animals are all birds, including eagle, hawk, and raven. The tarot suit of swords is associated with both air and east.

West

The west corresponds to water and autumn. Purple and blue are the traditional colors and the totem animals are water beasts, including swans, whales, and dolphins. The tarot suit of cups is associated with both water and west.

North, South, East, and West: a Ritual for Daily Life

You can purify your home every day and create sacred space for living a life of daily ritual. After cleaning or straightening your home, bless the rooms and ensure that you are surrounded with good energy. Take a bowl or cup of water and add a sprinkle of salt. Then anoint your fingers and forehead. Now turn to the east and say:

Powers of the East,
Source of the sun rising,
ring me hope and inspiration.

Sprinkle some water in the east, then turn to the south and say:

> *Powers of the South,*
> *Source of summer's warmth and light,*
> *Bring me joy and bounty.*

Sprinkle some water in the south, then turn to the west and say:

> *Powers of the West,*
> *Source of oceans and rivers,*
> *Bring me the power of the waves.*

Sprinkle some water in the west, then turn to the north and say:

> *Powers of the North,*
> *Source of the winter, place of the mountains, and*
> *the polestar,*
> *Bring me security and sight.*

Close this simple ritual by sprinkling the water and salt all around your home, especially on or around windows, windowsills, doorways, and thresholds where energy passes in and out as visitors arrive and depart. By doing this, you are cleansing and managing the energy of your space. After an argument or upsetting event, or even after a visit by a person who is in a foul mood, you can repeat this ritual to clear out the "bad energy."

Elemental Rituals: Water

The human body is made mostly of water, and our connection to this sacred element is primal. People are especially drawn to the ocean, whose water is a blend of minerals and water similar to the chemical mix of our blood. Have you ever noticed how blissful you can feel when you're at the beach? The negative ions produced by water are soothing and create an overwhelming sense of optimism. In the presence of water, we feel refreshed. The ocean tides are a rhythm of life and a regulating force of nature.

Water cleanses and restores us, determines our climate, enriches our crops and forests. Water has long been used in ritual and continues to this day to be employed by nearly every culture. In India, the sacred Ganges River cleanses the souls of Hindus from birth through death, when they often float off to eternity in a river burial. Christian baptisms are done with the sacrament of water. The Chinese deity Kuan Yin, goddess of compassion, offers spiritual seekers the comfort and solace of a holy lake. Aphrodite herself rose up from the ocean, and the Yoruban divinity, Ymoja (Yemaya in Brazil and Cuba), is believed to rule all the waters of the earth.

I was born with both my natal sun and moon in the astrological sign of Pisces. As a double Pisces, I receive much spiritual substance from water and turn to my element for succor. Water is the element that rules Pisces, Cancer, and Scorpio. It reconnects water folk with their native element and keeps them in tune with their true nature.

The Japanese have elevated water ritual to the level of an art form with baths, water meditations, water gardens, and tea ceremonies. Through the centuries, they have perfected the presentation of tea as an inventive and spiritual practice.

The following rituals concentrate on this life-sustaining and significant element.

Taking the Waters—a Releasing Ritual

Sarasvati is a Hindu goddess of the arts, and originally a river goddess. She is invoked by individuals seeking to improve the flow of their creativity and self-transformation.

A bath blessing that will both relax and purify you is a rare and wonderful thing. To prepare yourself, place 1 quart of rough sea salt or Epsom salts in a large bowl. Add the juice from 6 freshly squeezed lemons, ½ cup of sesame oil, and a few drops of rose and jasmine oils. Stir until the mixture is completely moistened. You can add more sesame oil if necessary, but do not add more lemon because it will make the mixture overly astringent and potentially irritating to your skin.

When your tub is one-third full, add one-quarter of the salt mixture under the faucet. Breathe in deeply ten times, inhaling and exhaling fully before you do this recitation. You may start to feel a tingling at the crown of your head. The water should still be running when you proclaim:

> *Sarasvati, O Harmonious One,*
> *Goddess and mistress, I ask your guidance.*
> *Remove from me any impurities*
> *Of heart, spirit, and mind. I open myself to you.*
> *My wish is to once again become whole,*
> *Free of pain, sadness, and all that is better in me.*

When the tub is full, it is time to step inside and breathe deeply ten more times. Repeat the prayer to Sarasvati, and use the rest of the salt to gently massage your body. Rest and rejuvenate as long as you like, allowing yourself to feel refreshed and renewed by the ministrations of this Hindu goddess of harmony and artistry from whom eloquence, inspiration, and blessings flow.

Designing Your Own Water Rituals

From the depths of your imagination, you can create a water ritual of your own by invoking other water deities. By inviting the energy of water into your sacred space, you will find the words will flow into you as you fashion ceremonial language appropriate to that god or goddess.

You can create your own ceremonies and spells to call forth the power of water for psychic development such as dream work, emotional balance, healing, creativity, joy, love, and letting go.

Water Deities

Lakshmi is also called Padma and is associated with all forms of wealth and abundance, both spiritual and material. It is said that Lakshmi can be found in gems and jewels, money, newborn babies, and in all cows. She is depicted floating on a lovely lotus blossom.

Naiads are freshwater nymphs that inhabit various bodies of water such as lakes, rivers, and springs. Naiads have the power to seduce, inspire, heal, and tell the future. You will do best by calling forth their gentle energy for healing rituals.

Poseidon is the Greek god of oceans and can use his might to create tidal waves, earthquakes, and typhoons. You should always appease Poseidon when you travel over water with an offering of olive oil; pour a few drops into the sea and you will enjoy smooth sailing all the way. His consort is Amphitrite, the Queen of the Sea.

Nereus, the "old man of the sea" from Greek mythology, is an oracle. You can invoke Nereus to inquire about the future, and for safety during travel by water.

Chaji: the Art of the Japanese Tea Ceremony

You might do well to go to a Japanese teahouse to fully experience the tea ceremony before you undertake one yourself, but don't be intimidated if you cannot. As with all ritual, your intention is the most important aspect. I am fortunate that I live in San Francisco, home of one of the last North American Japantowns. Thus I have several options for tea services in this unique shopping district, where there is a Japanese tea garden near a Shinto shrine. Following are the steps to take in the *Chaji*, a full tea presentation.

Establish a *chashits*, which is the special room for the ceremony. If you are like me and don't have a special room just for tea, clear out space in the living room and place pillows on the floor and set up a low table. I find it rather amusing that the stone basins whose purpose it is to provide cleansing water for the housemaster's hands and mouth are now sold as fancy garden ornaments for those modern folks who like a Zen look for their house. Establish a peaceful environment—no clutter; perhaps set out a lovely flower such as a single orchid or artfully arranged flowers in the high art form of Japanese flower arranging, *ikebana*. A Japanese teahouse has no distracting decor and is the ultimate in simplicity and serenity. One decoration, the exquisite scroll painting *kakemono*, is carefully chosen by the host. Choose a painting or drawing to represent the spiritual sense you want to suggest to your guests through the ceremony. I have friends who have done some *kanji* characters in the brush painting style to express the emotions they felt at that moment. A light and clean scented Japanese incense is the perfect energetic balancer and cleanser. Now you will take on the role of the host: the *teishi*, or housemaster.

Invite four people, the traditional and ideal number, and offer them hot water for the tea, referred to as *sayu*. The guests are to choose someone to act as the *hanto,* or "main guest." In formal Japanese tea ceremony, the host actually has a guest who is the *hanto.* The main guest is not set apart by hierarchy; it is just an arbitrary selection by the host to have a person with whom to engage first in the formalities of this high ritual. Also, there is an anteroom for a reception and a special flowerless garden that has been anointed with water for the purpose of offering a place for the guests to shrug off the cares and grime with which the world burdens them. This garden without flowers is the *roji,* or "dew ground." After leaving the mundane world behind, the guests go to a waiting bench called the *koshikake machiaii.* Complete silence reigns as the housemaster takes the guests through a symbolic gate in order to leave the material and physical world behind, and enter into the magical realm of the tea ceremony.

While the *Chaji* could easily take up its very one book, the way any Westerner can enjoy the spiritual aspects of tea is to receive the gift of tea from the master, pass it around, and share it with the other guests. The gift of tea is the gift of fire and water, yang and yin. Taking tea in this ritualized style is to help keep the world in balance, to escape the material world for a time, and then to return, refreshed and rebalanced.

Inspiration Infusions

Along with healing and energizing properties, herbal teas can aid the mind. Try the following blends:

- ✦ Bergamot dissipates negativity and uplifts.
- ✦ Basil lends a sense of serenity.
- ✦ Rosemary supports physical well-being.
- ✦ Orange creates sheer joy.

Earth Element Rituals

Earth is the ground beneath our feet, the solidity of *terra firma*. The goddess of this element is Gaia, as the Greeks named Mother Earth. Earth is a primal element of rock and stone, soil and tree, plant and flower. Calling forth the element of earth in your ritual work can help you put down roots to reinforce yourself and build a foundation under your hopes and dreams.

As I stated earlier, we are all part of the earth, and this is an important thought to ponder as you engage in the following rituals.

Getting Grounded Through Guided Meditation

Because the world we live in today is very much about getting in your head and staying there, many of us have to make a concentrated effort to become grounded and in touch with our bodies and the natural world around us.

Grounding is the technique for centering yourself within your being, getting into your body and out of your head. Grounding is the way to reconnect and balance yourself through the power of the element of earth. When you see someone driving past talking on their cell phone, you know that they are not grounded. For deep grounding, I recommend a creative visualization or, better yet, a group guided meditation.

Earth Day Ritual: The Sacred Grove

In much the same way that animals, stones, and stars were totemic to early peoples, so were trees. Greco-Roman spirituality had sacred groves, as did the Aborigines in Australia, Hindus in India, Germanic tribes, and the Celts of Europe. To the Celtic Druids, the oak was the major sacred totem tree.

Pliny the Elder pointed out that groves of trees were the first temples.

A wonderful way to celebrate our planet and engender the ideals of preservation and ecological sanctity of our precious resources is to return to the sacred grove. Essential elements necessary for the ritual are colored ribbons and colored markers.

Gather your friends on Earth Day, April 22, and go to a mutually agreed upon park, farm, or forest. Find the largest oak or largest tree with low-hanging branches and circle around it, holding hands while chanting:

> *We are the wisdom of the stars.*
> *The beauty of this green Gaia.*
> *To the planet that gives us life, we return the gift.*
> *We are one*
> *We are the stars and the stones and the sea.*
> *We are one.*

By casting the circle with voice and action, you create a boundary within which magic can take place. One by one, each member of the circle should speak a wish for universal healing, write the wish on a ribbon, and tie the ribbon on the tree. Each flutter of the breeze will speak of your hope and good wishes for our planet. If you are lucky enough to be on the property of a member of your circle, ask if you can leave the ribbons there as the mark of the sacred grove.

Walking Meditation

This is the simplest of rituals you can do every day of your life. As you walk, take the time to look and really see what is in your path. For example, my friend Eileen takes a bag with her and picks up every piece of garbage in her path. She does this as an act of love for the earth. During the ten years I have known her, she has probably turned a mountain of garbage into recycled glass, paper, and plastic. Goddess bless! This is one type of walking meditation. This very simple daily ritual honors the earth and helps preserve life for all beings.

Designing Your Own Earth Rituals

Drawing on the power of the earth, you can perform ceremonies of immense strength and richness to further your personal and spiritual goals. You can begin new projects, deepen your dreams, and ground yourself in nature. You can plant a magical garden with seeds of change. You can sculpt or carve a wooden or stone goddess for your altar. You can cook a sacred meal to serve after ritual work. You can perform rituals outdoors, celebrating the beauty of our planet, a gift we all share and must preserve.

Other earth elemental rites you can design on your own could include ceremonies for fertility, bodily health and strength, prosperity, property, success, and manifestation.

Earth Deities

In addition to Gaia, there are other gods and goddesses who can represent the element of earth. On your home altar or shrine, they can represent earth in your ritual work.

- **The Green Man:** the forest god who represents the power and divinity of nature.
- **Buddha:** He achieved enlightenment under the sacred Bodhi Tree.
- **Venus of Willendorf:** Her appealing and ample shape represents fertility and the feminine.
- **Artemis:** The huntress or woman warrior who travels with a pack of devoted dogs.

The Sacred Element of Fire

Fire inspires us as it seems to spring directly from the divine. Early people regarded fire as power, as a destroyer, and a regenerator. The sung invigorates us each day and we feed on his fire for passion, action, and zeal. Fire is the giver of light and warms us all, man, woman, child, and animal. Fire feeds the passions of the human soul. The fire of the sun warms our hearts and illuminates our imaginations.

Fire Rituals

Fire, giver of light, source of illumination and warmth, is a basis for the following rituals.

Maui Magic

Maui was the trickster god of Hawaii for whom the pacific island was named. Hawaiian peoples were given the gift of flame by the fire giantess herself, Mahuika. However, since it had been handed to them as a gift, the people did not know how to start a fire on their own. Maui visited in the night and stamped out all the fires because he was curious to see what would happen. All the islanders were scared to go to the cave and ask Mahuika for more fire, so the trickster took on the task. Once there, however, Maui made more mischief and swindled the not-so-gentle giantess into giving up nine of her ten fingers, the source of her sparks and flames. Once Mahuika figured out the ruse, Maui was incensed and Mahuika chased him with a wall of fire.

In order to escape the inferno of Mahuika's fire, Maui transformed into a hawk and flew away, using his power as a god to bring on rain to dampen the goddess's fire. Sadly, the storm brought on flooding and the giantess was drowned. Her last act of generosity to the people of Hawaii was turning her stack of firewood into a forest. Mollified, Maui taught the islanders how to spark fire from the wood.

Fire Making

Here is a ritual that requires diligence and patience. Fire making by rubbing sticks together is very difficult and time consuming, but the few folks I know who have accomplished it have certainly felt transformed.

I was inspired by the teachings of the incredible ritual designer, Luisah Teish, who told me she keeps a candle burning in her fireplace at all times to approach Maui's Magic Fire in another way. On the next full moon, gather a group and build a bonfire on the beach or a beautiful fire in a safety-certified fire ring in a park. Ask everyone to bring a glass-encrusted votive candle, preferably one of the seven-day candles you find at grocery stores or metaphysical shops. Begin a round of storytelling with the tale of Maui stealing fire. After you have told the story, light your own candle from the bonfire and say:

Thank you for the fire, Mahuika.

Next, go around the fire and let each participant tell a "fire story." This can be a personal story of fire, or another myth or legend. After each story, the storyteller lights a personal candle from the fire and gives thanks for the fire that warms us and keeps us alive.

Wishing Time: Brazilian Candomble Ritual

The Brazilian Candomble religion is now intertwined with Yoruban spirituality introduced to the New World via the slave trade. Yoruban spirituality offers many answers to personal problems and is a popular system of aid for people in trouble. The Yoruban entities are ready to lend a hand with broken hearts, illnesses, divorce, work woes, insomnia, betrayal, infertility, politics, luck—anything that concerns the human heart.

In Brazil, Candomble has adherents in every walk of life, not just the poor and downtrodden. Candomble is a "fiery" faith: candles and beach bonfires are very much a part of it. You will find shrines with brightly burning candles in the finest homes in Rio. Street shrines are a delightful aspect of the Brazilian culture. An extremely popular and powerful image is that of Xango, the storm god of lightning and thunder. Rich and poor alike have problems, and the spirits are there to help all. The beautiful beaches that run along the entire coast of Brazil are popular places for rituals and offerings. It is not uncommon to find candles glowing by the sea. This must be very pleasing indeed to their beloved mermaid goddess, Yemoja.

These accommodating spirits are called *orixas*. Whether public, as in the middle of a street, or privately in one's home, these offerings are all designed to attract and please the *orixas* when you need a favor. These offerings to the spirits are called *despachos*.

We all have times in our lives when we need help. Are you having difficulty with a coworker or your boss? Do you keep getting the flu all the time? Are you trying to quit smoking and can't seem to kick the habit? Do you need more money? Are you looking for love? Ask the *orixas*!

The following is a list of *orixas* and their correspondences:

* Esu's color is black. Esu has the power to bring messages, likes offerings of candy and toys, and is associated with the number three

* Ogum's color is green, and helps with getting jobs. Ogum's number is seven and he has a preference for cigars and rum.

- Oia-Iansa favors white, the number five, and is a protector. Eggplant is her preferred offering.

- Orunmila is in charge of all divination, prefers yellow and sweets, and favors the number sixteen. Offer yams and coca nuts.

- Oxala like white, the number eight, and brings peace. White cotton and white coconuts are the gifts to offer.

- Oxum favors yellow and is the divinity for love and marriage. Present Oxum with sweet honey and sweet cakes.

- Sonponno is the ruler of health and is connected with the color tan and the number seventeen. Corn and beans should be at Sonponno's shrine.

- Yemoja is the divinity who aids with fertility issues. Lucky number seven and bright blue are Yemoja's domain, and offerings should be sugar cane and the syrup made from it.

- Xando is the power and passion divinity and his color is bright red. With both four and six as totem numbers, he should be gifted with fruit. Bananas and red apples are best.

These are the steps for making an appeal to an *orixa* for aid:

1. Identify the *orixa* who is concerned with your problem.

2. Find an image of this *orixa*. These are often available at the local *botanica* or New Age store. While at the *botanica*, you should buy regular candles in the *orixa's* color and also "number candles" if possible. If you are invoking Ogum, for example, buy a seven-day burning candle, as Ogum's number is seven. Basically, you are matching up the above-listed correspondences customized to your need.

3. Stop at the market and get the offering of food or liquor for your divinity.

4. If you have a home altar, you should set up the shrine to your chosen *orixa* there. Another option is to find a safe place in your home or outside your home where you can burn candles for a long time with no threat of fire and where wind, nosy pets, or other disturbances cannot interfere. Take real care in the selection of your shrine space; if it were to be knocked down, your petition is likely to backfire!

5. Once you have selected your special shrine spot, place the representation of the *orixa* at the center and create a circle of candles around the deity. Make your offering by placing the food beside the icon. Never eat the food intended for the *orixa*. Do not make them mad. If you can, let the food offering stay there until it composts naturally.

6. Next, make your appeal in to the *orixa* through prayer and devotion. On a piece of paper, write down your true wish and heart's desire and place it under the representation of the *orixa*. Light each candle and leave the shrine so the *orixa* can come at leisure. Allow your *despacho* to take effect. Remain patient and allow the correct number of days to pass before you look for results.

When the ritual is finished, you should have your wish. Do not forget about the *orixa* who helped you. Keep the icon on your altar or mantel. You now have the favor of a god. Be thankful and keep making offerings occasionally to show your gratitude.

Designing Your Own Fire Rituals

Fire rituals are superb tools for personal transformation, but fire should be handled with great care and understanding of its volatility. Rituals for change, ceremonies invoking the warrior spirit, and rites for ardent passion all are rites associated with fire. Fire gives courage and sparks ideas. Rituals with candle magic are a daily fire ritual you can do to create positive changes in your life.

Rites using firepower could include those for creativity, love and lust, courage, ambition, mysticism, purgation and cleansing, and closure.

Fire Deities

+ **Shiva** is the Hindu lord of life. He performs a ritual dance within the circle of flames.

+ **Brigid** is an excellent example of how an old pagan goddess was adopted by Christianity. The Celtic tradition's great triple goddess was known as Brigantia in England, Brigindu in southern France, and Bride in Scotland. According to legend, Saint Brigid was a druid's daughter, and was baptized by Saint Patrick. Her name means "bright one" and she tended the undying fire of the sun. Her song of invocation, as befitting a fire goddess, is "Brigid, excellent woman, sudden flame, may the bright fiery sun take us to the lasting kingdom."

- ✦ **Durga,** the oldest and fiercest form of the Hindu goddess aspect Devi, sprang into being from the flames in the mouths of the gods. Even though born from them, she was stronger than them all and was given weapons and a lion with which to battle the demon Mahiso. Seizing the demon by the hair, she freed the world from his evil so others could live there. She also rules the intellectual realm.

- ✦ **Pele,** daughter of the Haumea, is the volcano goddess of fire and earth in Hawaii who first learned how to make fire. Luisah Teish tells of a personal encounter with her at a volcano in Maui in her book *Jump Up*. Many Pele stories involve the goddess appearing as an old woman who asks for a cigarette, then lights it with her magic.

The Element of Air

Air possesses the power of transformation. We often refer to the "winds of change." Air also uplifts the emotions and the spirit. Air is the sound of the song as it travels on the breeze. A breath of air refreshes and renews both body and soul. Air is the element associated with communication and the arts. Mastery of communication occurs through correct use of the power of air. Singing, talking, chanting, and conscious breathing are all invocations of air.

Air Rituals

Air, like all the other elements, is essential for living. Air is one of the easies elements to use in ritual, as we breathe it and use it when we speak and chant.

Murcha—The Euphoric Breath

Murcha in Sanskrit means "to retain," so *murcha* is the "retaining breath." *Murcha* will help you hold on to some of your natural energy that business drains away. Restore yourself through this ritual. *Pranayama* is the fine art of breathing and controlling the flow of oxygen in and out of the lungs. Conscious breathing can vastly improve your health and make you more alert. This is a yoga exercise for achieving a state of ecstasy through *pranayama*. Done properly, *murcha* will enhance your mental capacity, center you, and create a sense of euphoria.

Sit down on the floor or a mat and make yourself as comfortable as possible. Now close your eyes and calm yourself completely. Begin the process of *murcha* by taking a few mindful breaths. Breathe through your nose. Don't hold your breath; just breathe in and out in a natural manner, but remain aware of your breathing.

When you are ready, take a deeper breath through your nose and visualize the new air and oxygen traveling throughout your body, cleansing and relaxing you. Hold that deeper breath, bend your neck, and bring your chin as close to your lungs and chest as possible. Keep this position as long as you can do so comfortably. When you need to, raise your head again and slowly exhale through your nose. When your lungs are empty, repeat the *murcha* breath. Repeat this cycle of breathing five times only. After the fifth breath, notice how you feel and be "in the moment." Like most breathing meditations, you will experience a subtle sort of ecstasy with raised energy and a sense of bliss.

In *pranayama*, it is important to remember not to place any stress on your body. Don't hold your breath beyond your comfort level. To do so would be to go against the grain of the technique and teachings of *pranayama*.

With practice, you will notice you can hold your breath naturally and comfortably just a little bit longer each time. As with all things, *pranayama* yoga breathing gets better with practice. The beginning breath cleanses the pulmonary system and raises your energy level.

Grains of Nirvana—a Sand Mandala Ritual

Mandalas are sacred symbolic images traditionally used in Buddhism and Hinduism as aids for meditation. Mandalas have come into wider use in the West for healing, for spirituality, for art.

When His Holiness the Dalai Lama was in San Francisco, to honor his esteemed presence, the Asian Art Museum had a Tibetan cultural exhibit that was truly wonderful. One of the most moving aspects of the exhibit was the creation of an intricate, mosaic-like sand mandala by two Tibetan monks over a period of several days. Most astonishingly, at the end of the exhibit, the monks took the gorgeous, multihued masterpiece and simply threw it into the wind at Ocean Beach. We Westerners were thunderstruck. How could they possibly destroy this beautiful, spiritual art piece that took so long to create? The monks were quite jolly about it, laughing a lot and seeming quite unconcerned. They explained to the confused onlookers that "all of life is ephemeral and this act emphasizes nonattachment." While the sands are now mixed into the sands of the entire world, the wisdom associated with it has remained.

This six-step ritual taught by the Dalai Lama and his Tibetan monks has been handed down through centuries in the Himalayas. The process for making sand mandalas is a reflection of the concept of the "sacred circle." These mandalas are actually a way of "initiating" large groups of people, as the monks believe that Buddha intended enlightenment for all beings.

Preparation Rituals

Tibetan monks perform fairly intricate rituals prior to the construction of the mandala. They create sacred space with rites of purification, and bless the site where the mandala was made. Even the materials such as brushes, funnels, and sand receive blessings. Meditations upon the Buddha and other deities take place as the monks invite them to inhabit the mandala.

Mandala Designs

If you are feeling particularly ambitious, you can create the *Kalachkara Tantra,* or the "Wheel of Time," which is the sand mandala the Tibetan monks created in San Francisco. This mandala is an example of the Buddha's teachings that the Dalai Lama now shares with the Western world. However, you might not have days to devote to this ritual, and so you can design your own mandala instead. Other designs for mandalas include:

- ✦ **Sun:** Its rays are a representation of light, energy, and life. A sun mandala will represent the positive and celebrate your life, the spark and flame of existence.

- ✦ **Moon:** In all its phases, the moon represents the feminine and female power. Moon mandalas are wonderful for women to create in celebration of their own femininity and of womanpower throughout time. Any goddess mandala can include the symbol of the moon.

- **Heart:** A universal symbol of love, this sweet design would make an excellent blessing to a romantic relationship or a gift to loved ones.

- **Triangle:** It represents the Christian Holy Trinity and also Egyptian spirituality and wisdom.

- **Downward-Pointing Triangle:** It represents the "yoni yantra" and signifies the female, the element of water, and also signifies the mother and the ability to create. A mandala blessing for an expectant mother should include the downward-pointing triangle. Water signs Cancer, Scorpio, and Pisces would do well to honor themselves with this design.

- **Double Triangle or Hexagram:** In tantra, this represents all of creation, the conjunction of male and female energies. The concept of infinity is also represented by this symbol. A relationship mandala, especially in the sensual realm, will work well with double triangles. If you want to connect to the great universe, the symbol of infinity is essential. This symbol is ideal for creativity mandalas. In India, the double triangle indicates Kali in union with Shiva, and it is also the symbol for the heart chakra. If you want to create a mandala for blessing a relationship or to open your heart, the hexagram is an excellent choice. Combining the heart symbol and hexagram would be a powerful love mandala.

- **Pentagram:** Other names for the pentagram include the Wizard's Star, the Druid's Foot, the Witch's Cross, and the Star of Bethlehem. Wiccans have claimed the pentagram as their insignia. If you want to do a mandala for healing the earth, the pentagram will accomplish this quite nicely.

- **Square or Quadrangle:** It is the sign of the four directions, and also the four elements and the four seasons. The square of the day also indicates the four significant times of day—sunrise, noonday, sunset, midnight. For the ancient

Hindus, the square stood for order in the universe. You can use a square to invoke the four directions in this way, to honor the elements of air, earth, fire, and water, and also to mark sacred time for prayer and meditation.

- ✦ **Octagon or Double Square:** With its eight points, this is another symbol for divine order and unification It is a good symbol for peace on earth. Essentially an eight-pointed star, the octagon is a symbol for rebirth and renewal and the wheel of the year. The octagon is believed to have magical powers, as does the pentacle or pentagram, when drawn in one line. In this case, they are believed to indicate sacred space. An octagon is a very good symbol to include in a mandala when you are embarking on a new phase of your life—a new home, job, relationship, a "new you"—that can be blessed in this manner.

- ✦ **Knotwork and the "Knot of Eternity":** These are lovely symbols of unity. In Buddhist tradition, knotwork represents contemplation and meditation. Celtic knotwork symbolizes the eternal flow of energy and life.

- ✦ **Lotus:** This flower represents beauty, creation, renewal, and in Buddhism, the search for enlightenment. If the lotus has twelve petals, it represents the energy of the sun. If it has sixteen petals, it is the symbol for the moon. The most spiritual mandalas will likely contain the image of the lotus.

If you don't have access to a Tibetan temple space, you can create a sacred temple space in your own home. Ideally, your windows allow sacred light to fall upon the design. This is an artistic endeavor; you are making sacred art. If you do your best work at night, be sure to have adequate lighting. It is also a good idea to reduce the possibilities of distractions and interruptions. It is strongly suggested to turn off phones and television, to create as peaceful an environment as possible.

Bless the space in a fashion of your own choosing. Tibetan monks always use Tibetan incense and have images of Buddha to venerate his memory and teachings.

Clarify Your Intention

Why do you want to create a sand mandala? Your reason is your intention, and is the focus of your ritual. One basic guideline is that the creation of a sand mandala should be "for the greater good." Some examples of reasons to create a specific sand mandala include:

- ✦ To help create world peace
- ✦ To bring renewed health to body and spirit
- ✦ To bless a new home
- ✦ To bless and bring joy to all people in your life

Blessing the Supplies

Call upon the Buddha and beloved ancestors who have passed on to bless your materials. In this case, you have multiple packets of colored sand, readily available at any craft store, which you need to imbue with the energy of the divine. Simply place the packets on the surface of the mandala design you have chosen.

Hold your hand over the sand and the mandala design you have drawn and visualize the light of the universe and of the sun pouring through you and through your hands to the sand and the design. If you feel a personal connection to any benevolent spirits such as angels, the Buddha, or gods or goddesses, you should call upon them to also bless your efforts and the material with their sacred energy.

You may notice a warming of your hands as you continue concentrating "in the light." Invoke aloud or pray silently to your benevolent guardians to bless your endeavor.

Meditation

Tibetan monks also suggest doing a meditative movement, such as tai chi or yoga, to stretch and relax both body and mind prior to entering the intense mental stillness and physicality demanded by the construction of the sand mandala. Essentially, you are bent over for quite a long time in deep concentration, and you need to prepare yourself physically and mentally for this direction of your energies. Movement is a way of centering yourself.

In addition to the movement, you should also meditate and surround yourself with the energy of light and love. Sit on the floor, lotus fashion, and in a whispered chant, repeat the Sanskrit word *Om* over and over again. Manage your breathing, slowly and deeply. You will soon feel your heart and mind surrounded by energy. Now, focus on your intention again and ponder any new clarity of thought.

Painting with Sand

With your intention set clearly in your mind and being, pour sand into a funnel (or a small bag with a tiny hole in the bottom) and let it fall gently upon the design you have drawn, one color at a time, allowing the divine to guide you. If you are creating a specific image, you can copy its color and design; otherwise, allow creation and inspiration to flow through you. Creating the design slowly and carefully is key, but in case of accident a damp sponge applied with care will remove any random sand. It is important to remember that there are no "mistakes" in this art; you are in the safety of the sacred space you create with the help of the celestial.

When you have finished your sand mandala, you will see it and feel it and know it in your heart. However, physical completion of the sand mandala is not the end.

Dismantling Your Mandala

While dismantling the sand mandala is counterintuitive to the Western mind, it is actually the next step in the ritual. When you are ready, take some time to look at your mandala and contemplate the image you have created. Look deeply and quietly and "receive" any insights or messages during meditation.

Offer thanks to the divine beings who helped you in this ritual and who help you in your daily life. Now take a small brush and move the sand to the center of the mandala.

Scattering the Sand

When I learned the art of creating a sand mandala, the monks who taught me carried their sand to the Pacific Ocean. It is in accordance with the Tibetan tradition that the scattering take place at the nearest body of water, accompanied by chanting and song. If you have no water nearby, but there is a garden or park near your home, you might feel like performing the scattering aspect of the ritual there to keep the blessing energy nearby.

Close the ritual by dedicating the blessing energy of the mandala to the greater good of the universe.

Color Symbology for the Chakras and the Sand Mandala Ritual

First, root (base of spine)	red	security, survival
Second, sacral	orange	pleasure
Third, solar plexus	yellow	divine, personal power
Fourth, heart	green	abundance, love, serenity
Fifth, throat	blue	creativity, originality
Sixth, third eye	indigo	intuitiveness, perception
Seventh, crown	violet	holy bliss, all is one

Color Connection

Color is a form of energy that can be broken down by individual vibrations. We use colors in our homes and at work to affect moods. The right colors can calm, energize, or even romanticize a setting. Colors promote many desired states of being. Anyone using color is tuning in to the vibration frequency of that particular color. Some psychics have the skills and training to read your aura; they can literally see the energy radiating out from your body.

Other colors not in the spectrum or chakra exist in crystals and stones, and are significant in their own right: brown, gray, black, white, silver, and gold.

* **Brown:** the color of humility and poverty; represents safety and the home.

* **Gray:** the color of grief and mourning; symbolized resurrection in medieval times; gray is the first color the human eye can perceive in infancy.

* **Black:** protection and strength; fortifies your personal energies and gives them more inner authority; symbolizes fertile, life-giving, rich earth, and nourishing rain in Africa.

* **White:** purity, peace, patience, and protection; some cultures associate white with death.

* **Silver:** relates to communication and greater access to the universe; indicates a lunar connection or female energy.

* **Gold:** direct connection to God; facilitates wealth and ease.

The color spectrum is correlated with seven basic vibrations. These are the same vibrations that comprise the musical scale, and the same vibrations that are the foundation of our seven-N/vibration chakra system. The "lightest" vibrations are at the top and the "heaviest" vibrations are at the bottom. By now you should know that the color system is composed of seven colors, all visible in the rainbow—red, orange, yellow, green, blue, indigo, and violet. A great way to remember the colors is by their collective acronym, which sounds like a name: Roy G. Biv. Consult the following color guide when you are choosing a color for any aspect of your life.

Color management can help you on the most basic level each day. To combat feeling depressed, wear yellow to raise your energy level. If you have a business meeting and you want to put your colleagues at ease, wear earthy colors like brown or green. You can experiment with different combinations, too. Remember, the purpose here is to find your soul colors.

Color Guide

Color: Red

Chakra: N/A

Soul: Passionate and intense

Healing Characteristics and Associations: Security and survival; matters of the body; strong physical connection

Crystal Connection: N/A

Color: Rose Red

Chakra: Root

Soul: Loving

Healing Characteristics and Associations: Motherhood, home, grounding, money

Crystal Connection: Red gems and crystals aid in matters of the body. Jasper, amber, and agate in shades of red can help shy people feel stronger.

Color: Clear Red

Chakra: N/A

Soul: Angry

Healing Characteristics and Associations: Related to sense of smell

Crystal Connection: N/A

Color: Red Orange

Chakra: N/A

Soul: Passionate

Healing Characteristics and Associations: Sexual Passion

Crystal Connection: N/A

Color: Red Coral

Chakra: N/A

Soul: Vitality

Healing Characteristics and Associations: Skeleton and bones

Crystal Connection: N/A

Color: Pink

Chakra: N/A

Soul: Nurturer

Healing Characteristics and Associations: Boosts self-esteem

Crystal Connection: N/A

Color: Orange

Chakra: Sacral

Soul: Ambitious

Healing Characteristics and Associations: Hunger and sex; lucidity and orderliness; potency and immunity; stimulation and motivation

Crystal Connection: Orange stones can help home and build focused energy.

Color: Yellow
Chakra: Solar Plexus
Soul: Intellectual
Healing Characteristics and Associations: Personal power, freedom, control; fire; the eyes; mental activity
Crystal Connection: Yellow stones such as citrine carry healing energy and can help with nightmares and indigestion.

Color: Green
Chakra: Heart
Soul: Caring nurturer and healer
Healing Characteristics and Associations: Relationships; the heart and lungs; the element of air; sense of touch; will to live; balance of overall health
Crystal Connection: Green stones such as emeralds can represent healing and salvation, as well as closely guarded secrets; green is also the color associated with wood in Chinese astrology.

Color: Blue
Chakra: Throat
Soul: Teacher
Healing Characteristics and Associations: Communication, listening; intuition; the ears; creativity and mind control
Crystal Connection: Blue stones help maintain calm and protect the aura.

Color: Indigo
Chakra: Third Eye/Intuition

Soul: Spiritual Growth

Healing Characteristics and Associations: Opens third eye; promotes clear-headedness

Crystal Connection: Indigo stones can aid in psychic work

Color: Violet

Chakra: Crown/Entire Universe

Soul: Deep connection to the spirit

Healing Characteristics and Associations: Helps rid deep pain; works on deep tissue, hypersensitivity; promotes stability and contentment; secrecy

Crystal Connection: Amethysts are good for sensitivity issues. They keep energy from draining. Purplish agates guard stability and contentment.

Feather Messages: Symbols on the Wind

As you jog through the park or walk to work you might find a feather in your path. It could be a message. You might glean hidden meanings, for example, in the glistening iridescence of a raven's feather. Native peoples believed feathers to be gifts of healing or "feather medicine" from the Great Spirit. The wind is a form of the change-bringing element of air.

Another type of daily exercise in mindfulness is to actively look for feathers. There is much magic that can lie within something as small and light as this.

Crow Feathers: These indicate loss and mourning. Try not to be frightened but look at them as indicators of the cycles of life, death, and rebirth. You may lose someone you know, but you will also most likely greet a new friend or baby to complete the circle.

Hummingbird Feathers: These bring joy, beauty, and bliss. Take time out to have a good time and to share time with the people you love in your life. Follow your bliss!

Swan Feathers: These are the sign of grace. As swans mate for life, a swan feather can also mean a soul mate or good relationship is on the horizon.

Duck and Crane Feathers: These serve as prayer feathers for Native American people. They come from waterfowl, which are perceived as sacred birds. Finding a duck feather may mean you need to seek advice from a Native American teacher or experience healing from a medicine wheel.

Yellowhammer Feathers: These are the symbol for hearth and home. Seeing a yellowhammer feather in your path means you will have a happy new home. Most importantly, you will feel secure and loved within your family.

Roadrunner Feathers: These are a sign of the trickster. Beware! Finding one in your path either means you have the potential to be a magician, or you need to watch out that you aren't tricked, It is a symbol of duality.

Blue Jay Feathers: These are the bringers of light into darkness.

Robin Feathers: These are the sign of renewal and new personal growth, and are a good sign. Spring is coming both outside and inside you. It always means news is coming.

Magpie Feathers: These are just pain good medicine for any kind of illness. Magpies bring purification. If you find a magpie feather in your path, a friend who is sick will get better.

Scissortail Feathers: These represent the four directions. If you come across a scissortail flycatcher in your walk, you need to do a ritual invoking the four directions. It is a sign you are in need of grounding and should reconnect your spirit.

I suggest you keep a written record of your feather findings—where and when you find them. Secure a blank journal and a feather quill pen for your records. Meditate upon the meaning and the message the feather is bringing to you. Journal your thoughts and feelings. Years later, it will be fascinating to look back at the proof of divine providence in your life.

Designing Your Own Air Rituals

Rituals using the element of air can be a daily energy cleansing such as smudging with a sage stick or incense. You can call forth the power of the four winds, invoke the spirits of the air to inspire you, to surround and support you, and to communicate your wishes to the world at large.

Air Deities

Invocation of the spirit of the air for ritual brings the powers of the heavens to aid your ceremonies and ritual work. Birds and insects as well as the four winds will abet your spells.

* **Winged Isis,** the oldest of all Egyptian divinities, was believed to bear the souls of the dead to the place of eternal life.

* **Oya** is the Yoruban *orisha* of the wind who gives us the breath of life.

* **Nut** is the great sky goddess who covers and enwraps Geb, her younger brother the earth, with her body. She is the sky queen who is covered with stars, depicted as a lovely woman arched over the land in a constant posture of protection and service.

* **Norwan** is a goddess of light and air of the Wintun Native American tribe who brought nourishment to the world.

Known as "dancing porcupine woman," she dances all day until sunset.

Chapter Nine

CELEBRATING THE WHEEL OF THE YEAR: RITUALS FOR HOLIDAYS

Holiday time is a time when we all have rituals. As I write this, it is the Celtic New Year, which begins with Samhain, or All Hallow's Eve. I was fascinated with the media reports that Halloween has become the second biggest consumer holiday in North America. I believe this is indicative of people's thirst for celebratory times. As for other holidays, I look forward to the times when children have the equinoxes and solstices off from school, when we can observe the changing of the seasons and help people create memories.

As you know, holidays were created around the seasons of the year. Some of them celebrated springtime and the start of new growth, while others celebrated the harvest in preparation for the dark and chilly days of winter. Nearly all of our modern festivals and holy days have ancient roots in farming customs.

This chapter is intended to inform you about holidays, to teach you about ones you are unfamiliar with, and "spice up" those very special days you already observe. For ease and pure pragmatism, we use the traditional calendar year format to take a ritual tour through the Wheel of the Year. Some of these occasions may or may not correspond to the accepted definition of holiday; however, remember that these celebratory days are meant to be a springboard for your own "jump ups," as Luisah Teish calls ritual get-togethers. Use this chapter as inspiration to create your own holiday and help motivate yourself to honor the seasons and the progress of the year. Be sure to draw from the magical, meaningful correspondences discussed and listed in the appendix in the back pages of this book.

365 Days of Ritual

In this section, I have included a group of international celebrations and special birthdays grouped by month. This long list is intended to provide you with usual, ancient, and, in some cases, extremely obscure holidays to observe in your rituals and celebrations. Create your own unique set of celebration ceremonies with this lore. For example, March 11 is the day Johnny Appleseed died, so you could use this date to design a "seed exchange" or other spring rite with your circle. November 4 is Mischief Night in Great Britain, which sounds like an occasion for playfulness at its best. By researching various multicultural holidays, you can create newer, richer rituals. Choose from the hundreds of festivals and holy days to create your own one-of-a-kind set of glory days.

January

January 1, New Year's Day, *Gantan-sai* (Japan)

January 2, *Kakosome*, the Japanese Day of First Writing: Ancestry Day (Haiti)

January 3, Saint Genevieve Day

January 4, Our Lord of Chalma Day

January 5, Festival of Befana (Italian)

January 6, Epiphany, also known as Three Kings Day

January 7, Greek Orthodox Christmas

January 8, Midwife Day

January 9, Feast of the Black Nazarene

January 10, Seven Lucky Gods of Japan

January 11, Carmentalia, Day of Prophecy in Rome

January 12, *Seijin no Hi*, Coming of Age Day (Japan)

January 13, *Glaedelig Jul*, Norwegian Twentieth Day

January 14, Feast of the Donkey in Paris

January 15, Martin Luther King's birthday

January 16, Festival of Ganesha

January 17, San Antonia Abad

January 18, World Religion Day

January 19, Baha'i Feast of Sultan

January 20, Portuguese Breadbasket Festival

January 21, Saint Agnes Day

January 22, Burgundian Winemaker's Holiday

January 23, Buffalo Dancer's Holiday

January 24, Bolivian Ekeko Fair for Prosperity

January 25, Robbie Burns Night (Scotland)

January 26, Indian Independence Day

January 27, Mozart's Birthday

January 28, St. Thomas Aquinas Day

January 29, Martyr's Day (Nepal)

January 30, Three Bishops Day

January 31, Feast of Hecate (Ancient Rome)

Any discussion of rituals for the month of January must include New Year's Eve and New Year's Day. I remember the drama that ensued as people around the globe stood by to witness the sunrise on January 1, 2000, perceived as the beginning of the new millennium. While many other cultures observe their New Year at other times during the year, January 1 has also become a time of celebration, reflection, and an opportunity to embrace change.

For many millennia, indigenous peoples have celebrated their own New Year in unique ways. One common element is the use of fire rituals by North, Central, and South American peoples. The Pilgrims who arrived in what was to become New England observed and documented that the Iroquois and other tribes they encountered had a New Year's Council Fire, a time when the tribe gathered to review the past year, listen to the elders, and speak their hopes, dreams, and visions of the coming year.

In addition to your personal New Year's ritual with the significant people in your life, I recommend the Mayan Fire Ceremony as a powerful way to bring positive change of the New Year into your life.

The Mayan Fire Ceremony was considered to open a door or portal into the spirit world that held the promise of receiving the blessings of spirit—love, healing, prosperity, peace, and anything you need for personal transformation. This ritual is also an opportunity to pay respects and make homage to your ancestors and loved ones you have lost. For this reason alone, I suggest enacting the Mayan Fire Ceremony: our culture is losing the important connection to the older people in our lives. Involving them in the rituals, ceremonies, and passages of our lives could heal a cultural rift and bring deep wisdom to all. Mayan shamans could "read" the fire in a divinatory fashion, and I hear that some modern metaphysicians can do the same. If you are fortunate enough to know anyone with such skills, invite them to your fire ceremony to share what they divine from the flames.

January 1—Mayan Fire Ceremony

What you need:

- ✤ Candles in the following colors: red, yellow, green, blue, white, and black
- ✤ Herbs: tobacco, rosemary, lavender, cedar, sage, and rose petals
- ✤ Incense: copal, myrrh, or any resin-based incense
- ✤ 2 cups of sugar
- ✤ 1 chocolate bar per person
- ✤ Bells, rattles, drums, and other noisemakers
- ✤ A firepot, fireplace, or safe place for an outdoor fire, paper for your intention

The candle colors represent the six directions: north, south, east, west, up, and down (or sky and earth). They also represent the different people of the world.

Gather your friends together at dusk on New Year's Day and ask them to bring a colored candle (assign them a color), a noisemaker, and an open mind. Ask them also to write out what they want to purge from their life and bring the paper into the circle. The Mayan Fire Ceremony serves to bring positive new influences into our lives and also to dispel what no longer serves for good. This "letting go" can be anything. For me, one year ago, it was cancer, and this year it was too much clutter. For you, it could be an unhealthy relationship, a job that makes you miserable, or a cramped apartment.

Here are the steps to the ritual:

1. Build a fire at 5:00 p.m. and have it burning brightly as your guests arrive. Place a big bowl of herbs, flower petals, and incense near the fire.

2. Create a circle around the fire and ask the eldest in the group to slowly draw a circle of sugar around the fire.

3. When the elder has moved back into place in the circle, each person should light his or her candles from the fire and place it in the sugar circle, creating a mandala.

4. Ask the youngest person to lead the group in this chant:

My life is my own
I must but choose to be better,
Vital breath of life I breathe
No more pain and strife!
Wise ones, bring us health and life
Bring us love and luck
Bring us blessed peace
On this our New Year's Day.
Into the fire, we toss the old
Into the fire, we see our future
On this, our New Year's Day.
Harm to none and health to all!

Everyone should rattle and drum away, making merry and rousing the good spirits. The spirits of the wise elders will join you.

After the drumming, start around the circle, beginning with the eldest. Allow people to speak about what they want to release from their life, and have them toss their "letting go" paper into the fire. Then the eldest person should lead the group in a prayer for collective hopes for the coming year, and anyone who wants to add something should also speak out wishes for positive change, for themselves and for the world.

Thank the wise elders and ancestors for their wisdom and spiritual aid by throwing some chocolate into the fire. Be sure to keep some for members of the circle to share and enjoy. The Mayans held the belief that a plentitude of offerings to the ancestors would bring more blessings. They also believed that fire ceremonies helped support the planet and all the nations of the word. Gifts to the fire signal to the elders that they can return through the door and to the other world, until you call upon them for help in the future.

January 11, Carmentalia, Day of Prophecy

Romans observed this day of Carmenta, beloved for her prophetic powers and for her protection of motherhood. One of Rome's famed gates, the *Porta Carmentalis*, is dedicated to her. A fascinating detail of her lore is that the priests to this goddess never sacrificed animals because Carmenta forbade any kind of butchering. The ancient oracles always gave their prediction in verse, and this Arcadian deity did so as well. Her name comes from the same root as *Carmen*, which means "song," and indicates a spell as well as a prophecy. One legend tells that Carmenta was the mother of Evander, who brought the humanities with him, both the arts and the foundation of the Latin alphabet; another suggests that she was the mother of the alphabet. Only the priests of Carmenta were permitted to enter her innermost shrines. Roman women made sure they visited Carmenta's shrine during their pregnancies, especially on January 11, to hear the song spell sung for their new babies. This is a wonderful ritual for women to share so that they can know what to predict for the year to come.

Ritual for Carmentalia—Prophecies for the New Year

On January 11, gather a group of women together. Ask them to bring pens, paper, and offerings of fruit, flowers, or vegetables to Carmenta. Use these to build an altar, with the bounty placed around a black bowl filled with water that is used as the scrying mirror. Place candles around the room and turn down the lights.

Form a circle around the bowl and altar, and as each woman places her offering beside the bowl, she says aloud the name of her offering:

> *Pomegranate [or orange or lily, etc.], Goddess's herb,*
> *Perform for me enchantment superb.*
> *You give us grain and bread.*
> *Foretell for me the year ahead.*

After placing the offering to Carmenta on the altar, each woman should kneel over the mirror and look upon the water. Some people may see images, but oftentimes the information comes as an impression, thought, or meditative reflection. People should only share their visions if they feel the need to do so.

After everyone has had a turn, everyone should chant and sing together:

Daughters under this sun
Sisters under this moon
Tonight we receive your blessings
Carmenta, goddess great and good—
We thank you for the year to come.

Now open the circle and sit in silence for at least ten minutes, so that everyone present can record her impressions and visions from Carmenta in a journal. In years to come, if you and your circle of women decide to observe the Feast of Carmentalia annually, as I recommend, you can share and compare notes from prior years. This is a wonderful way to process the passages of your lives. Afterward, a feast is called for. The fruit and veggies from the altar should be consumed, and the flowers should decorate the dining table. Make sure to smudge very well with sage at the end of the evening, as remaining energies should scatter and not stay in the home. Water from the scrying bowl should be poured into the earth outside.

Clearing the New Year: Ganesha Mudras

The elephant-headed Ganesha is the Indian god who helps overcome all obstacles. What better way to start the New Year that with this mighty deity at your side? Ganesha is beloved in India, where he is also called *Vighnaharta*, the "Lord and Destroyer of Obstacles." When people seek success in work or school, they turn to this jolly elephant god. I keep a little bronze statue of a supine Ganesha on my computer.

Mudra is a type of yoga you do with your hands. It is also called "finger power points." This is a portable yoga that you can do anywhere—on the bus, on the place, at your desk, even walking down the street. This is a marvelous way to calm yourself and handle stress. Buddha statues are usually shown with the hands in a *mudra*.

The very easy *Ganesha mudra* begins by holding your left hand in front of your chest with the palm facing outward, away from your body. Bend your fingers. Grasp your left fingers with your right fingers bent, toward your body. Move the hands to the level of your heart, right in front of your chest. Exhale vigorously and gently try to pull your hands apart without releasing the grip. This will create tensions in your upper arms and chest area, exercising those muscles.

Now relax those muscles while inhaling. Repeat these steps six times, then place both your hands on your sternum in the Ganesha clasping position. Note the energy and heat you feel in your body. Now repeat six times with your hands facing in the reversed positions.

The *Ganesha mudra* opens the fourth chakra and gives us "heart"—courage, confidence, and good feelings toward others. It opens us up to new encounters and new, positive experiences. Performed once a day, this is a marvelous way to strengthen your upper body. It is also believed to open the bronchial tubes and stimulate that area.

February

February 1, Saint Brigid's Day

February 2, Candlemas

February 3, Folklore Day (South Korea)

February 4, Porridge Day in Latvia

February 5, Fiesta de la Alcaldesa (Sicily)

February 6, Waitangi Day (New Zealand)

February 7, Ghost Exorcising Festival (Tibet)

February 8, Youth Day (Congo)

February 9, Chingay Procession (Singapore)

February 10, World Marriage Day

February 11, Kurban Bairam (Islam)

February 12, Chinese New Year (moves according to the lunar calendar)

February 13, Parentalia (ancient Rome)

February 14, St. Valentine's Day

February 15, Lupercalia fertility festival (ancient Rome)

February 16, Heritage Day (Canada)

February 17, Tanis Diena, ancient Latvian festival honoring pigs

February 18, Spenta Armaiti festival of cultivators (Persian)

February 19, Copernicus birthday, 1473, revolutionary astronomer of the heliocentric theory—honor the sun!

February 20, Museum Day, commemorating to opening of New York's Metropolitan Museum

February 21, Feralia, Roman festival to honor the dead

February 22, St. Lucia's Day (Christian)

February 23, Terminalia, honoring the Roman god of boundaries

February 24, Gregorian calendar begins, as established by Pope Gregory XIII in 1582

February 25, Day of Nut (Ancient Egypt)

February 26, Purim

February 27, Ayyam I Ha, Day of Service and Giving (Baha'i)

February 28, Kalevala Day, commemorating the first publication of the Finnish mythological poem in 1835

February 29, Leap Day and Ladies Day

Although February is the shortest calendar month, it holds many rich festivals from several cultures. Celtic Pagans celebrate Imbolc, or Brigid's Day, as the first sign of spring in the Wheel of the Year. *Imbolc* translates as "in the milk," which reflects the lambing and calving season that begins around this time. The idea of purification also runs through February festivals such as Purim, Candlemas, and Lupercalia. Take the opportunity to start "spring cleaning" a bit earlier than you usually do to help chase away the winter blues. And of course, February holds Valentine's Day, a now-secular celebration of affection and friendship.

Chinese New Year

This most special holiday for Chinese all over the world is a "moveable feast," as it occurs on the second new moon after the shortest day of the year (the winter solstice, December 21) and lasts about two weeks. According to the Western calendar, this means the holiday begins sometime in either late January or early February. Tradition holds that homes must be cleaned from top to bottom in preparation for the festivities. On New Year's Eve, families get together for a banquet, and at this feast fish is the dish of delight, as the Chinese word for "fish" sounds like *yu*, or "great plenty." Red is the color of luck and all children receive red envelopes filled with money and bright, shining moon-like coins. Adults write "spring couplets" on red paper; these are short poems that are hung around the doorway to greet the New Year auspiciously. Oranges are placed around the house in bowls and plates and blooming plants adorn the home both indoors and out. All generations of the extended Chinese family, from great-grandmother to the tiniest toddler, stay up late playing games, telling stories, and making wishes for the New Year.

Hong Bao—an Ancient Feng Shui Custom

Essential elements: red envelopes, coins, and paper money. The Chinese call the red envelopes *lee sees.*

On the actual day of the Chinese New Year, go around to your neighbors, friends, and family with red envelopes containing money. If you are like me, bright, shiny coins are what you can easily afford to give instead of envelopes stuffed with paper money. With each gift, greet folks with *Gung Hey Fat Choy*, which means "Wishing you prosperity and health."

Give every child two *lee sees* because happiness comes in pairs. By taking care to provide the children you know with *lee sees*, you are making sure the next generation has good luck. Business owners also give *lee sees* to employees, important partners, and associates. When you hand a *lee see* to anyone you may have a grudge or grievance with, you should let go of the old feeling and refuse to drag the new you down with emotional baggage in the New Year.

Valentine's Day Observances: Attraction Altar

This is the first step to prepare for potential relationships and create a foundation for self-love in the truest sense. You can recreate your altar as a power source and a center from which to renew your erotic spirit. You can also concentrate your energy, clarify your intentions, and make your wishes come true. Incorporate a special element to enhance love in your life, for yourself, and for others. As always, the more you use your altar, the more powerful your spells will be.

Feng Shui for Love

Surely one of the main reasons for clearing space in your home and bedroom is to make room for a happy love life. Before you attempt to enhance your prospects for love, you need to improve the flow of *chi*, or life energy, in the environment where you express your love. Try any of all of the following to help you improve the chi:

- ✦ Remove all pictures of yourself where you are alone.
- ✦ Remove all empty cups, jars, vases, and bottles.
- ✦ Remove all photographs of past lovers, or at least relegate them to another room.
- ✦ Make sure that decorative accessories are in even numbers, not in odds or in triplets. This pertains to candles, frames, pillows, and lamps.
- ✦ Display special feng shui love symbols, such as an open red fan, a pair of crystal lovebirds, and two red hearts. On your bed, you should use rich, silky, and extremely comfortable fabrics and colors. Also be extravagant when it comes to

pillows—the more the merrier. But remember to have even numbers, not odd ones, which disrupt your "love chi."

Personal Ritual for Renewal: Bed Blessing

Turn back the bedspread to reveal fresh sheets. In a red cup, mix a half-teaspoon of jasmine oil and a half-teaspoon of rose oil. Hold it with both hands and speak:

> *In this bed, I show my love.*
> *In this bed, I share my body.*
> *In this bed, I give my heart.*
> *In this bed, we are as one.*
> *Here, my happiness lies as I give and live in total joy.*
> *Blessed be to thee and me.*

As you say, "Blessed be," flick drops of your bed blessing oil from your fingers all across the bed until the cup is empty. Now, lie down and roll around in the bed. After all, that is what it is there for!

Relationship Corner

As you walk into your bedroom, the relationship corner will be the back right corner. Your love and sex energy have to be nurtured there, and you might as well consider placing your altar there to serve as your personal erotic wellspring.

Look at this area with a fresh eye—what is cluttering your love corner with dead energy? Half-empty perfume bottles or near-empty cosmetic bottles could be impairing your relationship energy. You must clear unhappiness out of this space, clear the area of any clutter by getting rid of all unnecessary objects and tidying up.

To cleanse the area, ring a hand bell anywhere clutter has accumulated, giving special attention to your bed and pillows. Here are a few tips:

- ✤ Never bring old pillows into a new home. Old pillows can cause poor sleep and bad dreams. They can carry old sexual energy and can kill a relationship.
- ✤ Never place your bed in the center of a room, as this will cause anxiety and get in the way of a healthy sex life.
- ✤ Never have the foot of the bed facing the door, as this brings very bad luck.
- ✤ To keep your lovemaking fresh, always make the bed and change the linens often.

Place these objects in your bedroom to attract loving energy:

- ✤ 2 rose quartz crystals of equivalent size
- ✤ Pink, orange, or red fabric
- ✤ 2 red candles
- ✤ Images of two butterflies

New Moon Candle Consecration

If you are looking for love and feel like you need the physical release of sex, perform this rite and you will soon find a lover to satisfy your needs. On the night of the next new moon, take two pieces of rose quartz and place them on the floor in the center of your bedroom. Light two red candles and use this affirming chant:

> *Beautiful crystal I hold this night,*
> *Flame with love for my delight,*
> *Goddess of Love, I ask of you,*
> *Guide me in the path that is true.*

Harm to none as love comes to me.
This I ask and so it shall be.

Candlemas Ritual, February 2

Candlemas, the highest point between the winter solstice and the spring equinox, is also known as Imbolc, Brigid's Day, and the Feast of the Purification of the Virgin. Many Wiccans use this sabbat (holy day) as the special day to initiate new witches. Brigid, the Celtic goddess and saint honored on this day, is connected with both the elements of fire and water, both with powerful purificatory powers.

Essential elements for this Candlemas ritual are a cauldron, white candles, a bough of cedar, a small bough of pine, a small bough of juniper, a small bough of holly, incense, red cotton thread or yarn, a stone for an altar, and a bowl of water.

The leader of the circle should purify the circle with the fire of the incense while invoking the four directions to raise power. Place your altar stone north of the circle and place white candles on and around the altar. Cast the circle:

Face east and say:

Welcome, Guardians of the East, bringing your fresh winds, the breath of life. Come to the Circle of Candlemas.

Face south and say:

Welcome, Guardians of the South, bringing us heat and health. Come to the circle on Candlemas.

Face west and say:

Welcome, Guardians of the West, bringing the setting sun and light rains. Come to the circle on Candlemas.

Face north and say:

Welcome, Guardians of the North, brining life-bringing rains and snow. Come to the circle on Candlemas.

Meditating on the concept of purification, make a bouquet of the four branches and wrap it with the red cord. The red symbolizes Brigid's fiery aspect, while the four trees stand for purification. Bow with it to each of the four directions. Bow last to the north, over the altar stone, and say:

Bright Brigid,
Sweep clean our homes and spirits on this sacred day.
Purify our souls of the dullness of winter, and help us prepare for the light of summer.
Brigid of the white hands, Brigid of the golden curls,
Bless us all. So mote it be.

All respond:

So mote it be!

The ritual leader dips the branches in the water and sprinkles the circle, and the participants, saying:

Blessed Brigid, may your water heal us, and make us whole.

Leave the bouquet on the altar stone as an offering to Brigid.

March

March 1, Matronalia, Roman day of honor for all women

March 2, Saint Ceadda's Day

March 3, Hina Matsura, Japanese Doll Festival, a celebration of girlhood

March 4, Saint Casimir's Day, patron saint of Lithuania.

March 5, Navigium Isidis festival honoring Isis as navigator (Greco-Roman)

March 6, Kuan Yin's birthday (Buddhist)

March 7, Bird and Arbor Day, established 1909 by Luther Burbank

March 8, International Women's Day

March 9, Forty Saints Day in Romania

March 10, Tibet Day

March 11, Johnny Appleseed Day

March 12, *O-mitzutori*, "Receiving the Water Day" (Buddhist Japan)

March 13, Las Fallas Day in Valencia, bonfires to burn away the winter

March 14, Pi Day for mathematicians everywhere

March 15, Roman Ides of March; Japanese Phallus festival

March 16, Festival of Dionysus, the first day of the wild Roman Bacchanalia

March 17, Saint Patrick's Day; Roman Libernalia

March 18, Sheelah's Day in honor of Sheela-Na-Gig, goddess of fertility (Ireland)

March 19, San Giuseppe Day for Jesus's father

March 20, Spring equinox

March 21, No-Rus (Iranian New Year)

March 22, World Day of Water

March 23, Lildienas or Mara Day, named for the great goddess of Latvia

March 24, Feast of Saint Gabriel, patron saint of communications

March 25, The Annunciation, nine months before Christmas Day

March 26, Prince Kuhio Day, for the last royal prince of Hawaii

March 27, Easter, a moveable feast

March 28, Pesach, or Passover, a moveable feast

March 29, Festival of Ishtar (Babylonian)

March 30, Salus Day, also known as Hygieia, goddess of cleanliness, health, and the moon

March 31, Culture Day (Micronesia)

In March we see the more tangible signs of sprig—grass and trees begin to green, birds return from where they have wintered, and we breathe in the warmer breezes that herald summer ahead. Be careful, however—March can be a month of surprises and changes. Celebrate spring by bringing fresh flowers into your home, and take advantage of the first fruits and vegetables in the markets. March marks the vernal (or spring) equinox, one of only two days of the year where the hours of daylight and the night are balanced equally. The vernal equinox, like its partner, the autumnal equinox, exemplifies the concept of equilibrium and the idea that two halves create a whole: only with the darkness can light be seen and appreciated.

Ostara's Equinox: a Ritual for Spring

At this time, celebrate the festival of Ostara, the Saxon goddess who is the personification of the rising sun. Her totem is the rabbit. Legend has it that her rabbit brought forth the brightly colored eggs now associated with Easter. At this time the world is warming under the sun as spring approaches. Every plant, animal, man, and woman feels this growing fever for spring.

This ritual is intended for communities, so gather a group. Tell everyone to bring a "spring food" such as deviled eggs, salads with flowers in them, fresh broths, berries, mushrooms, fruits, pies, veggie casseroles, and quiches. Have the food table at the opposite side of the area away from the altar, but decorate it with flowers and pussy willow branches that are just beginning to bud. These are the harbingers of spring.

Essential elements for this ritual are an altar table; a cot; bay laurel leaves; bowls of water; multicolored crystals; candles; a jar of honey; fruits of yellow, red, white, and purple; musical instruments; and one bowl each of seeds, leaves, flowers, and fruit.

1. **Create your own Ostara altar in the middle of the ritual area by covering the table with a cloth of color that represents spring to you.** It could be a richly hued flowered cloth or a light green solid color. the cloth should represent new life. Scatter bay laurel leaves around the table. Place goddesses on the altar table, too, with Ostara at the center. Put colored eggs, chocolate rabbits, candles, and crystals around the goddesses. In the east, set a yellow candle and crystals of amber, gold, and yellow such as citrine or agate. Place yellow fruit such as pears or bananas in front of the candle as an offering to the

energies of the east. In the south, set a red candle and red and orange stones such as garnet or the newly available "rough rubies," which cost only a few cents each. Apples and pomegranates are excellent red food to place in front of the candle. In the west, set a purple candle with amethysts in front of it. Sweet plums are a perfect fruit to place in front of the candle. In the north, set a white candle and a clear quartz or white crystal. Honeydew melon is an appropriate selection for the fruit offering.

2. **Choose four representatives to invoke the directions.**

   - ✦ **East**—Everyone faces east. The representative for the direction should weave a story and create a vision that can be shared by all that is characterized by new beginnings, such as the rising of the morning sun. Spring is the time for new beginnings and growth in nature. The speaker can, for example, take the bowl of seeds and tell the tale of the seeds sprouting in the dark moist soil of Mother Earth. Pass the bowl of seeds around to everyone and urge them to take some seeds home to plant.

   - ✦ **South**—Everyone faces south. The speaker for this direction should invoke the power of the leaf. Leaves draw in the energy of the sun through photosynthesis and help keep an important cycle of life moving. Leaves grow throughout the summer season, drinking in the water of life and using the power of the sun for photosynthesis. Pass the bowl of leaves around the group.

   - ✦ **West**—Everyone faces west. The speaker for this direction should invoke the power of flowers. Flowers bud and bloom. They follow the sun and are some of nature's purest expressions of beauty. Flowers bring joy to people and many flowers become fruit. Pass the bowl of flowers to the group and urge everyone to take some.

- ⚜ **North**—Everyone faces the north. The speaker for the north should invoke fruit and harvest time. Fruit is the result of nature's generosity. Fruit also contains the seeds for our future. Pass the bowl of fruit around and suggest everyone take one and eat it, meditating on the glory and deep meaning it contains. If it is appropriate, you can also offer juice or wine as part of the fruit invocation. Wine is the glorious nectar of fruit.

3. **Now it's time for the ritual enactment. Everyone takes** a seat around the altar. Drummers should start to play a gentle rhythm. Chanting, singing, and ululating are also encouraged, however people feel comfortable expressing themselves.

4. **Each speaker should in turn light a candle and invoke the ancestors of the group.** Remembrances to people who have died in the past year are an important respect paid to the community at large.

5. **Next is the honoring of the moon. Ask people to speak** about the moon, reciting their favorite moon poems or moon memories.

6. **Anointing the third eye blesses your insight for the coming year.** Pass the bowls of water and laurel leaves around. Take a leaf and dip it in the water, then touch the wet leaf to your third eye. Pass the bowl on to the next person. When the bowl has made its way back to the ritual leader, sing and dance in celebration of spring. Everyone should get in a line and hold hands and dance around the circle like a plant moving and growing, flowering, and

fruiting. When the four speakers feel that the energy has reached a climax, each one should clap and say in turn:

And now it is done; now it is spring!

Then open the circle by saying together:

It is spring in the East, it is spring in the South, it is spring in the West, and it is spring in the North!

Mardi Gras or Carnival: a Moveable Feast

Mardi Gras means "Fat Tuesday," the last day before Lent, when Catholics were formerly forbidden to eat meat (or fat). Fat Tuesday is the day before Ash Wednesday, when the Lenten season begins. Depending on how early or late Easter is each year, Mardi Gras can be celebrated in March or April. The first Mardi Gras celebration was in New Orleans in 1827. In the olden times, people dressed in animal skin, pelted each other with bunches of flowers, and drank wine. Also called Carnival, this is a very important rite of spring and has traveled all over the world. It is perhaps most grandly celebrated in Brazil. Carnival and Mardi Gras last for days and involve parades, costumes, special foods, and much frolicking. This is an opportunity for you to choose what most appeals to you and create a gorgeous spring ritual.

April 1, April Fool's Day; Festival of Kali (Hindu)

April 2, International Children's Book Day

April 3, Birthday of the Buddha

April 4, Megalesia in Rome (from 204 BCE), celebrating the mother goddess, Cybele

April 5, Tomb-Sweeping Day in Taiwan, or *Quin Ming Jie*

April 6, First recorded solar eclipse in history, 684 BCE

April 7, World Health Day

April 8, *Hana Matsurei*, Flower Festival (Japan)

April 9, Feast of Glory for Baha'i faith

April 10, Anniversary of the first Arbor Day, 1872. Plant a tree!

April 11, Anniversary of when Haley's Comet was closest to Earth

April 12, Roman festival of Cerealia begins, honoring the grain goddess, Ceres

April 13, International Librarian's Day

April 14, Songkran Day, Thai New Year

April 15, Fordicia in honor of the Roman goddess Tellus

April 16, Anniversary of Gandhi's "Prayer and Fasting Day," 1919

April 17, Velvet Revolution in Czechoslovakia, deposing Communism

April 18, Friendship day in Brazil

April 19, Saint Dunstan's Day, Joan of Arc is declared a saint in 1909

April 20, Birthday of the Prophet Muhammad, *circa* 571 BCE

April 21, International Creativity Day

April 22, Earth Day

April 23, World Book Day

April 24, Astronomy Day

April 25, Festival of Robigalia, for the Roman goddess Robigus who protected crops from mildew

April 26, Birthday of Leonardo de Vinci (1452), painter

April 27, Freedom Day in South Africa

April 28, Floralia, the festival celebrating Flora, the Roman flower goddess

April 29, Greenery Day in Japan

April 30, Walpurgisnacht in Germany, May Eve

In April, many cultures honor the continuing growth seen in nature with such festivals as the Christian Easter, which celebrates the resurrection of the crucified Christ. This theme of resurrection is found in the mythology of many cultures, including Celtic mythology. In the spring, the Green Man, an avatar of the forests and fields, rises from his autumnal grave to stand tall once more.

Spring Fertility Symbols

Easter has become more and more a secular holiday, with families celebrating with chocolates, eggs, and rabbits. The symbol of the egg inspires us with the knowledge that new life will be born. The rabbit as a symbol of fertility arises not only from its incredible powers of reproduction, but from its ancient association with the lunar goddess of fertility and transformation. Folklore tells of the eggs of spring being laid by a bird until Oestre, a Teutonic goddess associated with the spring season, changed the bird into a hare that laid eggs.

Many of us engaged in Easter egg hunts as children. You can create a ritual for adults designed to recapture that joyous celebratory event and incorporating the various symbols associated with rebirth and fertility to bless new endeavors.

Floralia Hunt

This ritual blends the traditional egg hunt with a ceremony to honor Flora, the Roman goddess of flower. Essential elements for this ritual are baskets with handles (one for each guest), egg-shaped chocolates and sweets, or small hollow plastic eggs filled with blessings written on paper slips, and a vase. Ask each guest to bring a large dish of food for sharing, and to dress in light, flowing spring clothes and colors. Each guest must also bring a flower to represent a wish they have for a new project or endeavor they intend to embark on this year. This flower will be used to make an offering to Flora so that she may bless the project as it grows and develops. This flower can be chosen from the Language of Flowers list in the appendix on page 325. By carefully deciding on a certain type of flower, your guests can enhance the power of their spring wish.

Prepare for this ritual by deciding whether you will hold it inside or risk the whimsical weather of April outdoors. Consult your local weather channel, consult an almanac, and cross your fingers. If you choose to hold it outdoors, then scout out the area well to identify potential problem spots (low-lying areas that might be muddy, for example, or high-traffic areas where strangers might interfere, or even join in). Also mark off a perimeter to limit your hunt. Place sticks in the ground with bright ribbons tied to them to mark that perimeter, so that your guests know not to bother searching past that point. If you choose to hold the ritual inside, decide which rooms will be off-limits for your hunt.

Once you have your area set, take some time to write out various blessings and good wishes on slips of paper. Blessings might include, "Joy and happiness with every dawn," "May your love only increase," or "Wealth and abundance are yours." Tuck one blessing in each plastic egg, then gather all the eggs and blessings together and ask for Flora's benison upon them:

> *Flower queen,*
> *Princess of the spring,*
> *Lovely Maiden of garden and field,*
> *Bless these tokens and fill them with your goodwill.*
> *May those who receive them feel your love and*
> *bright beauty.*

Take your goodies and blessings and hide them in the space you have chosen. Be cunning, but don't make them too hard to find.

When your guests arrive, choose someone to stand in the north, the east, the south, and the west, then cast the circle.

Turn to the east. The speaker for the east should say:

> *Sacred breezes of the east,*
> *Bring us the gentle scent of Flora's blossoms.*
> *Flora, queen of spring, we welcome you.*

Turn to the south. The speaker for the south should say:

> *Sacred breezes of the south,*
> *Bless us with the vibrant color of Flora's blooms.*
> *Flora, queen of spring, we welcome you.*

Turn to the west. The speaker for the west should say:

> *Sacred breezes of the west,*
> *Bless us with the beauty of Flora's crop.*
> *Flora, queen of spring, we welcome you.*

Turn finally to the north, where the speaker for the north should say:

> *Sacred breezes of the north,*
> *Bless us with the abundance of Flora's bounty.*
> *Flora, queen of spring, we welcome you.*

Ask your guests to come up one by one, state a wish to Flora, and place their single flower in the vase. When everyone has made a spring wish, there will be a beautiful bouquet created for Flora.

Now hand your guests a basket each, and tell them to further seek Flora's blessings in the form of eggs, the symbol of fertility and new life. Laugh with your guests as they hunt high and low. Help the younger ones, or the ones who seem to be having difficulty finding any. Your guests should remember that this is not a traditional Easter egg hunt; the object is not to return with the largest collection of eggs. Instead, they are seeking Flora's blessings.

When everyone returns, have a spring picnic or buffet of potluck dishes, and whatever treats were hidden. Your guests may choose to share the written blessings they found aloud, or keep them secret. Enjoy the spring air, and remember that Flora has blessed your new projects.

May

May 1, May Day, Beltane

May 2, Last day of Ridvan, the Baha'i festival when no work can be done

May 3, Dia de la Crus, Day of the Holy Cross in Mexico and South America

May 4, Feast of Bona Dea, a Roman women's mystery rite

May 5, Mexico's Cinco de Mayo; Children's Day in Japan

May 6, National Day of Prayer (United States)

May 7, St. Nicola, pilgrimage of the Italian Christian hero

May 8, Festival of the Roman goddess of the mind, Mens, from whom Mensa takes its name

May 9, Lemuria, when Romans banished ghosts from their homes

May 10, Women's rights hero Victoria Woodhull is the first woman nominated for president in 1872

May 11, Anniversary of the year 330 CE, Roman ritual rededication of Byzantium to Constantinople

May 12, International Midwives Day

May 13, Portuguese Pilgrimage to Fatima

May 14, Mercuralia, Festival of Mercury

May 15, International Day of Families

May 16, French processions on Saint Honoratus Day, patron saint of all bakers

May 17, Norwegian Independence Day

May 18, International Museum Day

May 19, Holiday of Poetry (Turkmenistan)

May 20, Cuba's Independence Day

May 21, Anastenaria, Greek fire-walking festival

May 22, World Biodiversity Day

May 23, The American Civil War ends, 1865—celebrate national unity

May 24, Slovenian Sveti Kiril I Metodi

May 25, Ralph Waldo Emerson's birthday

May 26, Birth of Isadora Duncan (1878), self-proclaimed Dionysian ritual dancer and choreographer

May 27, St. Augustine of Canterbury Day, make a pilgrimage to a local shrine or holy place

May 28, John Muir founds the Sierra Club (1892)

May 29, Oak Apple Day in England

May 30, Memorial Day or Decoration Day

May 31, Flores de Mayo, last day of flowers, or May Day

Beltane Tryst

Beltane is the sexiest high holiday for witches and is anticipated all year. I always look forward to having a joyful "spree" every May. Witches begin to celebrate Beltane on the last night of April, and it is traditional for the festivities to last all night. This is a time for feasting, dancing, laughter, and lots of lovemaking. May Day is when revelers erect a beribboned Maypole and dance around it in gay garb followed by pagan picnicking and sexy siestas. Another bonus of Beltane is that this is the one day in the year when it is "officially OK" to enjoy sex outside your existing relationship. This is the day we look the other way.

First, serve a sensual feast of foods from the following list, called "Oral Fixations," along with beer, wine, ciders, and honeyed mead that you can make or obtain from a microbrewery. Gather some of spring's bounty of flowers— narcissus, daffodils, tulips, and my favorite, freesias, in your favorite colors. Set out candles in spring colors—yellow, pink, red, green, white, purple. With your arms extended, point to each of the four directions and say, "To the east, to the south, to the west, and to the north," and recite this Beltane rhyme:

> *Hoof and horn, hoof and horn,*
> *Tonight our spirits are reborn.*
> *Welcome joy to my home,*
> *Fill my friends with love and laughter.*
> *So mote it be.*

Oral Fixations

Food can be foreplay, a wonderful prelude to a night of love, feeding each other, and placing a little whipped cream and chocolate in strategic spots. I recommend consuming these aphrodisiacs for your pleasure:

- Almonds, or erotically shaped marzipan
- Arugula, also called "rocket seed"
- Avocado, referred to by the ancient Aztecs as the "testicle tree"
- Bananas and banana flowers
- Chocolate, quite rightly called "the food of the gods"
- Honey, as the term "honeymoon" came from a bee-sweetened drink served to newlyweds
- Nutmeg, the traditional aphrodisiac for Chinese women; eat enough and you will hallucinate
- Oysters, prized by the Romans for their effect and resemblance to female genitalia
- Strawberries, often mentioned in erotic literature
- Coffee, a stimulant for many things

- Garlic, the heat to light the flame of desire
- Figs, another symbol of ultimate femininity; just eating one is a turn-on
- Vanilla, captivating for both its scent and its flavor
- Wine drunk from each other's mouths can be quite erotic

Beltane Brew

Honeyed mead is revered as the drink of choice for this sexy Pagan holy day. It is an aphrodisiac, and with its sticky sweetness, it is perfect for dribbling on your lover's body and then licking it off. This is my special recipe for honeyed mead, handed down through generations of Celtic witches. You will need:

- 1 quart of honey
- 3 quarts of distilled water
- 1 packet of yeast
- Herbs to flavor

1. Mix the honey and water. Boil for five minutes. You can add the herbs to your liking, but I prefer a teaspoon each of clove, nutmeg, cinnamon, and allspice

2. Add a packet of yeast and mix. Put in a large container. Cover with plastic wrap and allow it to rise and expand. Store the mixture in a dark place and let it sit for seven days.

3. Refrigerate for three days while the sediment settles to the bottom. Strain and store in a colored glass bottle, preferably green, in a cool, dark place. You can drink it now, but it is even tastier after it has been aged for a period of at least seven months.

Nonalcoholic Mead

1 quart honey

3 quarts distilled water

½ cup lemon juice

1 sliced lemon

1 half-teaspoon nutmeg

Pinch of salt

Boil five minutes and then cool and bottle immediately. Keep in the fridge to avoid fermentation and enjoy.

June

June 1, Roman festival of Carna, goddess of doors and locks

June 2, US Congress granted citizenship and voter's rights to all Native Americans, 1927

June 3, Festival of Bellona, a Roman goddess of battle

June 4, First recorded Chinese solar eclipse (780 BCE)

June 5, Feast of St. Boniface

June 6, St. Fermin's Day in Spain, Running of the Bulls

June 7, Weaver's Festival in Japan

June 8, Founding of Islam *circa* 622 CE

June 9, Vestalia, Festival honoring the Roman goddess Vesta

June 10, Day of Anahita (Persian)

June 11, Feast of Saint Barnabus

June 12, *Dia dos Namorados*, Lovers' Day (Brazil)

June 13, Birth of the Muses

June 14, *Otaue Shinji*, Rice-Planting Festival in Japan

June 15, St. Vitus's Day

June 16, Bloomsday festival in honor of Irish author James Joyce with readings, breakfast, and a pilgrimage retracing the steps of Leopold Bloom

June 17, Iceland's Independence Day, 1944

June 18, High holy day for women's rights—Susan B. Anthony defies the law in 1872 by voting

June 19, Juneteenth

June 20, Day of Ix Chel (Mayan)

June 21, Midsummer

June 22, Rose Festival in England, Feast of Saint Alban

June 23, Jani, the major festival in Latvia

June 24, Feast of the Sun (Aztec)

June 25, Croatian Independence Day

June 26, Pied Piper Day, *circa* 1284

June 27, Stonewall, 1969, the day gays fought back

June 28, Constitution Day in Ukraine

June 29, Saint Peter's Day

June 30, Burial of Yarilo in Russia, a traditional rite of song, games, and dance

Juneteenth Celebration

Juneteenth is a beautiful example of a modern ritual that is reinvented and celebrated in a new and exciting way every year. Luisah Teish says this occasion celebrates "the flame as political power and divine inspiration." Juneteenth is held on June 19, the date when in 1865 the news of the Emancipation Proclamation finally reached the plantations in the states of Louisiana and Texas. While the actual law had gone into effect two years earlier in 1863, nobody told many of the slaves. When these duped slaves finally realized that they were free, it was a cause of great joy. Nowadays, there are festivals that celebrate the contributions by Africans to America and the world. Picnics, barbecues, singing, dancing, theater, games, and parades take place within the communities of the United States.

June 21, Summer Solstice

June is summer reaching its full glory. There have been many rites around the world to acknowledge the longest day of the year. The Japanese climb Mount Fuji at this time, for it is free of snow during two months in the summer. The Native American tribes of the Southwest and Great Plains hold ceremonies to honor the life-giving sun. Incan, Mayan, and Aztec midsummer rites honoring the sun gods were among their most important ceremonies.

Midsummer Day

Essential elements for a Celtic-inspired Midsummer ritual are a wooden wheel, fallen branches and firewood, multicolored candles, multicolored ribbons, food and drink, and flowers for garlands. This ritual should be performed outside, ideally on a hill or mountaintop, at dusk. Call the local fire department to verify the fire laws in your area. You will likely need a special permit to light a bonfire, and certain areas may be restricted. Always clear the grass and brush away from your fire area, and make sure to dig a shallow pit into the ground. Circle the pit with rocks to help mark the edge of the fire pit as well as to contain the accidental spread of fire. Have a fire extinguisher, a pail of sand, and water bottles nearby in case the fire gets out of control. One person not directly involved in the ritual should be on hand to watch the fire at all times. Make sure the fire pit is far enough away from surrounding trees and other landscape features to allow for a group to dance around it.

Lay the wooden wheel down in the circle of stones, and arrange the fallen branches and firewood around the edge of it. The wheel represents the turning of the year, and the sun on its daily and yearly cycle. Tie the colored ribbons on the nearest tree. While these preparations are being made, the priestess to lead the ritual should meditate in the area where the ritual will be held, connecting to the goddess. The gathered celebrants should weave garlands of flowers while the sun slowly sets. Just before the sun vanishes completely, the priestess should direct the gathered celebrants to ready their candles, or more ideally, torches. The priest lights them, declaring:

The fire festival is begun.
Under this longest day of the sun.
Let us go forth and make merry.
The god and goddess are here!

All say:

Blessed be!

The priest leads the celebrants into the circle where the priestess waits, and directs them to throw their torches and candles in the bonfire. The priestess raises her arms and invokes the Goddess:

Great Earth Mother and Lady of the Forest,
Be with us here and now!
On this night the Goddess reigns supreme.
On this, our night of our midsummer!

All say:

Blessed be!

All should dance in the direction of the sun (clockwise) around the fire, raise their arms, and clap and shout for joy for as long as they want. When people begin to tire, it is time for the feast. The priest directs the blessing of the food:

Blessed Lady of the Forest,
And old god and animals, spirits of the wild,
Bless this food and drink,
That it may strengthen us in your ways.

All say:

Blessed be!

Everyone should share in the refreshments and eat, drink, and make merry. Another round of dance and song is in order. When the bonfire has turned to ash, the priestess declares the ritual to be over and says:

> *Our revelry this day is done, dear one.*
> *Gods of the old and spirits of nature,*
> *We thank you for your blessings this night.*
> *This rite is done.*

All say:

> *Blessed be!*

Make certain the fire has completely gone out before you leave the ritual site. Soak the ashes with water and clean up the site. Always leave a natural area cleaner than you found it.

July

July 1, Climbing Mount Fuji Day in Japan

July 2, Palio de Siena, the legendary festival for the Italian horse race with feasts, blessings, and betting, founded in the Renaissance

July 3, Festival of Sothis (Ancient Egypt)

July 4, Festival honoring Pax, Roman goddess of peace

July 5, Tynwald Fair Day on the Isle of Man since 1079

July 6, Jan Hus Day in the Czech Republic

July 7, *Tanabata*, Japanese Weavers Festival; China's *Chi Nu* Feast for Milky Way

July 8, First actual Thanksgiving, Massachusetts's Bay Colony (1630)

July 9, Pilgrimage for Sempachfeier, retracing and re-enacting the 1386 battle between the Swiss and Austrians. Defend an issue about which you feel strongly, as the peaceful Swiss did.

July 10, Silence Day in India

July 11, Feast Day of Saint Olga, the first Russian Saint

July 12, Nadaam festival of horses, in Mongolia

July 13, Commemoration of the Departed (Japanese Buddhist)

July 14, Bastille Day (1789) in France

July 15, *Chang Yuan*, Festival of the Dead (China)

July 16, Feast for Our Lady of Carmel

July 17, Festival of Amaterasu, Japanese Sun Goddess

July 18, Saint Marina Day in Cyprus

July 19, Martyr's Day in Myanmar

July 20, National Moon Day (United States)

July 21, Horse's holiday in Rome, part of the Festival of Consualia

July 22, Saint Mary Magdalene's Feast Day

July 23, Rastafarian Celebration honoring Haile Selassie

July 24, Simon Bolivar Festival Day in South America

July 25, Incan holiday for Illyap, god of thunder and lightning

July 26, Birthday of Carl Jung and Robert Graves

July 27, Birthday of Osiris (Ancient Egypt)

July 28, Peruvian Independence Day (1821)

July 29, St. Martha Day in France, first celebrated in 48 CE

July 30, International Bog Day, celebrating the protection of wetlands

July 31, St. Ignatius's Day

The most appropriate rituals you can perform in the month of July are those in celebration of the sun.

Sirius, the Dog Star, rises in early July. The Egyptians knew this star as Sothis. In Egyptian mythology, Isis is Queen of Heaven, and Osiris, ruler of the underworld, is her husband and her brother. While these deities ruled, Egyptian culture thrived, advanced in the arts and science, and also grew in magic and religion. The Egyptians built great cities and became very powerful and renowned for the beauty of their civilization.

Isis is typically depicted as a beautiful winged woman. On her noble head is a crown with the disc of the sun gleaming golden. Veneration of Isis spread from Egypt to the Greeks, the Romans, and throughout the Hellenic world until her last temple was destroyed in the fourth century.

The palm tree is sacred to Isis and can be used in ritual. You can lay the palm leaves in your path and walk in procession. The palm has been used in various ways throughout the world in ritual. The following are some suggestions you can build upon in your own ritual design:

- In Cuba, folks sweep each other with palm branches that have been blessed with holy water in order to keep safe from evil spirits.
- Puerto Ricans weave palm leaves into crosses and use them as protective amulets. They also hang the palm crosses in their homes for abundance and to keep the home sacred.
- In Belgium, sections of palms are kept in the fields to ensure a copious harvest.
- The French decorate the graves of their beloved relatives with palm leaves that have been especially blessed for that purpose.
- In New Orleans, the residents plant palmetto palms beside a water fountain or pond on their property to bring money, love, luck, and good health.

Palm Leaf Protection Talisman

This simple ceremony blesses your home with the power of the sun and the protection of the palm leaf. Essential elements for this ritual are a palm leaf or front, incense, cup of water.

Take your palm leaf outside on a sunny day. Cast your sacred circle. Light the incense and pass the palm leaf through the smoke, saying:

By air and by fire I cleanse and consecrate you to the purpose of protection.

Touch your fingertips to the water, sprinkle a few drops onto the leaf, and say:

> *By water I cleanse and consecrate you to the purpose*
> *of protection.*

Lay the palm leaf on the ground, saying:

> *By earth I cleanse and consecrate you to the purpose*
> *of protection.*

Now hold the palm leaf up to the sun. Visualize the warmth and strength of the light permeating the palm leaf and filling it with power. Say:

> *Honored Sun,*
> *Beloved light of the day,*
> *Bless this palm with your protection and light.*
> *So mote it be!*

Pour the remaining water out onto the ground as an offering. When you return home, hang the palm leaf up over your front door.

August

August 1, Fiesta Day (Nicaragua)

August 2, Our Lady of the Angels Day (Costa Rica)

August 3, Drimes Day in Greece with offerings to the dead, all-night parties and bonfires in vineyards and orchards

August 4, Dom Perignon invents champagne in 1693—celebrate!

August 5, Grasmere Rush Bearing Festival in Cumbria, England, dating back to the medieval custom of weaving flooring for cathedrals

August 6, Peace Ceremony for World War II bombing of Hiroshima

August 7, Feast of Hathor (Ancient Egypt)

August 8, Dog Days in Japan, or Doyo

August 9, Nagasaki Peace Ceremony in Japan

August 10, Celebration of the Goddess of Reason, established 1793 in France

August 11, Puck Fair in Killarney, Ireland

August 12, International Youth Day

August 13, Feast of Vertumnus, god of seasons, gardens, and trees, in Rome

August 14, Ferragosto, Italy's traditional mid-August holiday

August 15, Feast Day of the Assumption of Mary

August 16, Saint Roch's Procession in France and Italy

August 17, Potunis in Italy; Marcus Garvey Day for Rastafarians

August 18, St. Helen's Day Pilgrimage

August 19, Roman Vinalia Rustica in honor of Venus since 293 BCE

August 20, *Szent Isvan Napja*, Day of St. Stephen, in Hungary

August 21, Consualia in honor of Consus, god of seeds, grain, and harvest

August 22, Feast of the Queenship of Mary, Star of the Sea, since 1954

August 23, Paper Costume Parade and Holy Bath Day in Portugal

August 24, St. Bartholomew's Day

August 25, Opiconsivia, festival to the goddess Ops

August 26, Feast day of Luonnatar, Finnish goddess of fertility

August 27, Birth of Isis

August 28, St. Augustine's Day to honor Augustine of Hippo (354–430), leading Christian theologian and Father of the Church

August 29, Festival of St. John, commemorating his death

August 30, Santa Rosa (Mexico); Saint Rose of Lima (Peru)

August 31, Anant Chaturdasi, a women's purification festival (Hindu)

The Romans honored Demeter, the grain mother and overseer of the harvest, during August. The Celts celebrated Lughnassadh in honor of Lugh, their god of many skills. Lughnassadh was adopted and adapted by the Christian church as Lammas ("Loaf-mass") and is still celebrated. The custom is that when the first grain is harvest, it must be baked into a loaf and offered to Lugh as thanks for healthy crops. Native Americans called August the Corn Moon, and the Franks referred to this time of year as *Aranmanoth*, The Corn Ears Month.

Lammas Day, August Eve Ritual

Essential elements for this ritual are wheat or barley, sheaves of grain, cauldron, water, one floating candle, one candle for each person present, and essential oils of rose, lavender, or other summer flowers.

To create the sacred space of the ritual, arrange the sheaves of grain in the four directions around a cauldron. Fill the cauldron three-quarters full with water and add essential oils of the flowers of summer. Cast your circle in the usual manner.

At this point, the leader of the ritual should light the candles and then hand them to each person and guide the participants to form a circle around the cauldron. Now the floating candle should be lit and placed in the cauldron by the leader, who says:

> *O Ancient Lugh of days long past,*
> *Be here with us now*
> *In this place between worlds,*
> *On this Lammas Day*

Rap three times on the cauldron and say:

> *Harvest is here and the seasons do change,*
> *This is the height of the year.*
> *The bounty of summer sustains us*
> *In spirit, in soul, and in body.*

Now the group circles five times around the cauldron. All present should then speak their gratitude for the gifts of the season, and the riches of the summer bounty. Storytelling, singing, and dancing should all be a part of this rite, and the leader determines when the rite is done by putting out the candles and proclaiming:

This rite is done!

Close the circle.

There are many ways you can create your own variations on Lammas Day celebrations with your own views on the summer season and how you show appreciation to nature and spirit. One lovely way to celebrate Lammas Day is to have a feast that begins and ends with gratitude and blessings for the good and wine with a place set and food served for the great godly guest, Lugh.

September

September 1, Greek New Year

September 2, St. Mama's Day in Cypress

September 3, Sukkot, Feast of the Tabernacles, a Jewish moveable feast celebrated around this time

September 4, Founders day of Los Angeles (1835), the "City of Angels," celebrated with processions, dance, rodeo, and Mass

September 5, Mother Teresa died in 1997

September 6, First day of the Hebrew calendar since 3761 BCE

September 7, Rificolne in Florence and Siena celebrating Cosimo de Medici's 1260 victory: a celebration with picnics, lantern processions, folk singing, and street dancing.

September 8, Water Festival honoring springs (Tibet)

September 9, Chrysanthemum Festival in Japan, *Choyo no Sekku, Kiky bo Seku*

September 10, St. Salvi Day, French bishop who died and came back to life in 574 BCE still celebrated with parades, feasts, and Mass

September 11, Coptic New Year in Egypt

September 12, National Grandparent's Day (United States)

September 13, Epulum Jova, The Great Banquet in Rome

September 14, First day of Greek Eleusinian Mysteries

September 15, Day to Respect the Aged (Japan)

September 16, Mexican Independence Day in Mexico (1810)

September 17, Feast of Hildegard of Bingen

September 18, Feast of Demeter (Ancient Rome)

September 19, International Talk Like a Pirate

September 20, International Day of Peace

September 21, Autumn equinox (on or around this day)

September 22, Birthdays of Bilbo and Frodo Baggins in The Lord of the Rings

September 23, *Shubun no Hi*, grave visiting day in Japan

September 24, *Schwenkenfelder*, German Thanksgiving

September 25, Rosh Hashanah, the movable Jewish feast of the New Year, occurs around this date

September 26, Saint Cyprian and Saint Justina's Day

September 27, Saints Cosmos and Damian's feast day, Arabian doctors

September 28, Birthday of Confucius, the great Chinese scholar (551–479 BCE)

September 29, Day of Saint Michael and All Angels (also known as Michaelmas)

September 30, the first book is printed with movable type, *The Gutenberg Bible*, 1452

The autumnal winds bring change as we begin harvesting and preparing for the future. We unpack the warm clothes and woolens, and start to winter-proof our homes, offices and cars. In our modern world, we go back to school and college. Vacations are over, and we go off to work with renewed spirits and goals. We now reap what we have sown throughout the year. Winter is also coming, the "scouring storm." To survive and thrive in the coldest times, we need to prepare by doing our inner work.

Rosh Hashanah: The Jewish New Year

This Jewish holiday is a moveable feast and occurs in September (sometimes in very early October). *Rosh* means "head" and *Hashanah* means "New Year." It is a rather somber holiday when participants pray for forgiveness and undertake ten days of penitence, ending in Yom Kippur, the Day of Atonement. During Rosh Hashanah, Jews begin their new year with a new outlook and hope of good health, a good year, and a long and happy life.

One ritual aspect of Rosh Hashanah is the sounding of the *shofar*, the ram's horn, by the rabbi. This custom is the signal for Jews to repent and think about their people and the current state of affairs with all Jews. Perhaps the most important aspect of this holiday is the three sets of prayers that are recited during the ten days that remind people of God's omnipotence, his response to the *shofar*, and that God always remembers good works and kindness.

You can use these Jewish themes of meditating on your current state of affairs, your family, and the blessings of the gods and angels in a fall equinox ritual.

Fall Equinox Ritual

Establish one room in your house as the temple. Ideally, it is the room in which you normally keep an altar or sacred shrine. In any case, you should create an altar in the center of the space. Place four small tables in the four corners of the directions and place four evenly spaced candlesticks between the tables. Place a loaf of freshly baked bread (bread you have made with your own hands is best) in the east, a bowl of apples in the south, a bottle of wine in the west, and a sheaf of wheat or a bundle of dried corn in the north. Upon the main altar, place a candle, a plate of sweet cakes and a goblet. Light incense and place it in front of the cakes. Before your ritual, take some time for contemplation. Think about what you have achieved during this busy year:

What have you done?

What do you need?

What remains to be done?

What are your aspirations?

Write down your thoughts and feelings and the answers to those questions. Read what you have written and ponder it. Look for continuing ideas or themes and make notes of these on a piece of paper. Next, take a calming and cleansing quiet bath, and snip a lock of your freshly washed hair and place it on the paper where you wrote your notes. Dress yourself in a robe and enter your temple space. Light the candle on the altar and use this candle to light all the other candles in the temple. Speak the traditional Hebrew words of self-blessing:

> *Ateh, Malkuth, Ve Geburah, Ve Gedulah, Le Olahm, Amen:*
> *Through the symbol of the pentagram in the name*
> *of Adonai.*

Repeat this facing each corner, and then face your altar and say:

> *In the east, Raphael; in the south, Michael; in the west,*
> *Gabriel; in the north, Uriel. Welcome to this place in the*
> *name of Melchisedek, the High Priest of the Godhead.*

Then go to the east and raise the loaf of bread as offering and say:

> *Raphael, Lord of the Winds of Heaven, bless this bounty*
> *born of sun and air and earth. Let us feed the hungry and*
> *bless the hand that gives it.*
> *Place the bread back into the bowl and go to the southern*
> *corner. Raise an apple as offering and state:*

Michael, protector of the weak and the oppressed,
bless this sun-ripened fruit and let it be not the fruit of
temptation but the fruit of our knowledge so we know
how to make our choices and understand the measure of
both good and evil.
Place the apple back into the bowl and go to the western
corner. Lift up the bottle of wine and say:
Gabriel, bringer of the word of God, bless this wine that
we may take into our body the wine of life shed by all
saviors since time began.

Place the bottle back on the western table. Turn to the north
and raise the corn or wheat as an offering and say:

Uriel, Lord of the Earth and all its bounty, bless this crop
that it may be plentiful all over the earth, that this may be
a year when all mankind will know the comfort of food
and hearth.
Now return to the altar in the center of the temple. Light
the incense and place some bread and the chalice of wine
on the altar. Dip a piece of bread into the blessing wine.
Proclaim:
Melchisedeck, priest of the most high God, in the desert
after the battle with the kings of Edom you brought bread
and wine to Abraham. In this communion shared between
man and priest of the most high God, a covenant was
made. I pray that this coming harvest makes bread for the
world. In token of the ancient custom, I take this bread and
wine into my body.
Now in this sacred place, guide and teach me, show me
how to pursue knowledge for the power of good. Help me
to grow in wisdom. Bless me. Bless those who share my
life. Bless all of those with whom I work. Bless this earth
and sweet, green world that gives us all the blessings we

enjoy—all the water and wine, all the corn and wheat, all
the joys of life in this body. Bless my home.

Take a lock of hair and light it from the candle and burn it in the bowl of incense and say:

This is the offering of myself.
In the east—blessings to Raphael.
In the south—blessings to Michael.
In the west—blessings to Gabriel.
In the north—blessings to Uriel.
Blessed be to all.

Now go around your temple space in reverse order and extinguish all candles. Then declare your temple closed. The common wisdom is that you should place the apples, bread, and wine in your garden as an offering the next day, as a blessing to all of nature.

Mexican Independence Day

September 16 is celebrated throughout Mexico as the day the Mexican Revolution began and it is actually now a bigger cause for celebration than Cinco de Mayo. As the legend goes, one day Father Hidalgo, an ordinary priest, began shouting from his pulpit, "Viva la Virgin de Guadalupe!" To the Mexican people of that era, this was an incitement to fight for freedom and be rid of Spanish rule. This cry spread across all of Mexico and stirred the people to great power. Unfortunately for the priest who initiated the movement in the name of Guadalupe, it resulted in his execution for treason against the Spanish government. While this was intended to shut the revolution down, it served only to infuriate the Mexican people who revolted and won their independence. This is a day to honor Father Hidalgo and revere Guadalupe with shrines, prayers, invocations, and candle burning.

The Orishas of Santeria

On September 22, 1862, Abraham Lincoln issued the Emancipation Proclamation. This is an excellent opportunity to celebrate freedom from oppression for the hardy and deeply spiritual Africans who kept their own religions alive despite the incredible odds against them.

African slaves brought their native religion with them wherever they went. African spirituality is based on nature—water, rivers, plants, seashells, and all the elements of the world around them. When the Africans came to the Catholic lands in Central and South America, their African deities were blended with Catholic saints to make an interesting new religion called Santeria. It was their way of keeping their African religion alive, and it has worked well. These *orishas* are spirit guardians, similar to those honored in Candomble. All of life is believed to come from one great creative force, Oloddumare. Practitioners of Santeria believe that everyone has one *orisha* as a guardian throughout his or her life.

- ✦ **Aganyu** corresponds to Saint Christopher. This volcano god is the father of Chango and whose mother is Yemmu. He can protect you from harm but only if you make your appeal through Chango.

- ✦ **Babalu-Aye** is associated with Saint Lazarus and is the deity to turn to for healing. He is one of the most beloved and needed of all the *orishas*. Babalu-Aye travels about with a bag of corn and offers healing and prosperity.

- ✦ **Chango** is a male god who corresponds to Saint Barbara. Chango holds major power. Red-coated and covered with cowry shells, Chango loves the good life—women, food, drink, dance, fire, lightning. He is the hot *orisha*. Call on Chango when you need passion in love.

✦ **Eleggua** corresponds to Saint Anthony, but he is a trickster who creates bewilderment in his wake. He is "all-knowing" and wants to be acknowledged first before any other *orisha*. Because order comes from chaos, it is believed that Eleggua brings us into wholeness.

✦ **Obatala** is a deity of both genders who corresponds to Our Lady of Mercy. He is a bringer of peace and purity, as evidenced by his white robes. Obatala teaches temperance and can help us control obsessive thoughts, anger, worry, and fear.

✦ **Ochosi** corresponds to Saint Norbert and is the hunter god who lives in the woods. He protects and helps hunters, is a healer, and helps with legal issues. Ochosi is the *orisha* to turn to if you need to relocate.

✦ **Oggun** corresponds to Saint Peter and is the warrior *orisha*, holding all metals under his domain. Call on Oggun when you need a job or if you need a protector.

✦ **Orunmila** corresponds to Saint Francis of Assisi and is the *orisha* of fate. He is "one who lives both in heaven and on earth." Since he holds all our fates in his hands, he can help us improve our destiny.

✦ **Oshun** corresponds to Our Lady of Charity and is a river goddess. She is the Santerian Venus and looks after affairs of the heart—love, marriage, and money. She gives us joy and abundance.

✦ **Oya** corresponds to Saint Teresa and is a deity of the dead. She is also a goddess of the winds and boundaries. Oya is a warrior and offers protection against death and is quite aggressive. She is married to Chango.

✦ **Yemaya** corresponds to Our Lady of Regla and is a goddess of the moon and of the ocean and the patroness of pregnancy. She is always depicted as a gorgeous goddess who helps girls make the passage to womanhood. Yemaya is one of the most popular *orishas*.

Autumn Equinox

Here is a wonderfully creative variation on this seasonal rite designed by Robin Heerens Lysne, the author of *Living a Sacred Life*. It is based on the Native American Muskogee Creek tribal story about the spider who weaves her web sack to catch the sun and bring it back to earth. Lysne suggests holding a potluck dinner followed by a story-telling session as the light begins to wane. While people tell their equinox or fall season stories and feelings, they should hold the end of a ball of yarn or string and toss the ball to the next person to signal that it is their turn. As people hold the yarn, they should wrap it once around their wrists. When the talking is done, you will have a web of people woven together. Make the web of life with the yarn, symbolizing the weaving of night, day, relationships, and the time of autumn. When you are finished, let yourselves be in the web and contemplate the meaning of your connections.

October

October 1, Beginning of Shinto "Godless" Month in Japan with pilgrimages to shrines temporarily abandoned by the gods and spirits

October 2, Old Man's Day in Hertfordshire, England, a day of charity and prayer

October 3, *Zhong Oiu Jie* is a moveable Chinese Moon festival celebrated around this time

October 4, Saint Francis Day, when pets are blessed

October 5, Pilgrimage to Zapopan in Jalisco, Mexico, celebrating the Virgin

October 6, Festival of Vishnu begins (Hindu)

October 7, United Nations Children's Day

October 8, *Okunchi* in Japan with a lucky lion dance parade

October 9, *Han'Gul*, Alphabet Day (Korea)

October 10, *Shuangshi Jie*, National Day in Taiwan, also called "Double Tenth Day," a festival of folk dancing, sword fighting, and martial arts

October 11, Medrinalia in Rome, the celebration of new wine

October 12, Fiesta de Nuestra Senora del Pilar in Spain

October 13, Fontinalia, Roman Festival in honor of Fons, son of Jupiter

October 14, Japanese Battle Festival, *Mega-kenka Matsuri*, celebrated with battle rites and reenactments since 201 CE

October 15, Festival of Mars (Ancient Rome)

October 16, World Food Day

October 17, Family Day (South Africa)

October 18, Heroes Day (Jamaica)

October 19, Our Lord of Miracles procession in Peru since 1687

October 20, Guru Har Rai Day for Sihks

October 21, Festival of the Black Christ in Panama, El Jesus Nazareno

October 22, *Cheung Yeung* (Hong Kong)

October 23, Swallows depart from Capistrano (and arrive back on March 19, St. Joseph's Day)

October 24, United Nations Day celebrated globally with school fairs, concerts, exhibitions, and banquets

October 25, Saint Crispin' Day (1415), immortalized in Shakespeare's *Henry V*

October 26, Quit Rent Day in Europe, celebrated with ceremonies, feasts, and presentations and token payment of rent with horseshoes

October 27, Feast of the Holy Souls

October 28, Meiji Festival in Tokyo featuring five days of performances, classical court dances, concerts and horseback-archery contests

October 29, Ringing of "Lost in the Dark" Church Bells in England

October 30, Angels' Night, also known as Devil's Night (United States)

October 31, Halloween, Samhain

Although October is the tenth month of the year, it comes from the Latin word for eight, as it was the eighth month in the Roman calendar. The Romans designated the month of October to honor Astraea, daughter of Zeus and Themis. Astraea lived on earth, but when mankind became too evil, she departed to the stars. The chilly air and biting winds of October symbolize her departure from earth. The Celts call October *Deireadh Fomhair*, and the Anglo-Saxons called it *Winterfelleth*, which translates to "winter is coming." The Franks linked October to the grape harvest and the pressing of new wine, calling it Vintage Month or *Windurmanoth*. Farmers in the seventeenth and eighteenth centuries in America called the October full moon the Hunter's Moon, and Native Americans refer to October as Second Summer, which is why we sometimes call it Indian Summer.

Chinese Harvest Mooncake

In China, the full or Harvest Moon in October is celebrated with mooncakes, which are offered to the Goddess Chang-O, the Lady in the Moon. This is the time when wheat and rice are harvested, making it an important time of thanksgiving for food to have on hand through the winter season.

The rice and the wheat are baked into cakes that look like the big round moon up in the sky and are used as offerings, along with melons and pomegranates, to the goddess. The women making the mooncakes put their intentions into them by whispering secret wishes into the batter. The unifying action of blending and mixing the tasty cakes represents family harmony. One sweet aspect of this ritual is the selection of a young girl to enter the "heavenly garden." At the ritual feast for the goddess of the Harvest Moon, this young lady becomes the prophet of her family and community, and she is urged to share her visions about the coming year and the prosperity of the village or the land. Feasting on mooncakes and other ritual foods is followed by games and singing under the bright light of Chang-O's moon.

Halloween Altar

On October 31, the veil is thinnest between the two worlds of the living and the dead. It is of vital importance to honor the dead. One way to do this is to create a special altar for this day, a tradition that comes down to us from the Celts among others. Create a new shrine just for this occasion with a chest or table in your home where people will see it and acknowledge your ancestors. On the altar, place photos, letters, and any mementos that will bring the energy of your late loved ones close.

Place candles on the altar and light them during twilight. While it may seem uncomfortable at first, talk to your ancestors and tell them about what is going on in your life. Share memories and speak about whatever you feel inspired to speak of—grief, hopes for the future, troubles, all you need to share. Take as much time as you need with this. Place the bowl of water with white flowers—gardenias are an excellent choice—on the altar and leave it overnight.

In the morning, say good morning and goodbye until next year. Then take the water and pour it in your front yard or outside near the front door of your home. You have communed with your beloved dead, and they are now free to leave and return to you next year. The water contains all the blessings and love from your ancestors whom you have honored and with the special altar, and you will receive their blessings and love every time you walk through your front door.

November

November 1, All Saints Day

November 2, All Souls Day, *Dia de los Muertos*

November 3, St. Hubert's Day, celebrated with a hunter's Mass

November 4, Mischief Night in England with bonfires and firecrackers, a "festival of chaos"

November 5, Guy Fawkes Day in England since 1605, also known as Bonfire Night

November 6, Leonhardi-ritt in Bavaria, for St. Leonard, patron saint of cattle

November 7, Mayan ghost banquet

November 8, *Fuigo Matsuri*, festival honoring Hettsui no Kami, Japanese goddess of the kitchen hearth

November 9, *Dia de Camana* (Peru)

November 10, Martin Luther's birthday (1483)

November 11, Remembrance Day, Armistice Day

November 12, Tesuque Feast Day for Pueblo Indians

November 13, Roman festival of Jupiter

November 14, South America's Little Carnival before Advent

November 15, Recycling Day (United States)

November 16, Festival of Bast (Ancient Egypt)

November 17, The Leonid meteor shower is visible on this day

November 18, Saint Plato's Day

November 19, Pilgrimage Day for Islam

November 20, *Ebisu-ko*, Japanese ceremony to the prophet god

November 21, Presentation of the Virgin Mary

November 22, St. Cecelia's Day, patron saint of musicians

November 23, St. Clement's Day, saint of blacksmiths

November 24, Feast of Burning Lamps for Isis and Osiris (Ancient Egypt)

November 25, Mange Yam, harvest festival (Haiti)

November 26, Thanksgiving if a Thursday and St. Peter of Alexandria Day

November 27, St. Maximus' Day in Provence

November 28, Baha'i Ascension of Abdul-Baha in 1892

November 29, St. Andrew's Eve, a night of fortune-telling in Europe

November 30, Saint Andrew's Day

Diwali in India: The Cluster of Lights Festival

Diwali, one of the most beloved holidays in all of India, is another moveable feast that generally takes place around mid-November. People will circumnavigate the globe to return home to be with their family during this special time. The Hindus treasure this late-autumn festival week and dress up their homes and themselves. All the streets and windows are brightly lit with special *diwali* lamps, small ceramic affairs filled with oil and cotton wicks that twinkle like stars, in every home and even on fences, garden walks, and porches.

Diwali is like a New Year, when everyone can start again, forgiving quarrels, wearing new clothes, and starting life anew with a fresh attitude and bright hopes. In the village and mountainous regions of India, bonfires are going strong, warming up the landscape along with fireworks that light up the night skies.

Diwali honors the victory of Rama, an avatar aspect of Vishnu who battled a ten-headed demon that stole Rama's wife,

Sita, with devotional music, lamp-lighting rituals, feasting, games, gambling, gift giving, and special foods, such as sweets, fruits, candies, and pastries that are constructed into temple-like towers.

Diwali Ritual

Diwali offers us the opportunity to vanquish our own demons and start anew. The symbols of light and sweetness are used here to represent the intention to replace resentment and bitterness with hope and balm. Essential elements of this ritual are plenty of candles, a new piece of clothing (such as a scarf) or a new item of jewelry, and a plate of sweet cakes, confections, or candy.

Light as many candles as you can in the room where you are performing this ritual. Create a circle of candles, and create sacred space by having a symbol of each element in your circle: a dish of salt or earth, a cup of water, incense, and a candle. Sit lotus-style in the center of your circle and relax in the flickering candlelight. Feel the center of your circle and relax in the flickering candlelight. Feel the presence of the four elements and the balance they create. Notice how warm and alive the room feels. Notice how the gentle, flickering candlelight makes you feel safe. Now think back to all the difficult situations you have experienced over the past year and think of the people who have angered or hurt you. Imagine them surrounded by the warm, loving candlelight, and say to each of them, one by one:

> *I release you. May the lights of Diwali bless you.*

As you release each person or situation, visualize their image melting into the candlelight. While the image fades from your mind's eye, place a bite of the cake or confection in your mouth. Allow the treat to dissolve, spreading its sweetness across your tongue. Visualize and feel that sweetness spreading through you, counteracting any of the traces of pain or bitterness that might remain. This is the sweetness that your new life holds, untainted by these bitter demons that have held you back.

When you have finished releasing your demons to the light, purify the new piece of clothing or item of jewelry by passing it through the smoke of the incense. Put on your new piece of jewelry of clothing, saying:

> *With this act, I declare the past gone, and see the future bright with hope.*

Stay within your circle of light as long as you desire. Leave some of the cake or sweets as an offering to the gods in thanks for your new life.

December

December 1, Festival of Pallas Athene (Ancient Greece)

December 2, Festival of Shiva (Hindu)

December 3, St. Xavier's Feast Day

December 4, International Hug Day

December 5, International Volunteers Day

December 6, St. Nicholas Day, precursor to St. Nick

December 7, Burning the Devil Night in Guatemala, *La Quema Del Diablo*

December 8, Festival of Ix Chel, Mayan lunar goddess

December 9, Virgin of Guadalupe first appears (1591)

December 10, International Human Rights Day

December 11, Pilgrimages at Tortuga, New Mexico

December 12, Pilgrimages at Guadalupe in Mexico, Nuestra Senora de Guadalupe

December 13, Saint Lucia Day in Sweden

December 14, Feast of St. John of the Cross

December 15, Consualia in Rome

December 16, Las Posadas in Mexico, procession commemorating the Holy Family's search for lodging

December 17, Saturnalia begins

December 18, Virgin of Solitude Day in Oaxaca, Mexico

December 19, Feast of Saint Boniface, the apostle of Germany

December 20, Commerce God Festival in Japan

December 21, Winter solstice

December 22, Saint Chaeremon Day

December 23, Laurentalia, Roman festival of hallowing the home

December 24, Mother Night (Anglo-Saxon)

December 25, Christmas Day

December 26, First day of Kwanzaa (Afro-American)

December 27, Freya's Day (Teutonic)

December 28, Holy Innocents Day (Mexico)

December 29, Saint Thomas of Canterbury's Day

December 30, Nia, or Purpose Night during the celebration of Kwanzaa

December 31, Hogmanay (Scotland)

Nearly every solar god is celebrated in December—Baal, Attis, Adonis, Apollo, Ra, Baldur, and Mithra, to name a few. Scots celebrate Hogmanay, a secular holiday with roots in the worship of the ancient solar god, Hogmagog. Yule is one of the pagan sabaats, or the eight holidays of the wheel of the year, and is celebrated on December 21, the shortest day of the year. The word *Yule* comes from the Germanic *jol*, and means midwinter. The old tradition was to have a vigil and a bonfire from dusk to dawn to make sure the sun does indeed rise again on this longest night of the entire year.

Chanukah: the Festival of Lights

Here we have another moveable feast, which is one of the most beloved of all Jewish holidays. As we know from the Roman historian, Tacitus, in the second century BCE Antiochus IV, the Seleucidian king, blocked all Jews from visiting their own temple on Mount Zion and tried to force them to sacrifice swine and eat the meat, which is against their religion. He also placed an edict commanding Jews, under penalty of death, to leave their sons uncircumcised. The stubborn and cruel Antiochus also invaded the Jewish temple on Mount Zion and installed a statue of Zeus therein. Many lives were lost in the struggle, but the Jewish resistance, led by Judah Maccabee, the "Jewish Hammer," overcame the Greek forces and reconsecrated the temple on the twenty-fifth day of the Hebrew month of Kislev in 165 BCE The triumphant Jews declared that this event should be remembered each year with a festival. Judah then lit the candelabra, or menorah, in the temple. The miracle of the menorah is that there was only enough lamp oil for one night but it lasted eight nights, thus the tradition of lighting a candle each day during Chanukah's eight nights. Feasting is also an important part of the ritual, with the customary latkes (fried potato pancakes) often topped with applesauce and sour cream.

Kwanzaa: December 26th

In 1966, a Black Studies professor at California State University in Long Beach, Maulana Ron Karenga, conceived Kwanzaa, which means "first fruit" in Swahili. Kwanzaa (December 26 to January 1) is very much a community ritual and begins with a gathering before an altar covered with the symbols of the season: corn; a woven mat; a unity cup; and an African flag of red, black, and green. Also on the altar are gifts made by the hand and a special Kwanzaa candleholder holding seven taper candles. The colors of the candles are red, for the blood of the people; black, for the people themselves; and green, for the land. Each night of the festival, a candle is lit commemorating and honoring the Seven Principles, Nguzo Saba, of Kwanzaa:

1. *Umoja* for unity
2. *Kujichagulia* for self-determination
3. *Ujima* for shared works
4. *Ujamaa* for shared monies
5. *Nia* for life purpose
6. *Kuumba* for creativity
7. *Imani* for faith

Winter Solstice Ritual, December 21

Winter solstice rituals traditionally celebrate the rebirth of the sun. In a safe place outdoors, build a bonfire and create a solstice altar to the east of it. Place a small cauldron with a candle in it on the altar, and surround it with mistletoe, ivy, and holly. Participants should also wear crowns woven from these evergreens. If it is too cold or snowy where you live, you can gather indoors and form a semicircle around the fireplace, or around the altar.

Begin the ritual by holding hands around the fire. Hum softly, gradually building the hum to a shout. This shout represents the cries of the Goddess giving birth once again to the sun, and to the new year. The ritual leader says:

> *All bow to the East! Hail to the newborn Sun, and to the Great Goddess who has brought him forth!*

Everyone bows to honor the Sun God and the Mother Goddess. The ritual leader chants:

> *Brigid,*
> *Diana,*
> *Morgan,*
> *Cerridwen,*
> *Heaven's Queen,*
> *By the light of this moon*
> *In this dark night,*
> *Teach us the mystery of rebirth.*

The ritual leader lights the candle in the cauldron while everyone else remains perfectly still. Now is the time when the Goddess will reveal herself privately to each participant. If you are outdoors, listen and look carefully for a sign. Traditional omens are a sudden wind, shooting stars, the screeching of an owl, and the appearance of a deer. Even if you are indoors by the fire, the Goddess will still make herself known in your heart. When the time feels right, the ritual leader says:

> *Queen of the Stars,*
> *Queen of the Moon,*
> *Queen of the Earth,*
> *Bringer of Fire,*
> *The Great Mother gives birth to this new year*
> *And we are her witnesses.*

Everyone shouts:

Blessed be!

Pass the lit cauldron to each participant so they can speak a blessing for the new year and the new sun. Place the cauldron with the candle back on the altar. The ritual leader closes the ritual with this final expression of gratitude to the Goddess:

Blessed be to the Mother Goddess
Thank you for the sun that gives us life
Without beginning and without end
Everlasting in Eternity.
This ritual is now done!

A toast to the new sun should take place with hot cider or mead, and warm festive foods.

Chapter Ten

DESIGNING YOUR OWN RITUALS: TRADITIONAL AND ALTERNATIVE

In this book are many examples of rituals, both traditional and alternative. In addition, there are ideas and suggestions for rituals of your own design. In creating your own rites and ceremonies, you can take many approaches. You can devise and enact new customs of your own invention. These new rituals can be pure, simple, uncomplicated events, or they can be incredibly elaborate. You decide. I urge you to avoid too much pomp. Too much planning, building, and painting of sets and excessive researching can create more stress than is really warranted, taking away from the meaning and distracting you from your true intention.

Participating in ritual can change your life. Even practicing one ritual can uplift and inspire you for years, and regular involvement can lead to spiritual riches. Ritual is soul work. Increasingly, with our hectic workday schedules, you may find yourself creating rituals and meditating alone, praying by yourself, and performing daily spiritual practices solo.

In addition to planning more intricate proceedings, you should also craft little on-the-spot private rituals that serve immediate spiritual needs. You can celebrate your gratitude to a deity that is special to you or light a candle and meditate at your altar on a holy day. Your rituals should reflect the ebb and flow of you outer life and your inner work.

This kind of ritual is simple and pure; I call it *real ritual*. Your spiritual pursuits should be a mix of simple, solo ceremonies and more complex ones that you perform alone or with others. The work of the soul is stimulated by interactions with others and grows in your time alone. Rituals enliven and add meaning to each day. Your simple daily ceremonies and practices are the individual threads that weave the fabric of your life rather like a tapestry quilt that grows thread by thread, stitch by stitch, and square by square. You need the threads, the patches, and the squares to hold together the tapestry of a rich, memory-filled, and meaningful life.

In this book, you have been provided with some of the great rituals of the world and many starting points for piecing together your own ceremonies. You can choose from the wealth of correspondences in the appendices to add layers of meaning, depth, and effectiveness, building your knowledge, expanding your experiences, and connecting you to the world's wise traditions. Also, by keeping a Book of Shadows or personal ritual journal, you will have your own set of measurements and memories of what has worked for you. The appendix gives ingredients that you can add to your ritual "recipe." Let's say you want to create a personal and private ritual to get a new job. You can look up the best time to do it in the Ritual Resources section and you will see that a Thursday new moon would be an optimum choice to perform such a ritual.

There are also different divinities you can choose from to call upon for help in this ritual, from jovial Jupiter to the very sympathetic and helpful Lakshmi, to name just two. There are also a variety of herbs and plants you can choose from to assist with money matters, along with correct colors for candles and essences for both incense and oils that supply abundance. When you create your new job ritual, therefore, you can select the right traditional correspondence that matches your need and you are halfway there.

Focus and attention concerning your intention are of equal importance. In terms of the language of your original ritual, you should write from your heart, which will ensure that the words will personally affect you and work for you. Believe in yourself and believe in your intention and the right words will flow. There is no exact science to writing rituals. Just match the words and correspondences to your intention, and you will be a creator of rituals.

It is natural that once you are completely comfortable working with the realm of existing rituals, you should begin to trust you own intuition and create your own. Listen to your inner voice and trust yourself. Correspondences are a start, but you must take a leap of faith and delve into the depths of your own psyche for rituals you create, enact, and share with the world.

While we know there is no exact science to ritual design, there is an art to it, and the knack is developed from participating in group rituals, learning from the experienced elders, performing private rituals, and endeavoring to craft rituals on your own for every season and reason. The art of creating rituals is the work of the heart, and while it is not always easy, it is the work of creating joy in your life. With each ritual, you are taking a step to a reality of your own creation. Rites and ceremonies serve many purposes in our lives. They can be designed to fulfill one person's wish, help a member of your spiritual circle, or help heal the entire world like the Dalai Lana's sand mandala ritual. There are no limitations to the scope of rituals you can design. Where there is need, you can supply intention and inspiration and, in so doing, spread bliss in your wake. Rituals can change the world, and your rituals will most certainly change your world. When you are designing ritual, you are really designing the life of your dreams.

Recording Your Rituals

In the chapter on tools for rituals, I recommend creating a Book of Shadows to keep notes on ceremonies you have participated in and witnessed. Your BOS can and should be a document of what works for you in terms of specifics—moon phases, colors, numbers, herbs, etc. You can greatly expand your BOS with notes on your ritual projects and your life as a work in progress. Here should be your musings, your writing of invocations, your hopes, and your intentions. I call this the "journal of the journey," and it can take any form of your imagination as long as it catches the deep truths of what you hope to accomplish.

Your ritual record need not be fancy, but it should be raw, honest, and real. Tell the stories of what *really* happened, mistakes and all. Those who are the most truthful and open will gain the most from their record of experience. Not every group ritual will be a smashing success—someone will be grumpy, someone else might say the words wrong, or you will all get nervous and forget what to do. Or nature may change your plans. For example, an outdoor full moon circles planed for a year may be driven indoors by a rainstorm that puts out the candles and wilts every spirit. Nevertheless, I am always encouraged and amazed to discover the so-called mistakes we learn most from. If everything is perfect, the ritual is more likely to slip from memory. Life itself is messy and bumpy. Think of the metaphor of the Navajo blanket in which the weaver, despite his skill, always makes one mistake. The metaphor is that life itself is not perfect, and the blanket should be reflective of life. That one "crooked thread" can be the strongest stitch holding the fabric together.

At one full moon weekend, a woman's circle organized by Z. Budapest started off badly when several women didn't show up, failing to help pay for the retreat house. The ever-resilient Z. only noted the resulting blessings. The women present created a coven of thirteen, a number sacred to the goddess. With fewer women, we could cook and clean up faster, leaving more time to hike in the woods and pray. During the first hike, we discovered a natural spring bubbling out of the side of the mountain. Inspired by this miracle of nature, we splashed and bathed and Z. created an on-the-spot goddess water rite. It was the highlight of the retreat, and an unexpected blessing. Pure magic was woven by Z's experienced hand with this crooked golden thread. By documenting and sharing the ritual stories, I have learned much about ritual and about myself in the process.

Chapter Eleven

ENERGY WORK: MANAGING ENERGY AND CREATING SACRED SPACE

Liz Ashling is a shamanic leader in Larkspur, California, who has worked with hundreds of people in her practice to help them live in balance and "awaken oneness." She has inspired the following meditation. This uniquely holistic approach to energy management provides the opportunity for deep inner work, since within sacred space you experience meaningful exploration to transform your life.

I suggest that you create a special space for yourself, a safe space for healing, such as an altar or healing sanctuary. You want to focus on what you wish to heal. You may wish to write out an intention list with your desires. While you hold your healing intention in your mind, begin to notice what would support your intention. It may be a picture of a healed person, a symbol, or a picture of a spiritual master such as St. Francis, the Blessed Mother, Kuan Yin, or the Buddha. Choose whomever you feel most connected with. Honor Mother Earth by placing a bowl of water on the altar as well as a white candle to banish bad energy. Use something to represent the element of fire and something to represent the earth: fresh flowers, crystals, and pictures of a sculpture of your animal allies and totems. If you have a permanent sacred place with an altar, simply add items with healing powers that match your healing intentions. The ritual of creating an altar provides support to your process.

Here is where you can apply your personal design and creativity. Tap into your intuition and let it be your guide in this sacred shrine. Altars may include a variety of items, such as minerals like rose quartz, amethyst, quartz crystal, turquoise, or any other minerals that promote healing and add supportive energy during your process. Some people use sage, evergreen, or cedar to prepare themselves and their space, asking to clear away earthly demands and confusion as they smudge. The result is the enhancement of listening to yourself, which leads to a deeper inner wisdom. Some people choose to use holy water or wear a gold cross as they do their healing process, while other place a glass bowl of blessed salt water on their altar to keep the space clear. Any of these can help to create sacred space and prepare you for your process. You may wish to play classical or soothing music in the background while you process. I prefer silence of my drum and rattles.

You should do the following exercises in silence, without interruption, and in a safe place. Once you have created your space, sit quietly without being disturbed for an hour or so. Turn off your phone and get comfortable. I suggest that you sit rather than lie down because you will be less likely to fall asleep. Now close your eyes and take a few deep breaths to quiet yourself. Note: I suggest that you read these exercises into a tape player, so you can simple close your eyes and listen to the process.

Guided Meditation

Close your eyes, take a deep breath in and let it go. Breathe in again, breathing in peacefulness and breathing out tension, breathing in joy, breathing out frustration, breathing in fresh air, breathing out staleness. Begin to imagine that you are sitting in a beautiful pyramid of golden light. The light within this pyramid totally surrounds your body. Take another deep breath, then let it go. Imagine that there is a mirror image of this pyramid beneath you grounding you into the earth, creating a structure of light all around you. Breathe in the light, feel its warmth, and relax.

Now image there is a ball of light at the top of the pyramid. Begin to bring this golden ball of light down through the top of your head through your crown area. Opening the crown chakra, located in the top of your head, allow the light to filter down through your crown into the center of your head and expand it out so that all the cells in your head become one with the light, relaxed yet alert. Now take another breath and, as you exhale, relax and let all the tension of the day drift away and become more and more relaxed with each breath you take. Now image the light moving in and out of the center of your forehead, opening up this energy center to the light. As you imagine this, feel the energy coming in and out of this area in the center of your forehead, opening up this energy center to the light. As you imagine this, feel the energy coming in and out of this area in the center of your forehead, opening this energy center for new awareness and clarity. Know that as you sit in sacred space and work with this guided meditation, this process will become easier for you.

Over time, you will develop new ways of sensing, feeling, or seeing the light energy, but for now, relax and allow this golden light to move from your head down to your throat...

allowing the light to massage your throat, opening up your throat to the light...readying your throat to speak your truth. When you feel each center opening, simply move to the next, breathing in and out. Imagine the light moving from the throat now down to the heart, bringing warmth and a golden glow to the heart center. Open your heart to its warmth by imagining your heart as a flower unfolding, opening to the warmth of the sun and your breath.

Stay here in the heart feeling yourself nurtured by the light. Notice the rhythm of your heartbeat...your rhythm, your vibration...and breathe. And now allow yourself to go deeper within the heat. Ask to go to your deeper heart, your soul heart, your wisdom heart...we all know this place...ask to go to this place and sit there with yourself. When you're ready, bring the golden light from the heart center to the upper belly and open up the solar plexus chakra to the light. Sit there for a while, feeling this energy center open. When you are ready, move on. Bring the light to the lower belly, opening this energy center, and sit there for a while. Now bring the light from the lower belly to the base of your spine, your root chakra, opening this energy center to the light. Once you feel your connection at the base of your spine, imagine a cord of light running from the base of your spine into the center of the earth, grounding you in the earth. Know now that you are connected to heaven and earth and yourself for all of your knowing.

This meditation is a powerful way to connect before each healing process. It opens and connects you to yourself, the divine and the earth, providing an inner connectedness that supports inner listening.

At this point, invite in your spiritual guides or guardians, if you have not already done so before entering into the guided meditation.

Calling guides and helpers is easy. Simply say, "Guardians from the light, please come to me and assist me on my healing journey." You may choose to know them and can say, "Show yourselves to me; let me know your presence." Sometimes a friend or loved one who has passed away will come, sometimes an old pet will appear, sometimes you may feel a touch on your shoulder or a loving presence. Trust these moments. You can always ask, "Who is with me from the light?" If you feel a strange presence that makes you uncomfortable, ask who it is or simply ask the energy to go to the light and leave your space now. If you are unaware of guides or elders that work with you, there are some exercises later to introduce you to your helpers. Your higher self and other higher beings, such as angels, must be called. They are always present, but to actively work with you they must be invited. I call them like this: "Angels, Archangels, please come and be with me now. I would like your presence with me for this healing. Higher Self, please work with me now." I also call all my guides and animal allies whenever I create my sacred space.

Casting the Sacred Circle and Calling the Four Directions

Native American culture honors and respects ancestors as guiding spirits. This ritual uses Native American–inspired invocations of your ancestors as your guides.

Before calling the sacred circle, prepare yourself and your space as previously described. You may choose to cast the circle using a drum or rattle as you speak, saying:

Grandmothers and Grandfathers, please come and create the sacred circle of light. Surround me in a circle of light. Thank you.

Grandmothers and Grandfathers of the north, I thank you for coming and I welcome the energy of the north, Great Spirit, the sacred Mountains, connection to our ancestors and the elders, and connection to our knowing, remembering, and our wisdom. I welcome White Buffalo here. Aho!

Grandmothers and Grandfathers of the east, thank you for coming, and I welcome the energy of the east, the golden doorway that leads to all levels of awareness and understanding. I connect to the rising sun, to the warmth of the sun, to new beginnings, to illumination, and to the light, for mental clarity. I welcome the spirit seeds of new ideas and the male energy to move forward. I welcome the energy of Eagle here. Aho!

Grandmothers and Grandfathers of the south, I welcome you and thank you for coming. I welcome the energies of the south, innocence and play and coming into the world from our child's wonder, our authentic self. I welcome the balance of lightheartedness. I welcome the energy of Coyote here. Aho!

Grandmothers and Grandfathers of the west, welcome. I give thanks to the energies of the west, the place of letting go of what no longer serves us, the place of diving deep

into the void, the darkness, Great Mystery, the place of the creative feminine and looking within. I welcome Bear here. Aho!

Grandmothers and Grandfathers of the Above World, I welcome you and the energies of Father Sky, the Cosmos, Star Beings, Light Beings, Ascended Masters, Angels, Archangels, and all who work with us from the light. Welcome. Aho!

Grandmothers and Grandfathers of the Below World, Great and Mother Earth, we welcome your mud, your beauty, and all our ancestors of the earth, the mineral kingdom, plant kingdom, animal kingdom, all creatures, and our relatives. We give thanks to you and all your vibrations and your wisdom. I welcome the nature spirits and align with the elements. Aho!

Grandmothers and Grandfathers at the Center of all being, we welcome you. I welcome the energy of love and well-being, the place that connects us all at heart. May we know our oneness and our unique gifts. Aho!

Once you have opened your chakras and created the sacred circle, you may call for a vision, pray for guidance, pray for healing, or choose to give thanks. This is a circle of light where you are connected to the divine source of love and light. Enjoy your journey. When you have completed your mission within the circle, open the circle by giving thanks to all who came to guide you, guides and totems, and all the energies of the directions.

Chapter Twelve

RITUALS FOR THE ROAD: MAKING YOUR OWN TALISMANS, AMULETS, CHARMS

Before you travel for work, study, and pleasure, it's good to create charms and talismans of power. You can also craft your own ritual tools from what you gather in your travels. Nature will often provide you with tools: shells, bark, and stones. In addition, you may also meet new spiritual teachers as you make your way on the pilgrimage that is life. Pay attention and you will learn much and receive many gifts.

A Medicine Wheel shamanic group run by Brooke Tarrant taught a group of drumming novices, myself included, how to make rattles and drums from recycled leather and sheepskin. In fact, all the materials we used to decorate our rattles and drums were found objects: crystals, sand, tiny shells, and sticks from the forest floor. Last, we used "feather medicine" and decorated the rattles with rawhide and found feathers, each with personal totemic meaning. With a final drumming circle and fire ceremony, we blessed the drums and rattles and each other. During the ceremony, we used both the new and old rattles and drums in some immensely powerful energy cleaning and healing. Even physical aches and pains were alleviated with these new tools. Rituals for the road should also be recorded in your Book of Shadows: what you find, who you meet, and what you create. When the spirit moves you, you should be creative. You can construct a sand mandala or take photographs on the beach to preserve your inspiration. One lovely custom from long ago: Upon your return home, create shadowboxes, which are really like little shrines of the sacred objects from the road.

Amulets

Amulets are protective adornments that date back to the beginning of human civilization. Evil eye amulets are perhaps the most globally popular, believed in most cultures to be capable of warding off a hex by reflecting it back to its origins. In some cultures, amulets were devoted to a god or goddess, and the wearer was protected by that divinity. Horns, hands, and the phallus have all been popular amulet shapes throughout history. We know from archaeological discoveries that the inhabitants of the ancient civilizations in Mesopotamia wore amulets. People in that time wore cylindrical seals covered in precious stones, as well as animal talismans to inherit the qualities associated with different animals.

Ancient Egyptian amulets are on display at museums everywhere. They used their amulets in elaborate burial practices. To make the charms, they used faience, which is glazed ground quartz that is usually colored blue-green. The Egyptian royals and priests also wore precious and semi-precious gems and crystals as amulets. The eye of Horus was the most significant, and usually this was made of lapis lazuli.

Other creations included the lapis lazuli scarab, symbolizing rebirth; the frog, symbolizing fertility; and the ankh, representing eternal life.

In the classical age, Romans wore amulets that were metal cylinders containing parchment inscribed with protective words.

The popularity of amulets extended beyond pagan people when organized religions embraced the idea. In medieval times, religious people would wear verses from the Torah, Bible, or Koran in amulets around their necks. Even today, many Catholics wear medals honoring saints. Celtic symbols and imagery pervade trendy shops as Wiccans and modern pagans have updated and re-popularized the wearing of amulets.

You can make your own amulets for yourself or friends. It is important that you believe your friends will truly benefit from amulets, and that they are aware of the special qualities and powers associated with these special charms. First, you must select a crystal associated with the desired energy. Hold the crystal in your hand until it gets warm, then visualize the specific power the stone is offering. If the amulet is for you, wear it as a pendant or tuck it in your pocket.

Stone: Amethyst
Powers: Prevents inebriation; helps with sobriety

Stone: Aquamarine
Powers: Guards against malevolent spirits; attracts wisdom; helps overcome fear of water/drowning

Stone: Bloodstone
Powers: Brings luck; wear while traveling

Stone: Carnelian
Powers: Keeps away evil sprits

Stone: Diamond
Powers: Brings good fortune; lends force to valor; should be worn touching the skin and works best as a gift

Stone: Emerald
Powers: Cancels out magician's power

Stone: Jade
Powers: Guards health of and protects, especially children; creates prosperity

Stone: Jasper
Powers: Aids in defense against venom of poisonous insects and snakes

Stone: Jet
Powers: Helps expel negativity, especially when set in silver

Stone: Moonstone
Powers: Brings fame and good fortune; wear while traveling

Stone: Turquoise
Powers: Good for a horse's gait when affixed to a bridle

All About Talismans

Talismans, like amulets, are decorative and magical objects. If you've ever read the story of King Arthur, you'll remember a supernatural sword, called Excalibur, which was given special powers by the Lade of the Lake. It is this sword, a talisman, which gives King Arthur magical powers.

Unlike amulets, which are passive protectors, talismans actively transform the wearer to hold certain powers. Crystals and gems already hold power, but with a talisman, special powers can be naturally occurring, or you can instill powers during a ritual. A talisman can be any object or symbol that you believe possesses mystical qualities.

Talismans are used for many different reasons. They can bring love, luck, wealth, and protect you from death or harm. For instructions on creating a talisman, consult a grimoire, or spell book. Here is a list of sacred stone shapes for amulets and pendulums when you are trying to figure out how you want to create ritual talismans and charms.

To maximize the power of the talisman that you design and make, consider the following tried and true suggestion: Keep in mind that this will work even better if you place the item on your altar to energize it. On a new moon night, light a candle that corresponds with your intention or hope. Green is for abundance, red is for power and love, blue is creative and spiritual vision. Burn the candle for one hour every evening.

I also like to create gifts of love for the special friends in my life. I like to gather seeds and herbs in my travels. If you create good luck talismans for your friends and loved ones, your good intentions will be repaid many times over. I keep a stock of tiny muslin drawstring bags on hand to make the talismans, but the talisman can be even more powerful if you sew the bag by hand and stuff the dried herbs and flowers inside. For a courage talisman, use mullein and borage; for safe travels, use comfrey; for protection, use snapdragon; for healing, use rue; for success, use woodruff; for strength, use mugwort; for beauty, use an acorn. In the appendix on page 320, there are many other options you can choose from in the Language of Flowers chart.

Keep these herbal talismans with you at all times and advise your friends to do the same. These bring good luck when you carry them in a purse, pocket, or even in a string around your neck.

Sacred Stone Shapes for Talismans and Amulets

Shape: Ankh-shaped stones
Use: Represent the key to life; develop creativity, wisdom, and fertility

Shape: Clusters
Use: Bring balance and harmony into your life

Shape: Diamond-shaped stones
Use: Attract riches; bring energy of wealth/abundance

Shape: Egg-shaped stones
Use: Give new ideas to wearer; denote creativity

Shape: Heart-shaped stones
Use: Promote romance, self-love; love energy

Shape: Holes that form naturally in stones
Use: Can see visions/spirits if you look through the hole by moonlight

Shape: Human body-shaped stones
Use: Bring energy and strength to whatever body part they look like

Shape: Obelisks
Use: Energy activators

Shape: Octahedrons

Use: Good for analysis, organization, healing; bring order to chaos

Shape: Pyramid-shaped stones
Use: Bring energy upward

Shape: Rectangular rocks and crystals
Use: Energy of God; symbolize male energy; protection; good for love/sex spells

Shape: Round stones
Use: Universe, the Goddess; spirituality, femininity, pregnancy; used in love spells to promote attraction

Shape: Square stones
Use: Bring prosperity; plenty; represent the earth

Shape: Triangular stones
Use: Protect wearers; guardians

Roadside Wisdom

Prosperity and purification go hand in hand. One of the greatest tools for purification is sage. While every metaphysical store has it in quantity, I highly recommend gathering or growing sage yourself. Aromatic sage dries quickly and can be bound into thick "smudge sticks," which you should keep at the ready in a fireproof clay dish. To make a smudge stick, take dried sage leaves and bind them with green and gold thread wound nine times around the bundles and knotted at each loop. Leave room for a handle at the base of the wand, where you wind and knot the green and gold threads thrice more. This will honor the three Fates who hold the thread of our destiny in their hands: Clotho spins the thread of life; Lachesis chooses its length and outcome; and Atropos cuts the thread.

Use your smudge stick at any time purification is in order, especially if you've moved, started a new job, bought a new car, or purchased any second-hand clothing or furniture. This will help remove any energy that might be clinging from the previous owner. Light your smudge stick and, moving clockwise, circle the area or items to be purified. Speak aloud:

> *Great Spirit, with this smoke, your blessed protection I invoke. Out with the bad, in with the good. Harm to none and blessings to all.*

As you travel through your life, you will acquire many sacred things, items which call to you and form part of your ritual equipment. By honoring those found items, you honor also your voyage, and Nature herself. Value these sacred things; they serve as your connection to your past, and your travels. The destination is often less important than the journey itself. The journey is the adventure that enables you to grow and gain in wisdom. Creating amulets and talismans and designing your own rituals are unique ways to fully experience your journey through life.

RITUAL RESOURCES: APPENDIX I

Dates and Times

This section contains lists and tables of information you can use to cast spells and work magic using dates, planets, goals, and astrological signs (if a date is listed as being both lucky and unlucky, the ritualist is free to make his or her own decision regarding personal practice).

Four Major Sabbats

Candlemas—February 2

Beltane—May 1

Lammas—August 1

Samhain—October 31

Four Lesser Sabbats

Vernal Equinox—March 20

Summer Solstice—June 24

Autumn Equinox—September 23

Winter Solstice/Yule—December 21

Lucky and Unlucky Dates

Month: January

Lucky Dates: 3, 10, 27, 31
Unlucky Dates: 12, 23

Month: February
Lucky Dates: 7, 8, 18
Unlucky Dates: 2, 10, 17, 22

Month: March
Lucky Dates: 3, 9, 12, 14, 16
Unlucky Dates: 13, 19, 23, 28

Month: April
Lucky Dates: 5, 17
Unlucky Dates: 18, 20, 29, 30

Month: May
Lucky Dates: 1, 2, 4, 6, 9, 14
Unlucky Dates: 10, 17, 20

Month: June
Lucky Dates: 3, 5, 7, 9, 13, 23
Unlucky Dates: 4, 20

Month: July
Lucky Dates: 2, 6, 10, 23, 30
Unlucky Dates: 5, 13, 27

Month: August
Lucky Dates: 5, 7, 10, 14
Unlucky Dates: 2, 13, 27, 31

Month: September
Lucky Dates: 6, 10, 13, 18, 30

Unlucky Dates: 13, 16, 18

Month: October
Lucky Dates: 13, 16, 25, 31
Unlucky Dates: 3, 9, 27

Month: November
Lucky Dates: 1, 13, 23, 30
Unlucky Dates: 6, 25

Month: December
Lucky Dates: 10, 20, 29
Unlucky Dates: 15, 26

Days, Planets, Colors, and Goals

Day: Sunday
Planet: Sun
Correspondence: Exorcism, healing, prosperity
Color: Orange, white, yellow
Incense: Lemon, frankincense

Day: Monday
Planet: Moon
Correspondence: Agriculture, animals, female fertility, messages, reconciliation, voyages
Color: Silver, white, gray
Incense: African violet, honeysuckle, myrtle, willow, wormwood

Day: Tuesday
Planet: Mars

Correspondence: Courage, physical strength, revenge, military honors, surgery, breaking negative spells

Color: Red, orange

Incense: Dragon's blood, patchouli

Day: Wednesday

Planet: Mercury

Correspondence: Knowledge, communication, divination, writing, business transactions

Color: Yellow, gray, violet, all opalescent hues

Incense: Jasmine, lavender, sweet pea

Day: Thursday

Planet: Jupiter

Correspondence: Luck, health, happiness, legal matters, male fertility, treasure, wealth, employment

Color: Purple, indigo

Incense: Cinnamon, musk, nutmeg, sage

Day: Friday

Planet: Venus

Correspondence: Love, romance, marriage, sexual matters, physical beauty, friendships, partnerships

Color: Pink, green, aqua, chartreuse

Incense: Strawberry, rose, sandalwood, saffron, vanilla

Day: Saturday

Planet: Saturn

Correspondence: Spirit, communication, meditation, psychic attack or defense, locating lost or missing persons

Color: Black, gray, indigo

Incense: Poppy seeds, myrrh

Sun Sign Correspondences

Birth Date: March 21 to April 19

Sun Sign: Aries

Lucky and Protective Stones and Minerals: Diamond, amethyst, topaz, garnet, iron, steel

Color: Red

Birth Date: April 19 to May 20

Sun Sign: Taurus

Lucky and Protective Stones and Minerals: Coral, sapphire, emerald, turquoise, agate, zircon, copper

Color: Azure

Birth Date: May 20 to June 21

Sun Sign: Gemini

Lucky and Protective Stones and Minerals: Aquamarine, agate, amber, emerald, topaz, aluminum

Color: Electric blue

Birth Date: June 21 to July 22

Sun Sign: Cancer

Lucky and Protective Stones and Minerals: Opal, pearl, emerald, moonstone, silver

Color: Pearl, rose

Birth Date: July 22 to August 22

Sun Sign: Leo

Lucky and Protective Stones and Minerals: Diamond, ruby, gold, sardonyx, chrysoberyl

Color: Orange

Birth Date: August 22 to September 23

Sun Sign: Virgo

Lucky and Protective Stones and Minerals: Jade, rhodonite, sapphire, carnelian, aluminum

Color: Gray blue

Birth Date: September 23 to October 23

Sun Sign: Libra

Lucky and Protective Stones and Minerals: Opal, sapphire, jade, quartz, turquoise, copper

Color: Pale orange

Birth Date: October 23 to November 22

Sun Sign: Scorpio

Lucky and Protective Stones and Minerals: Bloodstone, topaz, aquamarine, jasper, silver

Color: Dark red

Birth Date: November 22 to December 21

Sun Sign: Sagittarius

Lucky and Protective Stones and Minerals: Lapis lazuli, topaz, turquoise, coral, tin

Color: Purple

Birth Date: December 21 to January 20

Sun Sign: Capricorn

Lucky and Protective Stones and Minerals: Onyx, jet, ruby, lead, malachite

Color: Brown

Birth Date: January 20 to February 19

Sun Sign: Aquarius

Lucky and Protective Stones and Minerals: Aquamarine, jade, fluorite, sapphire, zircon, aluminum

Color: Green
Birth Date: February 19 to March 21
Sun Sign: Pisces
Lucky and Protective Stones and Minerals: Amethyst, alexandrite, bloodstone, stitchite, silver
Color: Ocean blue

Daytime Planetary Hours

Hour		Sun	Mon	Tues	Wed	Thurs	Fri	Sat
1	6/7 am	Sun	Moon	Mars	Mercury	Jupiter	Venus	Saturn
2	7/8 am	Venus	Saturn	Sun	Moon	Mars	Mercury	Jupiter
3	8/9 am	Mercury	Jupiter	Venus	Saturn	Sun	Moon	Mars
4	9/10 am	Moon	Mars	Mercury	Jupiter	Venus	Saturn	Sun
5	10/11 am	Saturn	Sun	Moon	Mars	Mercury	Jupiter	Venus
6	11/12 am	Jupiter	Venus	Saturn	Sun	Moon	Mars	Mercury
7	12/1 pm	Mars	Mercury	Jupiter	Venus	Saturn	Sun	Moon
8	1/2 pm	Sun	Moon	Mars	Mercury	Jupiter	Venus	Saturn
9	2/3 pm	Venus	Saturn	Sun	Moon	Mars	Mercury	Jupiter
10	3/4 pm	Mercury	Jupiter	Venus	Saturn	Sun	Moon	Mars
11	4/5 pm	Moon	Mars	Mercury	Jupiter	Venus	Saturn	Sun
12	5/6 pm	Saturn	Sun	Moon	Mars	Mercury	Jupiter	Venus

Nighttime Planetary Hours

Hour		Sun	Mon	Tues	Wed	Thurs	Fri	Sat
1	6/7 pm	Jupiter	Venus	Saturn	Sun	Moon	Mars	Mercury
2	7/8 pm	Mars	Mercury	Jupiter	Venus	Saturn	Sun	Moon
3	8/9 pm	Sun	Moon	Mars	Mercury	Jupiter	Venus	Saturn
4	9/10 pm	Venus	Saturn	Sun	Moon	Mars	Mercury	Jupiter
5	10/11pm	Mercury	Jupiter	Venus	Saturn	Sun	Moon	Mars
6	11/12 pm	Moon	Mars	Mercury	Jupiter	Venus	Saturn	Sun
7	12/1 am	Saturn	Sun	Moon	Mars	Mercury	Jupiter	Venus
8	1/2 am	Jupiter	Venus	Saturn	Sun	Moon	Mars	Mercury
9	2/3 am	Mars	Mercury	Jupiter	Venus	Saturn	Sun	Moon
10	3/4 am	Sun	Moon	Mars	Mercury	Jupiter	Venus	Saturn
11	4/5 am	Venus	Saturn	Sun	Moon	Mars	Mercury	Jupiter
12	5/6 am	Mercury	Jupiter	Venus	Saturn	Sun	Moon	Mars

Colors

This list can be useful when choosing candles for magical rituals or spells, tinting bath salts, or designing entire rituals around herbal products. Some differences of opinion do exist and color itself is a magical system. Use your instinct. Here is what each of the colors represents so that you can select the right ones for your magical ritual.

White: Protection, purification, peace, truth, binding, sincerity, chastity, happiness, exorcism, spirituality, tranquility

Red: Protection, strength, health, energy, vigor, lust, sex, passion, courage, exorcism, love, power

Black: Absorbing and destroying negativity, healing severe diseases, banishing, attracting money

Light Blue: Understanding, tranquility, healing, patience, happiness, overcoming depression

Dark Blue: Change, flexibility, subconscious mind, psychic perception, healing

Green: Finances, money, fertility, prosperity, growth, good luck, employment, beauty, youth, success in gardening

Gray: Neutrality, cancellation, stalemate

Yellow: Intellect, charm, attraction, study, persuasion, confidence, divination, psychic power, wisdom, vision

Brown: Working magic for animals, healing animals, the home

Pink: Love, honor, fidelity, morality, friendship

Orange: Adaptability, stimulation, attraction, encouragement, all legal matters

Purple: Power, healing severe disease, spirituality, medication, exorcism, ambition, business progress, and tension relief

Numbers

The following is based on the ancient Pythagorean system (on which modern-day numerology is based). If any number keeps appearing to you in various forms, pay attention to the meanings for that number.

One: Independence, new beginnings, self-development, oneness with life, individuality, progress and creativity

Two: A balance of yin and yang energies (the polarities) of the universe, self-surrender, putting others first, a dynamic attraction to one another, knowledge that comes from balancing the two opposites

Three: Trinity, mind-body-spirit, threefold nature of divinity, expansion, expression, communication, fun, self-expression, giving outwardly, openness and optimism (this number related to the Wiccan 3-by-3 law—whatever you send out, you will receive threefold)

Four: Security, foundations, four elements and the four directions, self-discipline through work and service, productivity, organization, wholeness

Five: Feeling free, self-emancipation, active, physical, impulsive, energetic, changing, adventuresome, resourceful, travel, curiosity, free soul, excitement, and change

Six: Self-harmony, compassion, love, service, social responsibility, beauty, the arts, generosity, concern, caring, children, balance, community service

Seven: Inner life and inner wisdom, seven chakras and seven heavens, birth and rebirth, religious strength, sacred vows, path of solitude, analysis, contemplation

Eight: Infinity, material prosperity, self-power, abundance, cosmic consciousness, reward, authority, leadership

Nine: Humanitarianism, selflessness, dedication of your life to others, completion, endings, universal compassion, tolerance, and wisdom

Master Numbers

In the Pythagorean tradition, master numbers were thought to have a special power and significance of their own.

Eleven: Developing intuition, clairvoyance, spiritual healing, other metaphysical faculties

Twenty-two: Unlimited potential of mastery in any area—spiritual, physical, emotional, and mental

Thirty-Three: All things are possible

A Full Moon By Any Other Name

Many of our full moon names come from medieval books of hours and also from North American Native Americana. Here are other, rarer names from these two traditions that you may want to use in your lunar rituals.

January: Old Moon, Chaste Moon
February: Hunger Moon
March: Crust Moon, Sugar Moon, Sap Moon, or Worm Moon
April: Sprouting Grass Moon, Egg Moon, Fish Moon
May: Milk Moon, Corn Planting Moon, Dyad Moon

June: Hot Moon, Rose Moon

July: Buck Moon, Hay Moon

August: Barley Moon, Wyrt Moon, Sturgeon Moon

September: Green Corn Moon, Wine Moon

October: Dying Grass Moon, Travel Moon, Blood Moon, Moon of Changing Seasons

November: Frost Moon, Snow Moon

December: Cold Moon, Oak Moon

Saturn's Return

The rhythm of the planets in each of our charts is also a determining factor. One astrological factor that determines when a woman becomes a crone is when she reaches her second Saturn Return, which is when Saturn returns for the second time to the place it occupied when she was born. Usually, this occurs sometime between the ages of fifty-four and fifty-eight. Because Saturn is the planet of wisdom, it is also a "teaching planet." Saturn moves slowly and gives us all time to grow into our wisdom. A good astrological natal chart can teach you much about yourself.

RITUAL RESOURCES: APPENDIX II

God and Spirit Correspondences

The following lists and tables contain information on magical goals and their related deities.

Deities and Their Domains

Agriculture: Adonis, Amon, Aristaeus, Baldur, Bonus Eventus, Ceres, Consus, Dagon, Demeter, Dumunzi, Esus, Gahanan, Inari, Osiris, Saturn, Tammuz, Thor, Triptolemus, Vertumnus, Yumcaa, Zochipilli

Arts: Athena, Ea, Hathor, Odin, Thor

Astrology: Albion

Cats: Bast, Freya

Childbirth: Althea, Anahita, Bes, Camenta, Cihuatcoatl, Cuchavira, Isis, Kuan Yin, Laima, Lucina Meshkent

Communications: Hermes, Janus, Mercury

Courage: Tyr

Dreams: Geshtinanna, Morpheus, Nanshe

Earth: Asia, Consus, Daghda, Enlil, Frigga, Gaea, Ge, Geb, Kronos, Ninhursag, Ops, Prithivi, Rhea, Saturn, Sif, Tellus

Fertility: Amnu, Anaitis, Apollo, Arrianrhod, Asherali, Astarte, Attis, Baal, Bacchus, Bast, Bona Dea, Boucca, Centeotle,

Cernunnos, Cerridwen, Cybele, Daghda, Demeter, Dew, Dionysus, Eostre, Frey, Freya, Frigg, Indra, Ishtar, Ishwara, Isis, Kronos, Ono, Lulpercus, Min, Mut, Mylitta, Ningirsu, Ops, Osiris, Ostara, Pan, Pomona, Quetzalcoatl, Rhea, Rhiannon, Saturn, Selkhet, Sida, Tane, Telepinu, Telluno, Tellus Mater, Thunor, Tlazolteotl, Yarilo, Zarpanitu

Good Luck and Fortune: Bonus Eventus, Daikoku, Fortuna, Ganesa, Jorojin, Laima, Tyche

Healing: Apollo, Asclepius, Bast, Brigid, Eir, Gula, Ixlilton, Khnos, Paeon

Journeys: Echua, Janus

Law, Truth, and Justice: Astraea, Maat, Misharu, Themis

Love: Aizen Myo-O, Alpan, Angus, Aphrodite, Asera, Astarte, Asthoreth, Belili, Creirwy, Cupid, Dzydzilelya, Eros, Erzulie, Esmeralda, Fenrua, Freya, Frigg, Habondia, Hathor, Inanna, Ishtar, Kades, Kama, Kivan-Non, Kubaba, Melusine, Menu, Minne, Mamaja, Odudua, Olwen, Oshun, Prenda, Rao, Sauska, Tlazoletotl, Turan, Venus, Xochipilli, Zochiquetzal

Lunar Magic: Aah, Anahita, Artemis, Asherali, Astarte, Baiame, Bendis, Diana, Gou, Hathor, Hecate, Ilmaqah, Ishtar, Isis, Jacy, Kabul, Khons, Kilya, Lucina, Luna, Mah, Mama Quilla, Mani, Menu, Metzli, Myestaa, Nanna, Pah, Selene, Sin, Soma, Taukiyomi, Thoth, Varuna, Yarikh, Yerak, Zamna

Marriage: Airyaman, Aphrodite, Aryan, Bes, Bah, Ceres, Errata, Frigg, Hathor, Hera, Hymen, Juno, Patina, Saluki, Svarog, Thalassa, Tutunis, Vor, Xochipilli

Music and/or Poetry: Apollo, Benten, Bragi, Brigid, Hathor, Odin, Orpheus, Thoth, Untunktahe, Woden, Xolotl

Reincarnation: Hera, Khensu, Ra

Sea: Amphitrite, Benten, Dylan, Ea, Enoil, Glaucus, Leucothea, Manannan Mac Lir, Neptune, Nereus, Njord, Paldemon, Phorcys, Pontus, Poseidon, Proteus, Shoney, Yamm

Shapeshifting: Freya, Volkh, Xolotl

Sky: Aditi, Anshar, Anu, Dyaus, Frigg, Hathor, Horus, Joch-Huva, Jupiter, Kumarbis, Nut, Obatala, Rangi, Svarog, Tane, Thor, Tiwaz, Ukko, Uranus, Varuna, Zeus

Sleep: Hypnos (also see the list of deities who rule over dreams)

Solar Magic: Amaterasu, Apollo, Atum, Baldur, Bochia, Dazhbog, Helios, Hiruku, Horus, Hyperion, Inti, Legba, Lugh, Mandulis, Mao, Marduk, Maui, Melkart, Mithra, Orunjan, Paiva Perun, Phoebus, Ra, Sabazius, Samas, Sams, Shamash, Sol, Surya, Texcatlipoca, Tonatiuh, Torushompek, Utto, Vishnu, Yhi

Vengeance: Nemesis

Wealth and Prosperity: Daikoku, Jambhala, Kuber, Plutus, Thor

Weatherworking: Adad, Acolus, Agni, Amen, Baal, Bragi, Burlash, Catequil, Chac-Mool, Chernabog, Donar, Fomagata, Ilyapa, Indra, Jove, Jupiter, Kami-Nari, Koza, Lei-Kung, Marduk, Nyame, Perkunas, Pillan, Pulug, Quiateot, Raiden, Rammon, Rudra, Shango, Sobo, Summanus, Taki-Tsu-Hilo, Tawhaaki, Tawhiri, Tefnut, Thor, Thunor, Tilo, Tinia, Typhoeus, Typhon, Yu-Tzu, Zeus, Zu

Wisdom: Aruna, Athena, Atri, Baldur, Brigid, Dainichi, Ea, Enki, Fudo-Myoo, Fugen Bosatsu, Fukurokuju, Ganesha, Minerva, Nebo, Mimir, Oannes, Odin, Oghama, Quetzalcoatl, Sia, Sin, Thoth, Vohumano, Zeus

Magical Intentions

The following words correspond to various planets and elements. See below to learn more.

Banishing: Saturn, fire

Beauty: Venus, water

Courage: Mars, fire

Divination: Mercury, air

Employment: Sun, Jupiter

Energy: Sun, Mars, fire

Exorcism: Sun, fire

Fertility: Moon, planet Earth

Friendship: Venus, water

Happiness: Venus, Moon, water

Healing and Health: Moon, Mars (to burn away disease), fire (the same), water

Home: Saturn, Earth, water

Joy and Happiness: Venus, water

Love: Venus, water

Money and Wealth: Jupiter, Earth

Peace: Moon, Venus

Power: Sun, Mars, fire

Protection: Sun, Mars, fire

Psychism: Moon, water

Sex: Mars, Venus, fire

Sleep: Moon, water

Spirituality: Sun, Moon

Success: Sun, fire

Travel: Mercury

Wisdom and Intelligence: Mercury, air

Elemental Dragons

Element	Manifestation	Cardinal Points	Dragon Name	Color
Earth	Land and Moonbeams	North	Grael	Clear Dark Green
Water	Oceans and Rivers	West	Naelyan	Blue
Air	Breezes and Wind	East	Sairys	Yellow
Fire	Sunbeams	South	Fafnir	Pure Red
Light Side of the Soul	Mother	N/A	N/A	White
Dark Side of the Soul	Father	N/A	N/A	Black

Elemental Spirits

Element	Spirit Name	Leader	Attracted By	Rulers Of
Earth	Gnomes or Trolls	Ghob	Salts and Powders	Riches and Treasure
Water	Nymphs or Undines	Neckna	Washes and Solutions	Plants and Healings
Air	Sylphs or Zephyrs	Paralda	Oils and Incense	Knowledge and Inspiration
Fire	Salamanders	Dijn	Fire and Incense	Freedom and Change

Wild Women

For your celebratory mask-making ceremonies, you can and should design your own wild woman images. You can also choose from a list of classical goddess images, such as:

- Peacock Woman is Juno whose totem is the royally plumed bird
- Winged Isis wears the sun disk on her head
- Medusa has snakes for hair
- Sphinx is an image of eternal mystery
- Saints are holy women with halos
- Mermaid goddesses wear tricorn crowns
- Imps and some underworld goddesses have horns
- Diana has the crescent moon on her head
- Fairies have butterfly-like wings and antennae at times
- Elves have pointed ears
- Dryads are tree nymphs with leafy crowns
- Anima Mundi, the "soul of the world," has a crown of stars

RITUAL RESOURCES: APPENDIX III

Herbs of the Gods and Goddesses

Herbs are a very direct way to connect to different divinities. You can use these energies in so many ways—gardens, potpourris, incenses, and teas. Always check with an herbalist or specialist before using them in anything you plan to ingest. Caution is always your best guide in herbology.

- Acacia: Buddha, Neith, and Osiris
- Aconite: Hecate, and Medea **(warning: toxic)**
- Agave: Mayauel (Aztec goddess of birth and death)
- All Heal: Hercules
- Anemone: Venus and Adonis
- Angelica: Archangel Michael and Atlantic
- Anise: Mercury and Apollo
- Azalea: Hecate
- Barley: Odin
- Basil: Lakshmi, Krishna, Vishnu, Erzulie (Haitian goddess of love)
- Belladonna: Bellona, Circe, Hecate, Atropos (the fate who cuts the thread) **(warning: toxic)**
- Benzoin: Venus and Nut (Egyptian vulture goddess and patroness of Thebes)
- Blackthorn: The Triple Goddess

- Broom: Blodeuwedd (Welsh goddess of spring)
- Catnip: Bast (Egyptian cat goddess) and Sekhmet (Egyptian lion-headed sun goddess)
- Centaury: Chiron
- Chamomile: Karnaya
- Coltsfoot: Epona
- Cornflower: Flora
- Cowslip: Freya
- Crocus: Venus
- Daffodil: Persephone
- Daisy: Artemis, Freya, Thor, Venue, and Zeus
- Dandelion: Brigid
- Dittany: Consus (Roman god of grain storage and council)
- Elecampane: Helen
- Eyebright: Euphrosyne (Greek goddess of mirth, one of the Charities)
- Fennel: Adonis
- Fenugreek: Apollo
- Ferns: Kupala (Polish water and mother goddess of the summer solstice, herbs, trees, and sex)
- Flax: Hulda (Teutonic fertility goddess)
- Garlic: Mars and Hecate
- Hawthorn: Hymen
- Heather: Venus and Isis
- Heliotrope: Apollo, Sol, Ra, and Helios
- Holly: Frau Holle (Scandinavian goddess of healing)
- Horehound: Horus

- Hyacinth: Artemis, Apollo, and Hyacinthus
- Iris: Isis, Hera, and Iris
- Ivy: Dionysus, Osiris, Attis
- Jasmine: Diana
- Jimsonweed: Apollo, Kwawar (Great Spirit and Creator of the Gabrielino Indians)
- Lady's Mantle: Benevolent Virgin Mary
- Lavender: Hecate, Hestia, and Cronos
- Leek: Thor and Jupiter
- Lettuce: Adonis
- Lily: Lilith, Ostara, Hera, and Astarte
- Lotus: Kuan Yin, Lakshmi, Osiris, Tara, Buddha, Brahma, Isis, Horus, Mercury
- Maidenhair Fern: Venus, Dis, and Kupala
- Mandrake: Hecate, Venus, Cronos, and Circe
- Marigold: Xochiquetzal (Aztec goddess of love, earth, flowers, dance, and games)
- Marjoram: Venus
- Meadowsweet: Blodeuwedd
- Mints: Mintha, Hecate, and Dis (Norse god of the Disablot, a midwinter drinking festival)
- Mistletoe: Zeus, Odin, Aeneas, and Balder
- Monkshood: Hecate, Cerberus (Hellhound of Greek Underworld) **(warning: toxic)**
- Moonwort: Selene, Thoth, Diana, Artemis
- Mosses: Tapio (Finnish forest god)
- Motherwort: All mother goddesses

- Mugwort: Artemis, Diana
- Mulberry: Athena
- Mullein: Odysseus and Circe
- Narcissus: Narcissus, Venus, Dis, Hades and Persephone
- Orchid: Bacchus and Orcus
- Orris root: Venus, Juno, Iris, Isis, and Osiris
- Osier: Hecate
- Parsley: Venus, Persephone
- Pennyroyal: Demeter
- Peppermint: Zeus
- Periwinkle: Venus
- Plantain: Venus
- Poppy: Diana, Persephone, and Ceres
- Primrose: Freya
- Purslane: Hermes
- Raspberry: Venus
- Reeds: Pan, Inanna
- Rose: Cupid, Venus, Demeter, Erato, Eros, Flora, Freya, Hathor, Holda, the Virgin Mary
- Rue: Mars
- Rush: Acis (Greek river deity)
- Rye: Ceres
- Sage: Consus and Zeus
- Sandalwood: Venus
- Saxifrage: Kupala
- Solomon's Seal: King Solomon

- Strawberry: Venus, Freya, Virgin Mary
- Sugar Cane: Kama, Eros
- Sunflower: Apollo, Demeter, Sol, Mary
- Tansy: Ganymede (cupbearer of Zeus)
- Tarragon: Lilith
- Thistle: Thor
- Trefoil: Olwen
- Verbena: Diana
- Vervain: Cerridwen, Demeter, Diana, Hermes, Isis, Thor, Mars, Jupiter, Juno, Hermes, Aradia (Italian goddess)
- Violet: Venus, Attis, Zeus and Io (Greek maiden and lover of Zeus)
- Water Lily: All water deities, Surya (Indian fire god and/or goddess)
- Wood Sorrel: St. Patrick
- Wormwood: Diana
- Yarrow: Achilles, The Horned God

Visionary Incense

You can access your intuitive and imaginative capabilities with this powerful incense:

2 cups of ground chicory root
1 cup of ground cloves
2 cups of cinquefoil

Mix and burn the herbs in your fireplace of in your home shrine while concentrating on a question you have or before you embark on a vision quest. Meditate deeply, clearing your mind of all distractions, worries, and thoughts of daily life. The smoke from the incense will cleanse your speech and your thoughts. Answers will come.

The Language of Flowers

Here is what each of the following flowers means so that you can select the right flowers for your ritual.

A

Abatina: Fickleness

Acacia: Chaste love

Acacia, Pink: Elegance

Acacia, Yellow: Secret love

Acanthus: The fine arts, artifice

Achillea Millefolia: War

Aconite, Crowfoot: Lustre

Aconite, Wolfsbane: Misanthropy

Adonis: Sorrowful remembrance

African Marigold: Vulgar minds

Agnus Castus: Coldness

Agrimony: Thankfulness, gratitude

Almond: Stupidity, indiscretion

Almond, Flowering: Hope

Almond, Laurel: Perfidy

Allspice: Compassion

Aloe: Grief, affection

Althea Frutex: Persuasion

Alyssum, Sweet: Worth beyond beauty

Amaranth: Immortality, unfading love

Amaranth, Cockscomb: Foppery, affectation

Amaranth, Globe: Unchangeable

Amaryllis: Pride

Ambrosia: Love returned

American Elm: Patriotism

American Linden: Matrimony

B

Bachelor's Buttons: Single blessedness

Balm: Sympathy

Balm, Gentle: Pleasantry

Balm of Gilead: Cure, relief

Balsam: Impatience

Balsam, Red: Touch me not, impatient resolve

Barberry: Sourness, sharpness, ill temper

Basil: Hatred

Bay Leaf: I change but in death

Bay Tree: Glory

Bay Wreath: Reward of merit

Bearded Crepis: Protection

Beech Tree: Prosperity

Bee Orchis: Industry

Bee Ophrys: Error

Begonia: Dark thoughts

Belladonna: Silence

Bell Flower, White: I declare against you

Betony: Surprise

Bilberry: Treachery

Bindweed, Great: Insinuation

Bindweed, Small: Humility

Birch: Meekness

Birdsfoot Trefoil: Revenge

Bitterweed, Nightshade: Truth

Black Poplar: Courage

C

Cabbage: Profit

Cacalia: Adulation

Calceolaria: Keep this for my sake

Calla Aethiopica: Magnificent beauty

Calycanthus: Benevolence

Camellia Japonica, White: Unpretending excellence

Chamomile: Energy in adversity

Campanula: Gratitude

Canariensis: Self-esteem

Canary Grass: Perseverance

Candytuft: Indifference

Canterbury Bell: Acknowledgement

Cardamine: Paternal error

Cardinal Flower: Distinction

Carnation, Red: Alas for my poor heart

Carnation, Striped: Refusal

Carnation, Yellow: Disdain

Catsus: Warmth

Catchfly: Snare

Catchfly, Red: Youthful love

Catchfly, White: Betrayal

Cedar: Strength

Cedar of Lebanon: Incorruptible

Cedar Leaf: I live for thee

Celandine: Joys to come

Centuary: Felicity

Cerebus, Creeping: Modest genius

Champignon: Suspicion

Crown, Imperial: Majesty, powerful

D, E

Daffodil: Regard

Daffodil, Great Yellow: Chivalry

Dahlia, Single: Good taste

Dahlia: Instability

Daisy, Double: Participation

Daisy, Garden: I share your sentiment

Daisy, One-Eyed: A token

Daisy, Party-colored: Beauty

Daisy, Red: Unconscious

Daisy, White: Innocent

Daisy, Wild: I will think of it

Dandelion: Oracle

Daphne Odora: Painting the lily

Darnel: Vice

Dead Leaves: Sadness

Dew Plant: A serenade

Diosma: Uselessness

Dittany of Crete: Birth

Dittany, White: Passion

Dock: Patience

Dodder of Thyme: Baseness

Dogsbane: Deceit, falsehood

Dogwood: Durability

Dragon Plant: Snare

Dragonwort: Horror

Dried Flax: Utility

Ebony Tree: Blackness

Eglantine or Sweet Briar: Poetry, I wound to heal

Elder: Zealousness

Elm: Dignity

Enchanter's Nightshade: Fascination, witchcraft

Endive: Frugality

Eschscholtzia: Sweetness

Eupatorium: Delay

Evergreen: Poverty

Evergreen, Thorn: Solace in adversity

Everlasting Pea: Lasting pleasure, an appointed meeting

F, G

Fennel: Worthy of all praise

Fern, Flowering: Fascination

Fern: Sincerity

Ficoides, Ice Plant: Your looks freeze me

Fig: Argument

Fig, Marigold: Idleness

Fig Tree: Prolific

Flax: Fate, domestic industry, I feel your kindness

Flax-leaved Golden Locks: Tardiness

Fleur-de-lis: Flame

Fleur-de-Luce: Confidence in heaven

Flower-of-an-Hour: Delicate beauty

Fly Orchis: Error

Fly Trap: Deceit

Fools Parsley: Silliness

Forget-Me-Not: True love

Foxglove: Insincerity

Foxtail Grass: Sporting

French Honeysuckle: Rustic beauty

French Marigold: Jealousy

Frog Ophrys: Disgust

Fritillary, Checquered: Persecution

Fullers Teasel: Misanthropy, importunity

Fumitory: Spleen

Fuchsia, Scarlet: Taste

Furze or Gorse: Enduring affection

Garden Anemone: Forsaken

Garden Chervil: Sincerity

Garden Marigold: Uneasiness

Garden Ranunculus: You are rich in attractions

Garden Sage: Esteem

Garland of Roses: Reward of virtue

Gentian: You are unjust

Germander Speedwell: Facility

Geranium, Dark: Melancholy

Geranium, Ivy: Bridal favor

Geranium, Nutmeg: An expected meeting

Geranium, Oak-leaved: True friendship

Geranium, Pencil-leaved: Ingenuity

Geranium, Rose or Pink: Preference

Geranium, Scarlet: Comforting

Geranium, Silver-leaved: Recall

Geranium, Wild: Steadfast piety

Gillyflower: Lasting beauty

Gladiolus: Strength of character

Glory Flower: Glorious beauty

Gloxinia: A proud spirit

Goats Rue: Reason

H, I, J

Hand Flower Tree: Warming

Harebell: Submission, grief

Hawkweed: Quick-sightedness

Hawthorne: Hope

Hazel: Reconciliation

Heartsease or Pansy: You occupy my thoughts

Heath: Solitude

Helenium: Tears

Heliotrope: Devotion

Hellebore: Scandal, calumny

Hemlock: You will be my death

Hemp: Fate

Henbane: Imperfection

Hepatica: Confidence

Hibiscus: Delicate beauty

Holly: Foresight

Holly Herb: Enchantment

Hollyhock: Fecundity

Honesty: Honesty, sincerity

Honey Flower: Love sweet and secret

Honeysuckle: Bonds of love, sweetness of disposition

Honeysuckle, Coral: The color of my fate

Honeysuckle, French: Rustic beauty

Hop: Injustice

Hornbeam: Ornament

Hortensia: You are cold

Houseleek: Vivacity, domestic economy

Houstonia: Content

Hoya: Sculpture

Humble Plant: Despotism

Hyacinth: Sport, game, play

Hyacinth, Blue: Constancy

Hyacinth, Purple: Sorrow

Hyacinth, White: Unobtrusiveness, loveliness

Hydrangea: A boaster, heartlessness

Hyssop: Cleanliness

Iceland Moss: Health

Ice Plant: Your looks freeze me

Imperial Montaque: Power

Indian Cress: Warlike trophy

Indian Pink, Double: Always lovely

Indian Plum: Privation

Iris: Message

Iris, German: Flame

Ivy: Friendship, fidelity

Ivy, Sprig of with tendrils: Assiduous to please

Jacobs Ladder: Come down

Japan Rose: Beauty is your only attraction

Jasmine, Cape: Transport of joy

Jasmine, Carolina: Separation

Jasmine, Indian: Attachment

Jasmine, Spanish: Sensuality

Jasmine, Yellow: Grace and elegance

Jasmine, White: Amiability

Jonquil: I desire a return of affection

Judas Tree: Unbelief, betrayal

Justicia: The perfection of female loveliness

K, L

Kennedya: Mental beauty

King-Cups: Desire of riches

Laburnum: Forsaken, pensive beauty

Lady's Slipper: Capricious beauty

Lagerstromia, Indian: Eloquence

Lantana: Rigor

Larch: Audacity, boldness

Larkspur: Lightness, levity

Larkspur, Pink: Fickleness

Larkspur, Purple: Haughtiness

Laurel: Glory

Laurel, Common in the flower: Perfidy

Laurel, Ground: Perseverance

Laurel, Mountain: Ambition

Laurestina: A token

Lavender: Distrust

Leaves, Dead: Melancholy

Lemon: Zest

Lemon Blossoms: Fidelity in love

Lent Lilly: Sweet disposition

Lettuce: Cold-heartedness

Lichen: Dejection, solitude

Lilac, Field: Humility

Lilac, Purple: First emotions of love

Lilac, White: Youthful innocence

Lily, Day: Coquetry

Lily, Yellow: Falsehood, gaiety

Lilly of the Valley: Return of happiness

Linden or Lime Tree: Conjugal love

Lint: I feel my obligation

Liquorice, Wild: I declare against you

Live Oak: Liberty

Liverwort: Confidence

Lobelia: Malevolence

Locust Tree: Elegance

Locust Tree, Green: Affection beyond the grave

London Pride: Frivolity

Lote Tree: Concord

Lotus: Eloquence

Lotus Flower: Estranged love

Lotus Leaf: Recantation

Love-in-a-Mist: Perplexity

Love-Lies-Bleeding: Hopeless, not heartless

Lucerne: Life

Lupin: Voraciousness

M, N, O

Madder: Calumny

Magnolia: Love of nature

Magnolia, Laurel-leaved: Dignity

Magnolia, Swamp: Perseverance

Mallow: Mildness

Mallow, Marsh: Beneficence

Mallow, Syrian: Consumed by love

Mallow, Venetian: Delicate beauty

Manchineel Tree: Falsehood

Mandrake: Horror

Maple: Reserve

Marigold: Grief, despair

Marigold, African: Vulgar minds

Marigold, French: Jealousy

Marigold, Prophetic: Prediction

Marjoram: Blushes

Marvel of Peru: Timidity

Meadow Lychnis: Wit

Meadow Saffron: My best days are past

Meadowsweet: Uselessness

Mercury: Goodness

Mesembryanthemum: Idleness

Mezereon: Desire to please

Michaelmas Daisy: Afterthought

Mignonette: Your qualities surpass your charms

Milfoil: War

Milkvetch: Your presence softens my pains

Milkwort: Hermitage

Mimosa, Sensitive Plant: Sensitiveness

Mint: Virtue

Mistletoe: I surmount difficulties

Narcissus: Egotism

Narcissus, Double: Female ambition

Nasturtium: Patriotism

Nemophila: I forgive you

Nettle, Common Stinging: You are cruel

Nettle, Burning: Slander

Night-blooming Cereus: Transient beauty

Night Convolvulus: Night

Nightshade: Falsehood

Oak Leaves: Bravery

Oak Tree: Hospitality

Oats: The witching soul of music

Oleander: Beware

Olive: Peace

Orange Blossoms: Bridal festivities, your purity equals your loveliness

Orange Flowers: Chastity

Orange Tree: Generosity

Orchid: A belle

Osier: Frankness

Osmunda: Dreams

Ox Eye: Patience

P, Q, R

Palm: Victory

Pansy: Thoughts

Parsley: Festivity

Pasque Flower: You have no claims

Patience Dock: Patience

Passion Flower: Religious superstition

Pea, Everlasting: An appointed meeting, lasting pleasure

Pea, Sweet: Departure, lasting pleasures

Peach: Your qualities like your charms are unequalled

Peach Blossom: I am your captive

Quaking Grass: Agitation

Quamoclit: Busybody

Queen's Rocket: You are the Queen of Coquettes, passion

Quince: Temptation

Ragged Robin: Wit

Ranunculus: You are radiant with charms

Ranunculus, Garden: You are rich in all relations

Ranunculus, Wild: Ingratitude

Raspberry: Remorse

Rye Grass, Darnel: Vice

Red Catchfly: Youthful love

Reed: Complaisance, music

Reed, Split: Indiscretion

Rhododendron, Rosebay: Danger, beware

Rhubarb: Advice

Rocket: Rivalry

S

Saffron: Beware of success

Saffron, Crocus: Mirth

Saffron, Meadow: My happiest days are past

Sage: Domestic virtue

Sage, Garden: Esteem

Sainfoin: Agitation

Saint John's Wort: Animosity

Salvia, Blue: I think of you

Salvia, Red: Forever thine

Saxifrage, Mossy: Affection

Scabicus: Unfortunate love

Scarlet Lychnis: Sunbeaming eyes

Schinus: Religious enthusiasm

Scilla, Blue: Forgive and forget

Scilla, Sibirica: Pleasure without alloy

Scilla, White: Sweet innocence

Scotch, Fir: Elevation

Sensitive Plant: Sensibility

Shamrock: Light-heartedness

Snakesfoot: Horror

Snowball: Bound

Snowdragon: Presumption

Snowdrop: Hope

Sorrel: Affection

Sorrel, Wild: Wit, ill-timed

Sorrel, Wood: Joy

Stephanotis: You can boast too much

Stock, Ten Week: Promptness

Stonecrop: Tranquility

Straw, Broken: Rupture of a contract

Straw, Whole: Union

Strawberry Blossom: Foresight

Strawberry Tree: Esteem, not love

Sumach, Venice: Splendor

Sunflower, Dwarf: Adoration

Sunflower, Tall: Haughtiness

T

Tamarisk: Crime

Tansy, Wild: I declare war against you

Teasel: Misanthropy

Tendrils of Climbing Plants: Ties

Thistle, Common: Austerity

Thistle, Scotch: Retaliation

Thorn, Apple: Deceitful, charms

Thorns, Branch of: Severity

Thrift: Sympathy

Throatwort: Neglected beauty

Thyme: Activity

Tiger Flower: For once may pride befriend me

Traveler's Joy: Safety

Tree of Life: Old age

Trefoil: Revenge

Tremella: Resistance

Trillium Pictum: Modest beauty

Truffle: Surprise

Tulip, Red: Declaration of love

Tulip, Variegated: Beautiful eyes

Tulip, Yellow: Hopeless love

Turnip: Charity

Tussilago, Sweet-scented: Justice shall be done you

V, W

Valerian: An accommodating disposition

Valerian, Greek: Rupture

Venus' Car: Fly with me

Venus' Looking Glass: Flattery

Venus Trap: Deceit

Verbena, Scarlet: Sensibility

Verbena, White: Pure and guileless

Vernal Grass: Poor, but happy

Veronica: Fidelity

Vervain: Enchantment

Vine: Intoxication

Violet, Blue: Faithfulness

Violet, Dame: Watchfulness

Violet, Sweet: Modesty

Violet, Yellow: Rural happiness

Virginia Creeper: Ever changing

Virgin's Bower: Filial love

Volkmannia: May you be happy

Walnut: Intellect, stratagem

Wallflower: Fidelity in adversity

Water Lily: Purity of heart

Watermelon: Bulkiness

Wax Plant: Susceptibility

Weigela: Accept a faithful heart

Wheat Stalk: Riches

Whin: Anger

White Jasmine: Amiability

White Lily: Purity and modesty

White Mullein: Good nature

White Oak: Independent

Whortleberry: Treason

Willow, Creeping: Love forsaken

Willow, Water: Freedom

Willow, Weeping: Mourning

Willow, Herb: Pretension

Willow, French: Bravery, humanity

Wisteria: I cling to thee

Witch Hazel: A spell

Woodbine: Fraternal love

X, Y, Z

Xanthium: Rudeness, pertinacity

Xeranthemum: Cheerfulness under adversity

Yew: Sorrow

Zephyr Flower: Expectation

Zinnia: Thoughts of absent friends

BIBLIOGRAPHY

Ahlquist, Cynthia. *Llewellyn's Magical Almanac.* St Paul: Llewellyn, 1996.

Budapest, Zsusanna. *The Holy Book of Women's Mysteries.* Berkeley: Wingbow, 1980.

Bulfinch, Thomas. *Bulfinch's Mythology.* New York: Modern Library, 1998.

Cicero, Marcus Tullius. *De Natura Deorum: The Nature of the Gods.* New York: Viking Press, 1985.

Cunningham, Nancy Brady. *A Book of Women's Altars.* Bottom: Red Wheel, 2002.

Driver, Tom. *The Magic of Ritual.* San Francisco: HarperSanFrancisco, 1991.

Eliade, Mircea. *Rites and Symbols of Initiation.* Dallas: Spring Publications, 1958.

Elk, Black. *Black Elk Speaks.* Lincoln: Bison Books, 2003.

Etheridge, J. W. *Targum of Onkelos and Jonathan Ben Uzziel on the Pentateuch with the Fragments of the Jerusalem from the Chaldee.* Hoboken: KTAV Press, 1969.

Fitch, Ed (published as Herman Slater). *A Book of Pagan Rituals.* York Beach: Weiser, 1978.

Frazer, James. *The Golden Bough.* New York: Avenel, 1981.

Gardner, Gerald. *The Meaning of Witchcraft.* Boston: Weiser, 2004.

Graves, Robert. *The White Goddess.* New York: Noonday Press, 1966.

Heerens Lysne, Robin. *Living a Sacred Life.* Berkeley: Conari Press, 1999.

Huizinga, Johan. *The Autumn of the Middle Ages.* Chicago: University of Chicago Press, 1997.

Kingma, Daphne Rose. *Weddings from the Heart.* Berkeley: Conari Press, 1994.

Knight, Brenda. *Gem Magic.* Gloucester: Fair Winds Press, 2004.

Mandela, Nelson. *Long Walk to Freedom.* Boston: Back Bay Books, 1995.

McKenna, Terence. *True Hallucinations.* San Francisco: HarperCollins, 1993.

Mongahan, Patricia. *The Book of Goddesses & Heroines.* St Paul: Llewellyn, 2004.

Rappaport, Roy. *Ritual and Religion in the Making of Humanity.* Boston: Cambridge University, 1999.

Roberts-Gallagher, Kim. *Daily Planetary Guide.* St. Paul: Llewellyn, 2004.

Silverwind, Selene. "Pagan Children and Ethics." *The Blessed Bee,* 2003

Smith, Steven. *Wylundt's Book of Incense.* York Beach: Weiser, 1989.

Teish, Luisah. *Jump Up.* Berkeley: Conari, 2000.

Walker, Barbara. *The Woman's Dictionary of Symbols and Sacred Objects.* San Francisco: Harper and Row, 1998.

Walker, Barbara. *Women's Rituals.* San Francisco: Harper and Row, 1986.

Mango Publishing, established in 2014, publishes an eclectic list of books by diverse authors—both new and established voices—on topics ranging from business, personal growth, women's empowerment, LGBTQ studies, health, and spirituality to history, popular culture, time management, decluttering, lifestyle, mental wellness, aging, and sustainable living. We were recently named 2019's #1 fastest growing independent publisher by *Publishers Weekly*. Our success is driven by our main goal, which is to publish high quality books that will entertain readers as well as make a positive difference in their lives.

Our readers are our most important resource; we value your input, suggestions, and ideas. We'd love to hear from you—after all, we are publishing books for you!

Please stay in touch with us and follow us at:
Facebook: Mango Publishing
Twitter: @MangoPublishing
Instagram: @MangoPublishing
LinkedIn: Mango Publishing
Pinterest: Mango Publishing

Sign up for our newsletter at www.mangopublishinggroup.com and receive a free book!

Join us on Mango's journey to reinvent publishing, one book at a time.